CHILTON BOOK COMPANY

REPAIR MANUAL

OLDS CALAIS
PONTIAC GRAND AM
BUICK SKYLARK
BUICK SOMERSET
1985-86

All U.S. and Canadian front wheel drive models

Vice President and General Manager JOHN P. KUSHNERICK
Editor-in-Chief KERRY A. FREEMAN, S.A.E.
Managing Editor DEAN F. MORGANTINI, S.A.E.
Senior Editor RICHARD J. RIVELE, S.A.E.
Senior Editor W. CALVIN SETTLE, JR., S.A.E.
Editor TONY MOLLA, S.A.E.

CHILTON BOOK COMPANY
Radnor, Pennsylvania
19089

SAFETY NOTICE

Proper service and repair procedures are vital to the safe, reliable operation of all motor vehicles, as well as the personal safety of those performing repairs. This book outlines procedures for servicing and repairing vehicles using safe, effective methods. The procedures contain many NOTES, CAUTIONS and WARNINGS which should be followed along with standard safety procedures to eliminate the possibility of personal injury or improper service which could damage the vehicle or compromise its safety.

It is important to note that repair procedures and techniques, tools and parts for servicing motor vehicles, as well as the skill and experience of the individual performing the work vary widely. It is not possible to anticipate all of the conceivable ways or conditions under which vehicles may be serviced, or to provide cautions as to all of the possible hazards that may result. Standard and accepted safety precautions and equipment should be used when handling toxic or flammable fluids, and safety goggles or other protection should be used during cutting.

Some procedures require the use of tools specially designed for a specific purpose. Before substituting another tool or procedure, you must be completely satisfied that neither your personal safety, nor the performance of the vehicle will be endangered.

Although information in this guide is based on industry sources and is as complete as possible at the time of publication, the possibility exists that the manufacturer made later changes which could not be included here. While striving for total accuracy, Chilton Book Company cannot assume responsibility for any errors, changes, or omissions that may occur in the compilation of this data.

PART NUMBERS

Part numbers listed in this reference are not recommendations by Chilton for any product by brand name. They are references that can be used with interchange manuals and aftermarket supplier catalogs to locate each brand supplier's discrete part number.

SPECIAL TOOLS

Special tools are recommended by the vehicle manufacturer to perform their specific job. Use has been kept to a minimum, but where absolutely necessary, they are referred to in the text by the part number of the tool manufacturer. These tools can be purchased, under the appropriate part number, from the Service Tool Division, Kent-Moore Corporation, 29784 Little Mack, Roseville, MI. 48066-2290, or an equivalent tool can be purchased locally from a tool supplier or parts outlet. Before substituting any tool for the one recommended, read the SAFETY NOTICE at the top of this page.

ACKNOWLEDGMENTS

The Chilton Book Company expresses its appreciation to the General Motors Corporation, Detroit, Michigan for their generous assistance.

Information has been selected from shop manuals, owners manuals, service bulletins and technical training manuals.

Manufactured in the United States of America
    66789   5432109

Chilton's Repair & Tune-Up Guide: Calais/Grand AM/Skylark/Somerset 1985–86
ISBN 0-8019-7657-X pbk.
Library of Congress Catalog Card No. 85-47958

CONTENTS

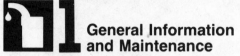

Quick Reference Specifications For Your Vehicle

Fill in this chart with the most commonly used specifications for your vehicle. Specifications can be found in Chapters 1 through 3 or on the tune-up decal under the hood of the vehicle.

Tune-Up

Firing Order_____

Spark Plugs:

    Type_____

    Gap (in.)_____

Torque (ft. lbs.)_____

Idle Speed (rpm)_____

Ignition Timing (°)_____

    Vacuum or Electronic Advance (Connected/Disconnected)_____

Valve Clearance (in.)

    Intake_____   **Exhaust**_____

Capacities

Engine Oil Type (API Rating)_____

    With Filter Change (qts)_____

    Without Filter Change (qts)_____

Cooling System (qts)_____

Manual Transmission (pts)_____

    Type_____

Automatic Transmission (pts)_____

    Type_____

Front Differential (pts)_____

    Type_____

Rear Differential (pts)_____

    Type_____

Transfer Case (pts)_____

    Type_____

FREQUENTLY REPLACED PARTS

Use these spaces to record the part numbers of frequently replaced parts.

PCV VALVE	OIL FILTER	AIR FILTER	FUEL FILTER
Type_____	Type_____	Type_____	Type_____
Part No._____	Part No._____	Part No._____	Part No._____

General Information and and Maintenance

HOW TO USE THIS BOOK

Chilton's Repair & Tune-Up Guide for the GM N-Body is intended to help you learn more about the inner workings of your vehicle and save you money on its upkeep and operation. All General Motors 1985-86 N-Body cars (Buick Somerset and Skylark, Oldsmobile Calais and Pontiac Grand Am) are covered in this book, with procedures specifically labeled as to the particular division when it makes a difference.

The first two chapters will be the most used, since they contain maintenance and tune-up information and procedures. Studies have shown that a properly tuned and maintained car can get at least 10% better gas mileage than an out-of-tune car. The other chapters deal with the more complex systems of your car. Operating systems from engine through brakes are covered to the extent that the average do-it-yourselfer becomes mechanically involved. This book will not explain such things as rebuilding the transaxle or differential for the simple reason that the expertise required and the investment in special tools make the task uneconomical. It will give you the detailed instructions to help you change your own brake pads and shoes, replace spark plugs or filters, and do many more jobs that will save you money, give you personal satisfaction, and help you avoid expensive problems. A secondary purpose of this book is a reference for owners who want to understand their car and/or their mechanics better. In this case, no tools at all are required.

Before removing any bolts, read through the entire procedure. This will give you the overall view of what tools and supplies will be required. There is nothing more frustrating than having to walk to the bus stop on Monday morning because you were short one bolt on Sunday afternoon. So read ahead and plan ahead. Each operation should be approached logically and all procedures thoroughly under-

stood before attempting any work. All chapters contain adjustments, maintenance, removal and installation procedures, and repair and overhaul procedures. When repair is not considered practical, we tell you how to remove the part and then how to install the new or rebuilt replacement. In this way, you at least save the labor costs. Backyard repair of such components as the alternator is just not practical.

Two basic mechanic's rules should be mentioned here. First, whenever the left side of the car or engine is referred to, it is meant to specify the driver's side of the car. Conversely, the right side of the car means the passenger's side. Secondly, most screws and bolts are removed by turning counterclockwise, and tightened by turning clockwise. Safety is always the most important rule. Constantly be aware of the dangers involved in working on an automobile and taking the proper precautions. See the section in this chapter "Servicing Your Vehicle Safely" and the SAFETY NOTICE on the acknowledgment page.

Pay attention to the instructions provided. There are 3 common mistakes in mechanical work:

1. Incorrect order of assembly, disassembly or adjustment. When taking something apart or putting it together, doing things in the wrong order usually just costs you extra time; however it CAN break something. Read the entire procedure before beginning disassembly. Do everything in the order in which the instructions say you should do it, even if you can't immediately see a reason for it. When you're taking apart something that is very intricate (for example a carburetor), you might want to draw a picture of how it looks when assembled at one point in order to make sure you get everything back in its proper position. We will supply exploded views whenever possible. When making adjustments, especially tune-up adjust-

ments, do them in order; often one adjustment affects another, and you cannot expect even satisfactory results unless each adjustment is made only when it cannot be changed by any other.

2. Overtorquing (or undertorquing). While it is more common for overtorquing to cause damage, undertorquing can cause a fastener to vibrate loose causing serious damage. Especially when dealing with aluminum parts, pay attention to torque specifications and utilize a torque wrench in assembly. If a torque figure is not available, remember that if you are using the right tool to do the job, you will probably not have to strain yourself to get a fastener tight enough. The pitch of most threads is so slight that the tension you put on the wrench will be multiplied many, many times in actual force on what you are tightening. A good example of how critical torque is can be seen in the case of spark plug installation, especially where you are putting the plug into an aluminum cylinder head. Too little torque can fail to crush the gasket, causing leakage of combustion gases and consequent overheating of the plug and engine parts. Too much torque can damage the threads, or distort the plug, which changes the spark gap. There are many commercial products available for ensuring that fasteners won't come loose, even if they are not torqued just right (a very common brand is "Loctite ®"). If you're worried about getting something together tight enough to hold, but loose enough to avoid mechanical damage during assembly, one of these products might offer substantial insurance. Read the label on the package and make sure the product is compatible with the materials, fluids, etc. involved before choosing one.

3. Crossthreading. This occurs when a part such as a bolt is screwed into a nut or casting at the wrong angle and forced. Crossthreading is more likely to occur if access is difficult. It helps to clean and lubricate fasteners, and to start threading with the part to be installed going straight in. Then, start the bolt, spark plug, etc. with your fingers. If you encounter resistance, unscrew the part and start over again at a different angle until it can be inserted and turned several turns without much effort. Keep in mind that many parts, especially spark plugs, use tapered threads so that gentle turning will automatically bring the part you're threading to the proper angle if you don't force it or resist a change in angle. Don't put a wrench on the part until it's been turned a couple of turns by hand. If you suddenly encounter resistance, and the part has not seated fully, don't force it. Pull it back out and make sure it's clean and threading properly. Always take your time and be patient; once you have some experience, working on your car will become an enjoyable hobby.

TOOLS AND EQUIPMENT

Naturally, without the proper tools and equipment it is impossible to properly service your vehicle. It would be impossible to catalog each tool that you would need to perform each or every operation in this book. It would also be unwise for the amateur to rush out and buy an expensive set of tools on the theory that he may need one or more of them at some time.

The best approach is to proceed slowly, gathering together a good quality set of those tools that are used most frequently. Don't be misled by the low cost of bargain tools. It is far better to spend a little more for better quality. Forged wrenches, 10 or 12 point sockets and fine tooth ratchets are by far preferable to their less expensive counterparts. As any good mechanic can tell you, there are few worse experiences than trying to work on a car or truck with bad tools. Your monetary savings will be far outweighed by frustration and mangled knuckles.

Begin accumulating those tools that are used most frequently; those associated with routine maintenance and tune-up. In addition to the normal assortment of screwdrivers and pliers you should have the following tools for routine maintenance jobs (your N-body uses both SAE and metric fasteners, but most are primarily metric):

1. SAE/Metric wrenches/sockets and combination open end/box end wrenches in sizes from ⅛ in. (3mm) to ¾ in. (19mm); and a spark plug socket (13⁄16 in.) If possible, buy various length socket drive extensions. One break in this department is that the metric sockets available in the U.S. will all fit the ratchet handles and extensions you may already have (¼, ⅜, and ½ in. drive).

2. Jackstands—for support;

3. Hydraulic floor jack—for raising and lowering the vehicle;

4. Oil filter wrench;

5. Oil filter spout—for pouring oil;

6. Grease gun—for chassis lubrication;

7. A container for draining oil;

8. Many rags for wiping up the inevitable mess;

9. Battery terminal and clamp cleaner.

In addition to the above items there are several others that are not absolutely necessary, but handy to have around. These include oil dry, a transmission funnel and the usual supply of lubricants, antifreeze and fluids, although these

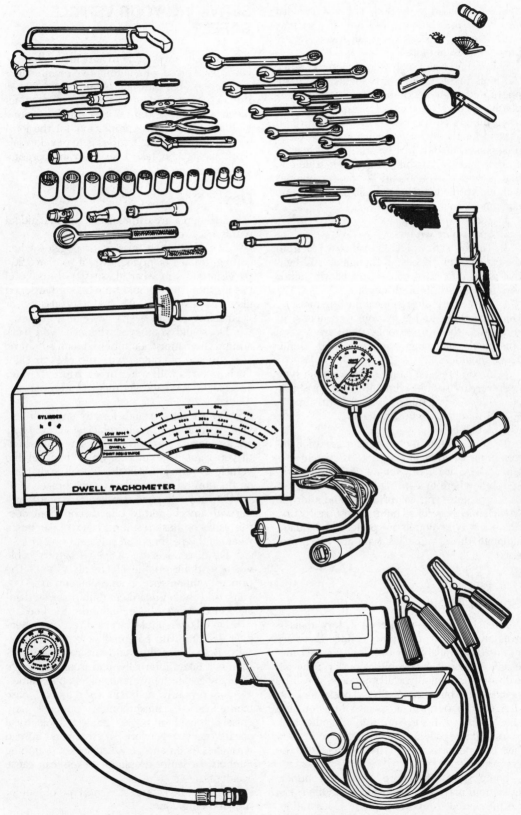

You need only a basic assortment of hand tools for most maintenance and repair jobs can be purchased as needed. This is a basic list for routine maintenance, but only if your personal needs and desire can accurately determine your list of tools.

The second list of tools is for tune-ups. While the tools involved here are slightly more sophisticated, they need not be outrageously expensive. There are several inexpensive tach/dwell meters on the market that are every bit as good for the average mechanic as a $100.00 professional model. Just be sure that it goes to at least 1200–1500 rpm on the tach scale and that it works on 4, 6 and 8 cylinder engines with electronic ignition. A basic list of tune-up equipment could include:

1. Tach-dwell meter;
2. Spark plug wrench;
3. Timing light (a DC light that works from the car's battery is best, although an AC light that plugs into 110V house current will suffice at some sacrifice in brightness);
4. Wire spark plug gauge/adjusting tools;

Here again, be guided by your own needs. In addition to these basic tools, there are several other tools and gauges you may find useful. These include:

1. A compression gauge. The screw-in type is slower to use, but eliminates the possibility of a faulty reading due to escaping pressure;
2. A manifold vacuum gauge;
3. A test light;
4. An induction meter. This is used for determining whether or not there is current in a wire. These are handy for use if a wire is broken somewhere in a wiring harness.

As a final note, you will probably find a torque wrench necessary for all but the most basic work. The beam type models are perfectly adequate, although the newer click type are more precise.

Special Tools

Normally, the use of special factory tools is avoided for repair procedures, since these are not readily available for the do-it-yourself mechanic. When it is possible to perform the job with more commonly available tools, it will be pointed out, but occasionally, a special tool was designed to perform a specific function and should be used. Before substituting another tool, you should be convinced that neither your safety nor the performance of the vehicle will be compromised.

Some special tools are available commercially from major tool manufacturers. Others can be purchased from Kent-Moore Corporation, 29784 Little Mack, Roseville, MI, 48066-2290.

SERVICING YOUR VEHICLE SAFELY

It is virtually impossible to anticipate all of the hazards involved with automotive maintenance and service but care and common sense will prevent most accidents. The rules of safety for mechanics range from "don't smoke around gasoline," to "use the proper tool for the job." The trick to avoiding injuries is to develop safe work habits and take every possible precaution.

Dos

• Do keep a fire extinguisher and first aid kit within easy reach.

• Do wear safety glasses or goggles when cutting, drilling or prying, even if you have 20–20 vision. If you wear glasses for the sake of vision, then they should be made of hardened glass that can serve also as safety glasses, or wear safety goggles over your regular glasses.

• Do shield your eyes whenever you work around the battery. Batteries contain sulphuric acid; in case of contact with the eyes or skin, flush the area with water or a mixture of water and baking soda and get medical attention immediately.

• Do use safety stands for any undercar service. Jacks are for raising vehicles; safety stands are for making sure the vehicle stays raised until you want it to come down. Whenever the vehicle is raised, block the wheels remaining on the ground and set the parking brake.

• Do use adequate ventilation when working with any chemicals. Like carbon monoxide, the asbestos dust resulting from brake lining wear can be poisonous in sufficient quantities.

• Do disconnect the negative battery cable when working on the electrical system. The primary ignition system can contain up to 40,000 volts, and the on-board computer can be damaged or destroyed by arcing under the hood.

• Do follow manufacturer's directions whenever working with potentially hazardous materials. Both brake fluid and antifreeze are poisonous if taken internally, and freon turns into a deadly gas in the presence of an open flame.

• Do properly maintain your tools. Loose hammerheads, mushroomed punches and chisels, frayed or poorly grounded electrical cords, excessively worn screwdrivers, spread wrenches (open end), cracked sockets, slipping ratchets, or faulty droplight sockets can cause accidents.

• Do use the proper size and type of tool for the job being done.

• Do when possible, pull on a wrench handle rather than push on it, and adjust your stance to prevent a fall.

• Do be sure that adjustable wrenches are tightly adjusted on the nut or bolt and pulled so that the face is on the side of the fixed jaw.

• Do select a wrench or socket that fits the nut or bolt. The wrench or socket should sit straight, not cocked.

• Do strike squarely with a hammer—avoid glancing blows.

• Do set the parking brake and block the drive wheels if the work requires that the engine be running.

Don'ts

• Don't run an engine in a garage or anywhere else without proper ventilation—EVER! Carbon monoxide is poisonous; it takes a long time to leave the human body and you can build up a deadly supply of it in your system by simply breathing in a little every day. You may not realize you are slowly poisoning yourself. Always use power vents, windows, fans or open the garage doors.

• Don't work around moving parts while wearing a necktie or other loose clothing. Short sleeves are much safer than long, loose sleeves and hard-toed shoes with neoprene soles protect your toes and give a better grip on slippery surfaces. Jewelry such as rings, watches, fancy belt buckles, beads or body adornment of any kind is not safe working around a car. Long hair should be hidden under a hat or cap.

• Don't use pockets for toolboxes. A fall or bump can drive a screwdriver deep into your body. Even a wiping cloth hanging from the back pocket can wrap around a spinning shaft or fan.

• Don't smoke when working around gasoline, cleaning solvent or other flammable material.

• Don't smoke when working around the battery. When the battery is being charged, it gives off explosive hydrogen gas.

• Don't use gasoline to wash your hands; there are excellent soaps available. Gasoline contains additives that can enter the body through a cut, accumulating in the body until you are very ill. Gasoline also removes all the natural oils from the skin so that bone dry hands will suck up oil and grease.

• Don't service the air conditioning system unless you are equipped with the necessary tools and training. The refrigerant, R-12, is extremely cold and when exposed to the air will instantly freeze any surface it comes in contact with, including your eyes. Although the refrigerant is normally non-toxic, R-12 becomes a deadly poisonous gas in the presence of an open flame. One good whiff of the vapors from burning refrigerant can be fatal.

A NOTE ABOUT TERMINOLOGY

There are a few descriptive words uses in connection with the N-Body cars which may be new to you. First is the term "N-Body" itself. The explanation for this, used to collectively describe the Buick Somerset and Skylark sedan, Oldsmobile Calais and Pontiac Grand Am, is quite simple. All GM cars have code names, used within the corporation to describe a body size series. For example, the full size, rear drive cars are known as B-Bodies. The N-Body is one of the newest front wheel drive models, and was first introduced in 1985. If this is your first front wheel drive car, you may not be familiar with the terms "transaxle," "halfshaft," or "constant velocity joint."

In a front wheel drive car, the transmission and differential share a common housing and the front axles (halfshafts) are driven by this unit. Thus, a "transaxle" is a combination transmission/differential/drive axle. The N-Bodies use a manual transaxle as standard equipment and an automatic as an option.

"Halfshafts" are drive axles. The term came about as a way to describe the two shafts which emerge from the transaxle case and connect to the front wheels, transmitting power from one to the other. In a conventional front engine/rear drive car, a driveshaft is used to transmit the power from the transmission to the drive axle. Thus, in a front wheel drive, where there are two driveshafts, each one becomes half of a driveshaft, or a halfshaft.

A "constant velocity joint" is a variation on a conventional universal joint. Differences between them lie in the greater flexibility of the constant velocity joint and its ability to transmit power at an angle without fluctuations in speed (hence "constant velocity"). Two constant velocity joints are used on each halfshaft, one at each end.

Because the N-Body is primarily an all-metric car, there are a few metric terms with which you should be familiar. Newton-meters (Nm) are the metric equivalent of foot-pounds, a measurement of torque. Millimeters are abbreviated to "mm;" liters are "L." Celcius temperatures are, of course, abbreviated to "C" and in all cases conventional English equivalents are given in the text along with the metric values.

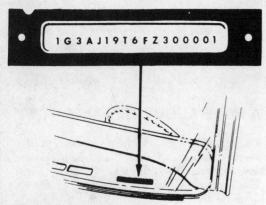

VIN number plate location

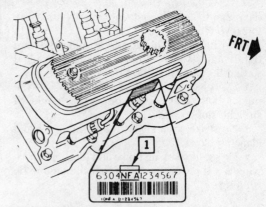

3.0L engine identification plate

SERIAL NUMBER IDENTIFICATION

It is important for servicing and ordering parts to be certain of the vehicle and engine identification. All numbers are stamped on various plates or pads, located in different places on the car and engine. The body number plate is attached to the front tie bar behind either the right or left headlamp, or on the upper radiator support in the engine compartment on some models; on other models, a service parts identification label is attached to the underside of the trunk lid.

Vehicle Identification Number (VIN)

The VIN is a 17 digit number visible through the windshield on the driver's side of the dash

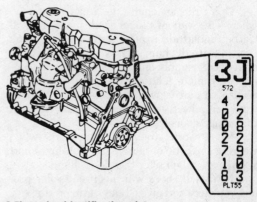

2.5L engine identification plate

and contains the vehicle and engine identification codes. See the accompanying charts for an interpretation of what the numbers mean.

VEHICLE IDENTIFICATION NUMBER (VIN)

It is important for servicing and ordering parts to be certain of the vehicle and engine identification. The VIN (vehicle identification number) is a 17 digit number visible through the windshield on the driver's side of the dash and contains the vehicle and engine identification codes. It can be interpreted as follows:

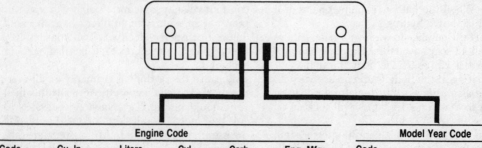

Engine Code						Model Year Code	
Code	Cu. In.	Liters	Cyl.	Carb	Eng. Mfg.	Code	Year
U	151	2.5	4	TBI	Pont.	F	1985
L	183	3.0	V6	MFI	Buick	G	1986

The seventeen digit Vehicle Identification Number can be used to determine engine application and model year. The 10th digit indicates the model year, and the 8th digit identifies the factory installed engine.
TBI–(Throttle body injection)
MFI–Multi-Port Fuel Injection

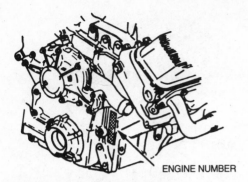

Serial number location on V6 engine

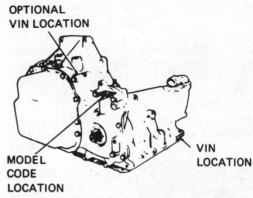

Serial number location on automatic transaxle

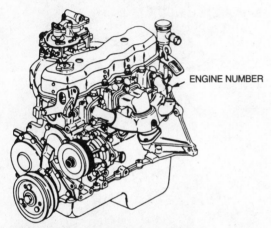

Serial number location on 4 cyl engine

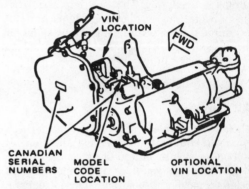

Automatic transaxle number locations for Canadian models

Engine Identification

See the accompanying illustrations for the locations of various engine identification numbers. Most engine numbers are stamped on a pad just below the cylinder head or on a plate attached to a valve cover.

Transaxle Identification

Manual transaxle model identification is either stamped into the transaxle case or on a paper label attached to the case. If the label is missing or unreadable, use the service parts information label to determine which transaxle was installed in your vehicle. The serial number plate for the automatic transaxle is located on the rear side of the transaxle case, above the left drive shaft opening.

ROUTINE MAINTENANCE

Routine maintenance is the self-explanatory term used to describe the sort of periodic work necessary to keep a car in safe and reliable working order. A regular program aimed at monitoring essential systems insures that all the car's components are functioning properly and will continue to do so until the next inspection. By following a regular maintenance program, small problems can be prevented from becoming major repair bills. A regular maintenance program can also pay dividends by keeping repair costs at a minimum, extending the life of the car and enhancing resale value, should you ever decide to part with your N-Body.

The Somerset, Skylark, Calais and Grand Am require less in the way of routine maintenance than earlier GM models, but a very definite maintenance schedule is provided by General

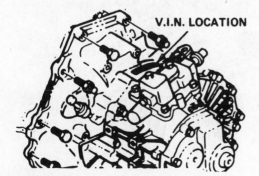

Serial number location on 5 speed transaxle

Motors and must be followed to keep the new car warranty in effect and to keep the vehicle working properly. The "Maintenance Intervals" chart contained in this chapter outlines the routine maintenance which must be performed according to intervals based on either accumulated mileage or time. Your N-Body also came with an owners manual that outlines the maintenance schedule provided by GM. Adherence to these schedules will result in a longer life for the car and will, in the long run, save you money.

The checks and adjustments in the following sections generally require only a few minutes of attention every few weeks and the services to be performed can generally be accomplished in a morning. The most important part of any maintenance program is regularity. The few minutes or an occasional morning spent on these seemingly trivial tasks will forestall or eliminate major problems later.

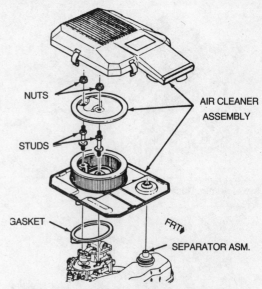

4 cyl air cleaner assembly—Grand Am shown

Air Cleaner

The air cleaner element is a dry paper type. If equipped with port fuel injection, the element will be rectangular instead of the familiar round type. Make sure you have the correct element before removing the old one. Do not operate the vehicle for any length of time without the air cleaner in place. The air cleaner element should be replaced every 30,000 miles (15,000 miles if the car is used in dusty conditions or driven daily in heavy traffic) as follows:

1. Depending on the type of air cleaner housing used, remove the wing nut(s) or bolts or release the locking clips on the air cleaner and lift off the lid or separate the housing halfs.

2. Lift out the old air cleaner element.

3. Before installing a new filter element, wipe out the inside of the air cleaner housing with a

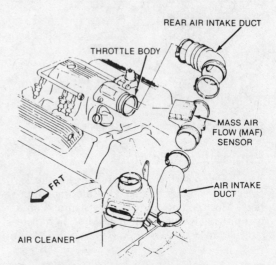

V6 air cleaner assembly on Buick models

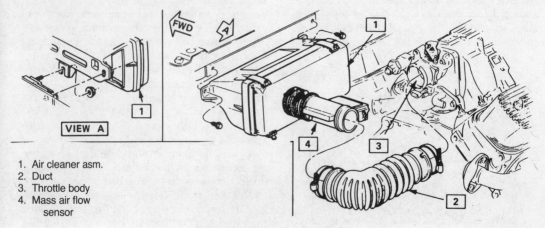

1. Air cleaner asm.
2. Duct
3. Throttle body
4. Mass air flow sensor

Typical V6 air cleaner assembly

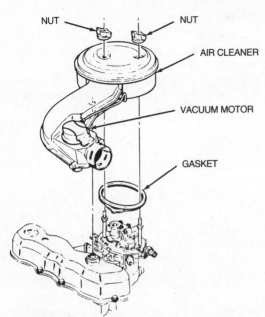

NUT

NUT

AIR CLEANER

VACUUM MOTOR

GASKET

Typical 4 cyl air cleaner assembly—Oldsmobile and Buick models

damp cloth and check the lid gasket for a tight seal.

4. Install a new filter into the housing and replace the wing nut, bolts or fasten the retainer clips.

NOTE: *On models equipped with port fuel injection, it is particularly critical that the air cleaner housing be fastened properly to prevent air leaks which could cause starting or driveability problems. Make sure the lid or housing halfs are fastened properly and sealed.*

PCV Valve

The Positive Crankcase Ventilation (PCV) valve must be replaced every 30,000 miles. Details

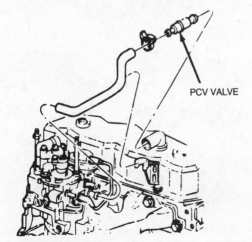

PCV VALVE

Typical 4 cyl PCV valve

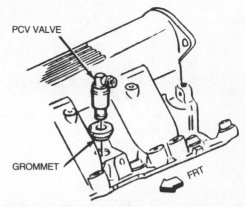

PCV VALVE

GROMMET

FRT

Typical V6 PCV valve location

on the PCV system, including system tests, are given in Chapter Four. Depending on the engine, the valve is either located in a rubber grommet in the intake manifold or valve cover, or in-line in a hose leading from the valve cover to the intake manifold. Replacement is a simple matter of pulling the PCV valve from its grommet or removing it from the hose and replacing it with a new part. Do not attempt to clean a PCV valve using solvent; if its operation is in question, it should be replaced.

PCV Filter

Four cylinder engines have a PCV filter located in the air cleaner housing which must be replaced at 30,000 mile intervals. Remove the air cleaner housing lid and slide back the retaining clip on the filter. Pull the old filter from the air cleaner and replace it with a new part.

Evaporation Control System Canister Filter

All models have a charcoal canister located in the engine compartment as part of the Evaporation Control System (ECS) which is designed to trap fuel vapors. Details on this system can be found in Chapter Four. Every 30,000 miles (or 24 months), the filter on the bottom of the vapor canister must be changed. Cut the interval in half if the vehicle is operated under dusty conditions or driven regularly in heavy traffic.

1. Locate the canister in the engine compartment. It is held in place at the base by two bolts. Unbolt and lift the canister without disconnecting any of the hoses.

NOTE: *If there is not enough slack in the hoses to allow you to lift the canister, label them before removal. It is important to reconnect the vapor canister hoses properly.*

2. Turn the canister over. The filter is in-

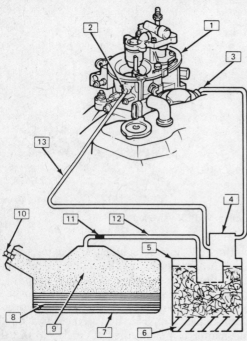

1. TBI
2. Canister purge port
3. Vacuum signal
4. Purge valve
5. Vapor storage canister
6. Purge air
7. Fuel tank
8. Fuel
9. Vapor
10. Pressure-vacuum relief gas cap
11. Vent restricter
12. Fuel tank vent
13. Purge line

Typical 4 cyl evaporative control system

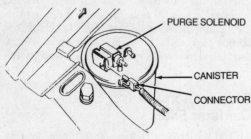

Typical V6 charcoal canister

stalled in the bottom and can simply be pulled out.

3. Install a new filter into the bottom of the vapor canister.

4. Reconnect any hoses removed during removal, being careful to install them in their original locations.

5. Install the canister.

The ECS hoses should be inspected for cracks, kinks or breaks at the time of filter replacement. If replacement hoses are necessary, use only those designed for this purpose, usually marked "EVAP". This type of hose is available from your local dealer or parts store.

Battery

All N-Body cars use a maintenance-free battery as standard equipment, eliminating the need for periodic fluid level checks and the possibility of specific gravity tests. Nevertheless, the battery does require some attention.

Once a year, the battery terminals and the cable clamps should be cleaned. Remove the

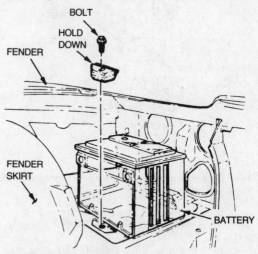

Typical battery mounting

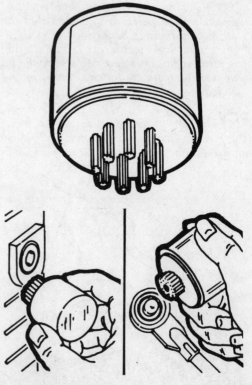

A special tool is available for cleaning the side terminals and clamps

side terminal bolts and the cables (negative cable first) and clean the cable clamps and battery terminals with a wire brush until all corrosion, grease, etc. is removed and the metal is shiny. It is especially important to clean the inside of the clamp thoroughly, since a small deposit of foreign material or oxidation will prevent a sound electrical connection and could inhibit charging or starting ability. A special battery brush is available for cleaning side terminals and clamps.

Before installing the cables, loosen the battery hold-down clamp, lift out the battery and check the battery tray. Clear it of any debris and check it for soundness. Rust and corrosion should be wire-brushed away and the metal coated with anti-rust paint. Replace the battery and tighten the hold-down clamp securely, but be careful not to overtighten and crack the battery case.

After the clamps and terminals are clean, install the terminals (positive cable first), then apply a thin external coat of grease to retard corrosion. Check the cables while cleaning the clamps, looking for frayed or broken insulation. If the cable has frayed ends or excessive corrosion is present, it should be replaced with a new cable of the same length and gauge.

CAUTION: *Keep flame or sparks away from the battery as it gives off explosive hydrogen gas. Battery electrolyte contains sulfuric acid. If you should get any on your skin or in your eyes, flush the affected area with plenty of clear water. In the case of eye contact, seek medical help immediately. It's also a good idea to wear some sort of filter when wire brushing excessive corrosion to avoid inhaling dust particles.*

TESTING MAINTENANCE-FREE BATTERY

The sealed top battery cannot be checked for charge in the normal manner, since there is no provision for access to the electrolyte. To check the condition of the battery, locate the indicator "eye" on top of the battery case. If the eye is dark, the battery has enough fluid; if the eye is light, the battery is low on fluid and must be replaced. If a green dot appears in the middle of the eye, the battery is sufficiently charged. It may be necessary to tip the battery from side-to-side to get the green dot to appear after charging. Never disconnect the battery with the key ON or the engine running as serious computer damage will occur.

Drive Belts

BELT TENSION ADJUSTMENT

Every 12 months or 15,000 miles, check the water pump, alternator, power steering pump and air conditioning compressor drive belts for proper tension. Look for signs of wear, fraying, separation, glazing and so on and replace the belts as required. It should be noted that modern fanbelts will often not show any signs of wear and the prudent owner will replace them every 24 months or 30,000 miles as a matter of routine maintenance.

Belt tension should be checked with a gauge made for the purpose. If a gauge is not available, tension can be checked with moderate thumb pressure applied to the belt at its longest span midway between pulleys. If the belt has a free span less than twelve inches, it should deflect approximately 1/8–1/4 inch. If the span is longer than twelve inches, deflection should range between 1/8–3/8 inch. To adjust the belt:

1. Loosen the driven accessory's pivot and mounting bolts.

2. Move the accessory toward or away from the engine until the tension is correct. You may use a wooden hammer handle or broomstick as a lever, but do not use any metallic prybar.

3. Tighten the bolts and recheck the tension. If new belts have been installed, run the engine for a few minutes, then recheck the belt tension adjustment. It is better to have belts too loose than too tight, because overtight belts

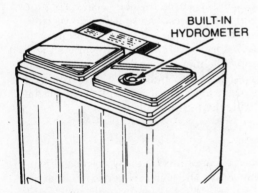

BUILT-IN HYDROMETER

Location of indicator on sealed battery

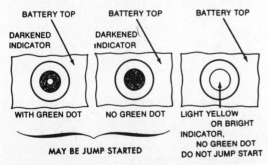

BATTERY TOP — DARKENED INDICATOR — WITH GREEN DOT

BATTERY TOP — DARKENED INDICATOR — NO GREEN DOT

MAY BE JUMP STARTED

BATTERY TOP — LIGHT YELLOW OR BRIGHT INDICATOR, NO GREEN DOT — DO NOT JUMP START

Check the appearance of the charge indicator on top of the battery before attempting a jump start; if it's not green or dark, do not jump start the car

HOW TO SPOT WORN V-BELTS

V-Belts are vital to efficient engine operation—they drive the fan, water pump and other accessories. They require little maintenance (occasional tightening) but they will not last forever. Slipping or failure of the V-belt will lead to overheating. If your V-belt looks like any of these, it should be replaced.

Cracking or weathering

This belt has deep cracks, which cause it to flex. Too much flexing leads to heat build-up and premature failure. These cracks can be caused by using the belt on a pulley that is too small. Notched belts are available for small diameter pulleys.

Softening (grease and oil)

Oil and grease on a belt can cause the belt's rubber compounds to soften and separate from the reinforcing cords that hold the belt together. The belt will first slip, then finally fail altogether.

Glazing

Glazing is caused by a belt that is slipping. A slipping belt can cause a run-down battery, erratic power steering, overheating or poor accessory performance. The more the belt slips, the more glazing will be built up on the surface of the belt. The more the belt is glazed, the more it will slip. If the glazing is light, tighten the belt.

Worn cover

The cover of this belt is worn off and is peeling away. The reinforcing cords will begin to wear and the belt will shortly break. When the belt cover wears in spots or has a rough jagged appearance, check the pulley grooves for roughness.

Separation

This belt is on the verge of breaking and leaving you stranded. The layers of the belt are separating and the reinforcing cords are exposed. It's just a matter of time before it breaks completely.

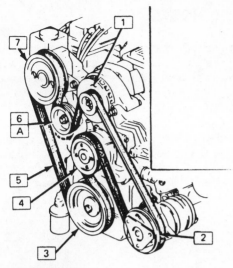

1. Generator pulley
2. A/C compressor
3. Crankshaft balancer
4. Water pump pulley
5. Serpentine belt
6. Belt tensioner
7. P/S pump pulley
A. Rotate drive belt tensioner in direction of arrow in order to install or remove drive belt.

Serpentine drive belt routing with A/C

will lead to bearing failure, particularly in the water pump or alternator. However, loose belts place an extremely high impact load on the driven component due to the whipping action of the belt.

NOTE: *Some engines use a single, serpentine belt to drive all accessory components. Adjustment of this type of belt is maintained by a spring-loaded tensioner. Never attempt to force the tensioner in order to tighten a serpentine belt.*

Hoses

Upper and lower radiator hoses and all heater hoses should be checked for deterioration, leaks and loose hose clamps every 15,000 miles. To remove the hoses, allow the engine to cool completely, then drain the radiator.

CAUTION: *When draining the coolant, keep in mind that cats and dogs are attracted by the ethelyne glycol antifreeze, and are quite likely to drink any that is left in an uncovered container or in puddles on the ground. This will prove fatal in sufficient quantity. Always drain the coolant into a sealable container. Coolant should be reused unless it is contaminated or several years old.*

Loosen the hose clamps at each end of the hose to be removed, then work the hose back and forth while twisting to slide it off its connec-

tion. If the hose seems tight, or stuck due to corrosion, use a razor knife to slice the connection end and peel the hose free. Do not use excessive force on the radiator connections or you may break the solder bead and cause a leak which requires removing the radiator to repair. Position the hose clamp about ¼ in. from the end of the new hose and tighten them securely. Do not overtighten the hose clamps.

Cooling System

Once a month, the engine coolant level should be checked. This is quickly and easily accomplished by simply looking at the level of coolant in the recovery tank (the translucent tank mounted next to the radiator and connected to the filler neck by a small hose). As long as coolant is visible in the tank between the "Full Cold" and "Full Hot" marks, the radiator level is correct.

If coolant is needed, a 50/50 mix of ethylene glycol-base antifreeze and clear water should always be used for additions, both winter and summer. This is imperative on cars with air conditioning; without the antifreeze, the heater core could freeze when the air conditioning is used. Add coolant to the recovery tank through the capped opening and make additions only when the engine is cold. The radiator cap should be checked at the same time as the coolant level. Inspect the gasket for any obvious tears, cracks or swelling, or for any signs of incorrect seating in the radiator neck.

CAUTION: *To avoid injury when opening the radiator, cover the cap with a thick cloth and wear a heavy glove to protect your hand. Turn the radiator cap slowly to the first stop and allow any residual pressure to vent (indicated when the hissing noise stops) before pressing down and removing the cap completely.*

FLUSHING THE COOLING SYSTEM

The cooling system should be drained, flushed and refilled every two years or 30,000 miles, according to the manufacturer's recommendations. However, many mechanics prefer to change the coolant every year as cheap insurance against corrosion, overheating or freezing.

CAUTION: *When draining the coolant, keep in mind that cats and dogs are attracted by the ethelyne glycol antifreeze, and are quite likely to drink any that is left in an uncovered container or in puddles on the ground. This will prove fatal in sufficient quantity. Always drain the coolant into a sealable container. Coolant should be reused unless it is contaminated or several years old.*

HOW TO SPOT BAD HOSES

Both the upper and lower radiator hoses are called upon to perform difficult jobs in an inhospitable environment. They are subject to nearly 18 psi at under hood temperatures often over 280°F., and must circulate nearly 7500 gallons of coolant an hour—3 good reasons to have good hoses.

A good test for any hose is to feel it for soft or spongy spots. Frequently these will appear as swollen areas of the hose. The most likely cause is oil soaking. This hose could burst at any time, when hot or under pressure.

Swollen hose

Cracked hoses can usually be seen but feel the hoses to be sure they have not hardened; a prime cause of cracking. This hose has cracked down to the reinforcing cords and could split at any of the cracks.

Cracked hose

Weakened clamps frequently are the cause of hose and cooling system failure. The connection between the pipe and hose has deteriorated enough to allow coolant to escape when the engine is hot.

Frayed hose end (due to weak clamp)

Debris, rust and scale in the cooling system can cause the inside of a hose to weaken. This can usually be felt on the outside of the hose as soft or thinner areas.

Debris in cooling system

1. Allow the engine to cool completely and remove the radiator cap.

2. With the radiator cap removed, start and idle the engine until heat can be felt in the upper radiator hose, indicating that the thermostat has opened. Move the heater controls to the maximum HEAT position to allow the heater control valve to open.

3. Stop the engine and open the drain cock located at the bottom of the radiator. Be careful as the coolant will be hot.

4. Close the radiator drain cock and refill the cooling system with clear water. A cooling system flushing compound and/or cleaner can be added if desired.

5. Start the engine and allow it to warm up again, then turn the ignition OFF.

6. Open the radiator drain cock again, then flush the system by slowly adding fresh water through the radiator until the water from the drain cock runs clear.

7. Clean the coolant recovery tank. Remove the cap (leaving the hoses in place) and then remove the recovery tank and drain it of any coolant. Clean the tank with soap and water, then rinse with clear water and reinstall.

8. Close the drain cock and fill the radiator with a 50/50 mix of ethylene glycol base antifreeze and water to the base of the filler neck. Fill the recovery tank with the same solution to the "FULL HOT" mark and install the recovery tank cap.

9. Start and run the engine until the upper radiator hose is hot again (radiator cap still off), then top off the radiator with the 50/50 mix until the coolant level again reaches the bottom of the filler neck.

10. Turn the engine off and install the radiator cap, aligning the arrows on the cap with the overflow tube on the filler neck. Turn off the heater and check for leaks.

Air Conditioning

The air conditioning system requires no routine maintenance, except for periodic belt tension adjustment as described earlier. The A/C system should be operated for at least five minutes every week (even during the winter) to circulate the lubricating oil within the system and to prevent the various seals from drying out. The factory-installed air conditioning unit has no sight glass for checking the refrigerant level. Due to the potentially hazardous service procedures, it is recommended that all air conditioning repair and maintenance be left to a qualified technician.

NOTE: *This book contains simple testing procedures for your N-Body's air conditioning system. More comprehensive testing, diagnosis and service procedures may be found in CHILTON'S GUIDE TO AIR CONDITIONING SERVICE AND REPAIR, book part number 7580, available at most book stores and auto parts stores, or available directly from Chilton Co.*

SAFETY PRECAUTIONS

There are two particular hazards associated with air conditioning systems and they both relate to the refrigerant gas commonly known as Freon or R-12. First, the gas is an extremely cold substance. When exposed to air, it will instantly freeze any surface it comes in contact with, including your eyes. The other hazard relates to fire. Although normally non-toxic, refrigerant gas becomes highly poisonous in the presence of an open flame. One good whiff of the vapor formed by burning refrigerant can be fatal. Keep all forms of fire (including cigarettes) well clear of the air conditioning system. Any repair work to an air conditioning system should be left to a professional. DO NOT, under any circumstances, attempt to loosen or tighten any fittings or perform any work other than that outlined here.

Checking for Oil Leaks

Refrigerant leaks show up only as oily areas on the various components because the compressor oil is transported around the entire system along with the refrigerant. Look for oily spots on all the hoses and lines, and especially on the hose and tube connections. If there are oily deposits, the system may have a leak and you should have it checked by a qualified repairman.

NOTE: *A small area of oil on the front of the compressor is normal and no cause for alarm.*

Checking Compressor Belt Tension

Refer to the section in this chapter on "Drive Belts".

Cleaning The Condenser

Periodically inspect the front of the condenser for bent fins or foreign material (dirt, bugs, leaves, etc.) If any cooling fins are bent, straighten them carefully with needle nose pliers. You can remove any debris with a stiff bristle brush or hose.

Windshield Wipers

For maximum effectiveness and longest element life, the windshield and wiper blades should be kept clean. Dirt, tree sap, road tar and so on will cause streaking, smearing and blade deterioration if left on the glass. Wash

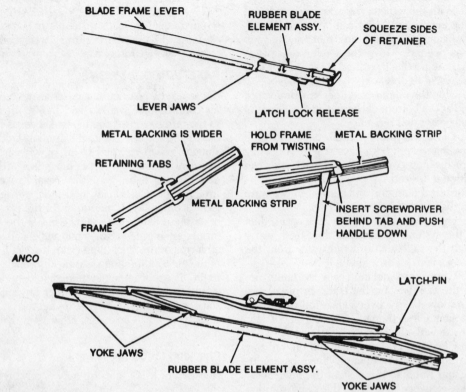

TRICO

BLADE FRAME LEVER

RUBBER BLADE ELEMENT ASSY.

SQUEEZE SIDES OF RETAINER

LEVER JAWS

LATCH LOCK RELEASE

METAL BACKING IS WIDER

RETAINING TABS

HOLD FRAME FROM TWISTING

METAL BACKING STRIP

METAL BACKING STRIP

FRAME

INSERT SCREWDRIVER BEHIND TAB AND PUSH HANDLE DOWN

ANCO

LATCH-PIN

YOKE JAWS

RUBBER BLADE ELEMENT ASSY.

YOKE JAWS

The rubber wiper element can be changed without replacing the entire blade assembly. Your N-Body may have either one of these blades

the windshield with a commercial glass cleaner, then wipe the wiper blades with the damp cloth when finished to remove deposits on the rubber.

Inspect the blades for signs of deterioration and replace any that are found to be cracked, broken or torn. Replacement intervals vary with usage, but ozone deterioration usually limits blade life to about one year. If the wiper pattern is smeared or streaked or if the wiper chatters when moving across the glass, replace the blades with refill elements available. The elements should always be replaced in pairs.

WIPER REFILL REPLACEMENT

Normally, if the wipers are not cleaning the windshield properly, only the refill has to be replaced. The blade and arm usually require replacement only in the event of damage. It is only necessary (except on Tridon refills) to remove the arm or the blade to replace the refill, though you may have to position the arm higher on the glass. You can do this by turning the ignition switch on and operating the wipers. When they are positioned where they are accessible, turn the ignition switch off. There are several types of refills and your vehicle could

have any kind, since aftermarket blades and arms may not use exactly the same type refill as the original equipment. The original equipment wiper elements can be replaced as follows:

1. Lift the wiper arm off the glass.
2. Depress the release lever on the center bridge and remove the blade from the arm.
3. Lift the tab and pinch the end bridge to release it from the center bridge.
4. Slide the end bridge from the wiper blade and the wiper blade from the opposite end bridge.
5. Install a new element and be sure the tab on the end bridge is down to lock the element in place. Check each release point for positive engagement.

Most Trico styles use a release button that is pushed down to allow the refill to slide out of the release jaws. The new refill slide in and locks in place. Some Trico refills are removed by locating where the metal backing strip or the refill is wider. Insert a small screwdriver blade between the frame and the metal backing strip. Press down to release the refill from the retaining tab.

The Anco style is unlocked at one end by

squeezing two metal tabs, and the refill is slid out of the frame jaws. When the new refill is installed, the tabs will click into place, locking the refill. The polycarbonate type is held in place by a locking lever that is pushed downward out of the groove in the arm to free the refill. When the new refill is installed, it will lock in place automatically.

The Tridon refill has a plastic backing strip with a notch about an inch from the end. Hold the blade (frame) on a hard surface so that the frame is tightly bowed. Grip the tip of the backing strip and pull up while twisting counterclockwise. The backing strip will snap out of the retaining tab. Do this for the remaining tabs until the refill is free of the arm. The length of these refills is molded into the end and they should be replaced with identical types. No matter which type of refill you use, be sure that all of the frame claws engage the refill. Before operating the wipers, be sure that no part of the metal frame is contacting the windshield.

Tires

INFLATION PRESSURE

Tire inflation is the most ignored item of auto maintenance. Gasoline mileage can drop as much as .8% for every 1 pound per square inch (psi) of under inflation. The air pressure should be checked weekly to ensure maximum fuel economy and tire life. Check the tire pressure (including the spare) regularly with a pocket type gauge. Kicking the tires won't tell you a thing, and the gauge on the service station air hose is notoriously inaccurate.

The tire pressures recommended for your car are usually found on the door post or in the owner's manual. Ideally, inflation pressure should be checked when the tires are cool. When the air becomes heated it expands and the pressure increases. Every 10° rise (or drop) in temperature means a difference of 1 psi, which also explains why the tire appears to lose air on a very cold night. When it is impossible

Tread wear indicators will appear as bands across the tread when the tire is due for replacement

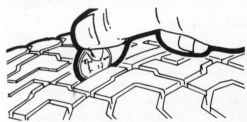

You can use a penny for tread wear checks; if the top of Lincoln's head is visible in two adjacent grooves, the tire should be replaced

Inexpensive gauges are also available for measuring tread wear

to check the tires "cold," allow for pressure build-up due to heat. If the "hot" pressure exceeds the "cold" pressure by more than 15 psi, reduce your speed, load or both. Otherwise internal heat is created in the tire. When the heat approaches the temperature at which the tire was cured during manufacture, the tread can separate from the body. Before starting a long trip with lots of luggage, you can add about 2–4 psi to the tires to make them run cooler, but never exceed the maximum inflation pressure on the side of the tire.

CAUTION: *Never counteract excessive pressure build-up by bleeding off air pressure (letting some air out). This will only further raise the tire operating temperature.*

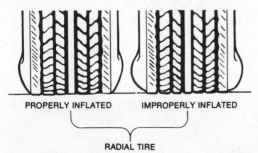

PROPERLY INFLATED   IMPROPERLY INFLATED

RADIAL TIRE

Don't judge a radial tire's pressure by its appearance. An improperly inflated radial tire looks similar to a properly inflated one

TREAD DEPTH

All tires have 8 built-in tread wear indicator bars that show up as ½ in. wide smooth bands across the tire when ¹⁄₁₆ in. of tread remains. The appearance of tread wear indicators means that the tires should be replaced. In fact, many states have laws prohibiting the use of tires with less than ¹⁄₁₆ in. tread. You can check your own tread depth with an inexpensive gauge or by using a Lincoln head penny. Slip the Lincoln penny into several tread grooves. If you can see the top of Lincoln's head in 2 adjacent grooves, the tires have less than ¹⁄₁₆ in. tread left and should be replaced. You can measure snow tires in the same manner by using the "tails" side of the Lincoln penny. If you can see the top of the Lincoln memorial, it's time to replace the snow tires.

TIRE ROTATION

Tire wear can be equalized by switching the position of the tires about every 6000 miles. Including a conventional spare in the rotation pattern can give up to 20% more tire life, but the smaller "Spacesaver" spare tires cannot be rotated since they are designed for emergency use only. Studded snow tires should not be rotated, and radials should be kept on the same side of the car (maintain the same direction of rotation). The belts on radial tires get set in a pattern. If the direction of rotation is reversed, it can cause rough ride and vibration.

> NOTE: *When radials or studded snows are taken off the car, mark them, so you can maintain the same direction of rotation. Torque the wheel nuts to 80 ft. lbs. (110 Nm).*

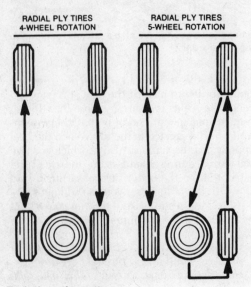

Typical rotation patterns

TIRE STORAGE

Store the tires at proper inflation pressure if they are mounted on wheels. All tires should be kept in a cool, dry place. If they are stored in the garage or basement, do not let them stand on a concrete floor, set them on strips of wood.

Fuel Filter

Fuel Injected Engines

All models equipped with fuel injection use a pressurized fuel system. Any time the fuel system is serviced, the fuel pressure must be relieved before attempting to remove any fuel lines. The fuel filter is located on the rear crossmember of the vehicle, near the fuel tank, mounted in-line by two screw-type fittings. Before loosening the fuel connections, first remove the fuel pump fuse from the fuse box, then start and run the engine until it stalls. Crank the starter for three seconds to make sure all fuel pressure is relieved from the system, then turn the ignition OFF and replace the fuse. If this procedure is not followed, the fuel will spray when the connections are loosened. Always use a backup wrench when removing or installing fuel connections and make sure the O-rings are installed properly. Tighten the fuel fittings to 22 ft. lbs. (30 Nm).

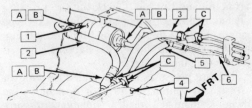

1. Fuel filter
2. Fuel Feed hose
3. Fuel return hose
4. Fuel tank
5. Vapor hose
6. Rear brake crossover pipe
A. 30 N·m (22 ft. lbs.)
B. Use backup wrench at all screw couple locations also make sure a good "O" ring is installed at these locations
C. Lubricate hose ends for installation

Typical fuel filter installation

FLUIDS AND LUBRICANTS

Fuel

N-Body cars with gasoline engines are designed to use only unleaded gasoline, with an

Capacities

Year	Eng. V.I.N. Code	Engine Displacement (Cu. In.)	Eng. Mfg.	Crankcase Quarts		Transaxle Pints		Gas Tank Gal	Cooling System Qts	
				w/filter	wo/filter	5 speed	Auto.		w/heater	w/AC
'85–'86	U	4-151	Pont.	3	3	5.3	8②	13.6	7.8	7.9
	L	6-183	Buick	①	4	5.3	8②	13.6	7.8	7.9

① Fill to mark on dipstick
② 12 pts. if drained completely

octane rating of at least 87. Using leaded gasoline can damage the emission control system by decreasing the effectiveness of the catalyst in the catalytic converter and by damaging the oxygen sensor which is part of the Computer Command Control System. Do not use gasolines containing more than 5 percent methanol even if they contain cosolvents and corrosion inhibitors. Although gasolines containing 5 percent or less methanol and appropriate cosolvents and inhibitors for methanol may be suitable for use in your car, General Motors does not endorse their use, at this time.

Engine Oil

Engine oils are labeled on the containers with various API (American Petroleum Institute) designations of quality. For gasoline engines, make sure that the oil you use has the API designation "SF", either alone or shown with other designations such as SF/CC or SF/CD. Oils with a label on which the designation "SF" does not appear should not be used.

Engine oil viscosity (thickness) should be considered according to temperature weather conditions. Lower viscosity engine oils can provide better fuel economy; however, higher temperature weather conditions require higher viscosity engine oils for satisfactory lubrication. When selecting an oil viscosity, consider the

range of temperature your car will be operated in before the next oil change.

OIL LEVEL CHECK

At every fuel stop, check the engine oil in the following manner:

1. Park the car on a level area.
2. The engine oil may be either hot or cold when checking the oil level. However, if it is hot, wait a few minutes after the engine has been shut off to allow the oil to drain back into the oil pan. If the engine is cold, do not start it before checking the oil level.
3. Open the engine compartment and locate the dipstick. Pull the dipstick from its tube, wipe it clean and reinsert it.

NOTE: *Make sure the dipstick is fully seated when checking the oil level to assure accurate readings.*

4. Pull the dipstick out again and while holding it horizontally, read the oil level. The oil level should be above the "ADD" line but not above the "FULL" line. Do not overfill.

OIL AND FILTER CHANGE

The milage figure given in the "Maintenance Intervals" chart are the General Motors recommended intervals for oil and filter changes assuming average driving. If your car is being driven under dusty conditions, or used regularly for trailer towing, cut the milage intervals in half. The same thing goes for cars driven in stop-and-go traffic or for only short distances.

Always drain the oil after the engine has been running long enough to bring it to operating temperature. Hot oil will flow easier and more contaminants will be removed along with the oil than if it were drained cold. You will need a large capacity drain pan which you can purchase at any auto store. Another necessity is containers for used oil. You will find that plastic bottles such as those used for detergents, bleaches etc., make excellent storage jugs. One ecologically desirable solution to the used oil disposal problem is to find a cooperative gas station owner who will allow you to dump your used oil into his tank. Do not, under any circumstances, dispose of used engine oil by

Engine oil viscosity chart

GASOLINE FUELED

ITEM NO.	TO BE SERVICED	WHEN TO PERFORM Miles (Kilometers) or Months, Whichever Occurs First	The services shown in this schedule up to 48,000 miles (60,000 km) are to be performed after 48,000 miles of the same intervals															
		MILES (000)	3	6	9	12	15	18	21	24	27	30	33	36	39	42	45	48
		KILOMETERS (000)	5	10	15	20	25	30	35	40	45	50	55	60	65	70	75	80
1	Engine Oil & Oil Filter Change*	Every 3,000 mi. (5 000 km) or 3 mos	•	•	•	•	•	•	•	•	•	•	•	•	•	•	•	•
2	Chassis Lubrication	Every other oil change		•		•		•		•		•		•		•		•
3	Carb. Choke & Hose Insp.*	At 6,000 mi. (10 000 km) and then every 30,000 mi (50 000 km)		•								•**						
4	Carb or TBI Mounting Bolt Torque*	At 6,000 mi. (10 000 km) only	•**															
5	Eng. Idle Speed Adj. (Some Models)*		•**															
6	Vac. or Air Pump Drive Belt Insp.*	Every 30,000 mi. (50 000 km) or 24 mos.										•**						
7	Cooling System Refill*											•						
8	Wheel Brg. Repack (Rear Wheel Drive Cars Only)	See explanation for service interval																
9	Transmission/Transaxle Service																	
10	Vac. Advance System Insp. (Some Models)*	Every 30,000 mi. (50 000 km)										•						
11	Spark Plug and Wire Service *											•**						
12	PCV Valve Insp.*											•						
13	EGR System Service*	Every 30,000 mi. (50 000 km) or 36 mos.										•						
14	Air Cleaner & PCV Filter Repl.*											•**						
15	Eng. Timing Check*											•						
16	Fuel Tank, Cap & Lines Insp.*	Every 30,000 mi. (50 000 km)										•						
17	Thermostatically Controlled Air Cleaner*											•						

Follow Schedule II if, as a general rule, the car is driven on a daily basis for several miles (km) and none of the above conditions apply.

GASOLINE FUELED

ITEM NO.	TO BE SERVICED	WHEN TO PERFORM Miles (kilometers) or Months, Whichever Occurs First	The services shown in this schedule up to 45,000 miles (75,000 km) are to be performed after 45,000 miles at the same intervals					
		MILES (000)	7.5	15	22.5	30	37.5	45
		KILOMETERS (000)	12.5	25	37.5	50	62.5	75
1	Engine Oil Change*	Every 7,500 mi. (12500 km) or 12 mos.	•	•	•	•	•	•
	*Filter Change†	At first and every other oil change or 12mos.	•		•		•	
2	Chassis Lubrication	Every 7,500 mi. (12500 km) or 12 mos.	•	•	•	•	•	•
3	Carb. Choke & Hose Insp.*	At 7,500 mi. (12500 km) and 30,000 mi. (50000 km)	•			•**		
4	Carb. or TBI Mounting Bolt Torque*	At 7,500 mi. (12500 km) only	•**					
5	Eng. Idle Speed Adj. (Some Models)*		•**					
6	Vac or Air Pump Drive Belt Insp.*	Every 30,000 mi. (50000 km) or 24 mos.				•**		
7	Cooling System Refill*					•		
8	Wheel Brg. Repack (Rear Wheel Drive Cars Only)	Every 30,000 mi. (50000 km)				•		
9	Transmission/Transaxle Service	See explanation for service interval						
10	Vac Advance System Insp. (Some Models)*	Every 30,000 mi. (50000 km)				•		
11	Spark Plug and Wire Service *					•**		
12	PCV Valve Insp.*					•		
13	EGR System Service*	Every 30,000 mi. (50000 km) or 36 mos.				•		
14	Air Cleaner & PCV Filter Repl.*					•**		
15	Eng. Timing Check*					•		
16	Fuel Tank, Cap & Lines Insp.*	Every 30,000 mi. (50000 km)				•		
17	Thermostatically Controlled Air Cleaner*					•		

Follow Schedule I if the car is operated under one or more of the following conditions:

- Operating when outside temperatures remain below freezing and when most trips are less than 4 miles (6 km); or
- Idling for extended periods and/or low speed operation such as in door-to-door delivery;

Also follow Schedule I when:

- Towing a trailer;
- Operating in dusty areas; or
- Using the car in taxi, police car, delivery or daily rental service.

FOOTNOTES: *An Emission Control Service.
**In California, these are the minimum Emission Control Maintenance Services an owner must perform according to the California Air Resources Board. General Motors, however, urges that all Emission Control Maintenance Services shown above be performed. To maintain the other new car warranties, all services shown should be performed.

Typical gasoline engine maintenance schedule

dumping it down a convenient drain. This not only pollutes the environment, it is a violation of federal law. Used engine oil is also suspected of being a carcinogenic (cancer-causing) substance. Avoid prolonged skin contact and/or wearing oil-soaked clothing while working on the vehicle.

General Motors recommends changing both the oil and filter during the first oil change and the filter every other oil change thereafter. For the small price of an oil filter, its cheap insurance to replace the filter at every oil change. One of the larger filter manufacturers points out in its advertisements that not changing the filter leaves a quanity of dirty oil in the engine, which could be as much as a quart on some models. This claim is true and should be kept in mind when changing your oil. Change your oil as follows:

1. Run the engine until it reaches normal operating temperature.

2. Jack up the car and support it safely with jackstands.

3. Slide a drain pan under the oil pan.

4. Loosen the drain plug. Turn the plug out by hand. By keeping an inward pressure on the plug as you unscrew it, oil won't escape past the threads and you can remove it without being burnt with hot oil.

5. Allow the oil to drain completely and then install the drain plug. Be careful not to over-tighten the plug and strip the threads in the oil pan.

6. Using a strap wrench, remove the oil filter. Keep in mind that it's holding dirty, hot oil.

7. Empty the old filter into the drain pan and dispose of the filter.

8. Using a clean rag, wipe off the filter adapter on the engine block. Be sure that the rag doesn't leave any lint which could clog an oil passage.

9. Coat the rubber gasket on the new filter with fresh oil. Spin it onto the engine by hand; when the gasket touches the adapter surface give it another ½–¾ turn. Do not overtighten or you may crush the gasket and cause it to leak.

10. Refill the engine with the correct amount of fresh oil.

11. Check the oil level on the dipstick. It is normal for the level to be a bit above the full mark. Start the engine and allow it to idle a few minutes.

CAUTION: *Do not run the engine above idle speed until it has built up oil pressure, indicated when the oil light goes out.*

12. Shut off the engine, allow the oil to drain for a minute, and check the oil level. Check around the filter and drain plug for any leaks and correct as necessary.

Automatic Transaxle

FLUID RECOMMENDATION AND LEVEL CHECK

The automatic transaxle fluid level should be checked at each engine oil change. When adding or changing the automatic transaxle fluid use only fluid labeled Dexron®II.

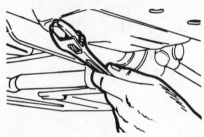

The oil drain plug is located at the lowest point of the oil pan

Use an oil filter strap wrench to remove the oil filter; install the new filter by hand

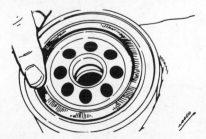

Apply a thin film of clean oil to the new filter gasket to prevent it from tearing upon installation

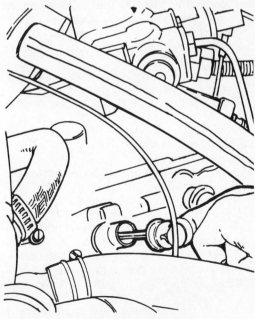

Automatic transaxle fluid dipstick and filler hole location

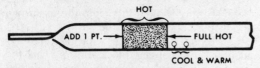

Automatic transaxle dipstick markings

1. Set the parking brake and start the engine with the transaxle in "P" (Park).

2. With the service brakes applied, move the shift lever through all the gear ranges, ending in "P" (Park).

NOTE: *The fluid level must be checked with the engine running at slow idle, the car level and the fluid at least at room temperature. The correct fluid level cannot be read if you have just driven the car for a long time at high speed, city traffic in hot weather or if the car has been pulling a trailer. In these cases, wait at least 30 minutes for the fluid to cool down.*

3. Remove the dipstick located at the rear end of the engine compartment, wipe it clean, then push it back in until the cap seats.

4. Pull the dipstick out and read the fluid level. The level should be in the cross-hatched area of the dipstick.

5. Add fluid using a long plastic funnel in the dipstick tube. Keep in mind that it only takes one pint of fluid to raise the level from "ADD" to "FULL" with a hot transaxle.

DRAIN AND REFILL

Under normal operating conditions, the automatic transmission fluid only needs to be changed every 100,000 miles, according to General Motors, unless one or more of the following driving conditions is encountered. In the following cases the fluid and filter should be changed every 15,000 miles:

a. Driving in heavy traffic when the outside temperature reaches 90°F.

b. Driving regularly in hilly or mountainous areas.

c. Towing a trailer.

d. Using a vehicle as a taxi or police car or for delivery purposes.

Remember, these are factory recommendations, and in this case are considered to be minimum. You must determine a change interval which fits your driving habits. If your vehicle is never subjected to these conditions, a 100,000 mile change interval is adequate. If you are a normal driver, a two-year/30,000 mile interval will be more than sufficient to maintain the long life for which your automatic transaxle was designed.

NOTE: *Use only fluid labeled Dexron®II. Use of other fluids could cause erratic shifting and transmission damage.*

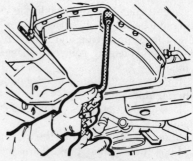

Many late model vehicles have no drain plug. Loosen the pan bolts and allow one corner of the pan to tilt slightly to drain the fluid

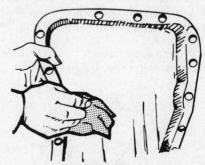

Clean the pan thoroughly with gasoline and allow to air dry completely

Install a new gasket on the pan

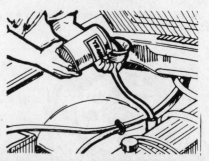

Fill the transmission with the required amount of fluid. Do not overfill. Start the engine and shift through all gears. Check the fluid level and add fluid if necessary

1. Jack up the vehicle and support it safely with jackstands.

2. Remove the front and side pan bolts.

3. Loosen the rear bolts about four turns.

4. Carefully pry the oil pan loose and allow the fluid to drain.

5. Remove the remaining bolts, the pan, and the gasket or RTV sealant. Discard the old gasket.

6. Clean the pan with solvent and dry it thoroughly, with compressed air.

7. Remove the strainer and O-ring seal.

8. Install a new strainer and O-ring seal, locating the strainer against the dipstick stop.

NOTE: *Always replace the filter with a new one. Do not attempt to clean the old one.*

9. Install a new gasket or RTV sealant then tighten the pan bolts to 12 ft. lbs.

10. Lower the car and add about 4 quarts of Dexron®II transmission fluid.

11. Start the engine; let it idle. Block the wheels and apply the parking brake.

12. Move the shift lever through the ranges. With the lever in Park, check the fluid level and add as necessary.

NOTE: *The transmission fluid currently being used may appear to be darker and have a strong odor. This is normal and not a sign of required maintenance or transmission failure.*

Manual Transaxle

The fluid in the manual transaxle should be changed at the interval specified in the "Maintenance Intervals" chart, or more often if the car is driven under severe conditions. You may want to change it if you purchased your N-Body used or if it has been driven in water deep enough to reach the transaxle case.

1. The fluid should be hot before being drained. If the car is driven until the engine is at normal operating temperature, the fluid should be hot enough.

2. Remove the filler plug from the left side of the transaxle to provide a vent.

3. The drain plug is located on the bottom of the transaxle case. Place a pan under the drain plug and remove it.

CAUTION: *The fluid will be HOT. Press up against the threads as you loosen the plug to prevent leakage.*

4. Allow the fluid to drain completely. Check the condition of the plug gasket and replace it if necessary. Clean the plug and install it with the gasket, tightening until it is snug. Do not overtighten.

5. Fill the transaxle with fluid through the filler hole in the left side. Use only Dexron®II automatic transmission fluid to fill the transaxle. Do not use conventional manual transmission lubricants. You will need a long necked funnel or a funnel and hose to pour through. Check the lubricant capacity in the "Capacities" chart; do not overfill.

6. The transaxle fluid should come right up to the edge of the filler hole. You can stick your finger in to verify this level, but watch out for sharp threads.

7. Replace the filler plug. Dispose of the old fluid in the same manner as used engine oil. Road test the car, stop on a level surface and recheck the fluid level.

Brake Master Cylinder

The brake fluid reservoir is part of the brake master cylinder, and is located under the front engine compartment lid, on the driver's side of the car. Check the fluid level each time your engine oil is changed. It should be noted that brake fluid can absorb moisture from the air, which reduces effectiveness and can corrode brake parts once in the system. Never leave the master cylinder cover off any longer than necessary. If the brake fluid level is constantly

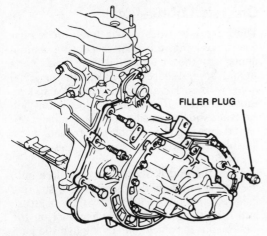

FILLER PLUG

Manual transaxle filler plug

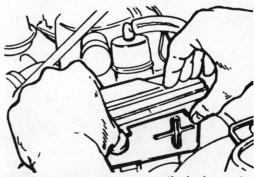

Use thumb pressure to remove the brake master cylinder cover

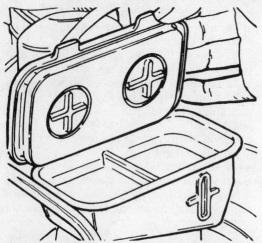

Proper brake fluid level; non-power brakes do not have the see-through window on the side of the reservoir

proved power steering fluid, NOT transmission fluid.

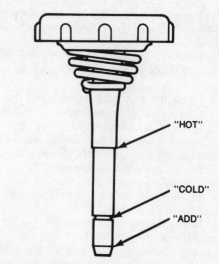

Power steering dipstick markings

low, the system should be checked for leaks, but it is normal for the fluid level to drop about ⅛ inch for every 10,000 miles of brake pad wear.

FLUID LEVEL CHECK

The master cylinder reservoir cover is retained by a bail wire. To remove the wire, pry it off with a screwdriver or other suitable tool. The levels in both the front and rear chambers must be maintained at a point about ¼ inch below the top of the chamber. Delco Supreme No. 11 or other DOT 3 specification brake fluid is used in most cars; add as necessary. Note, however, that some cars may come filled with silicone based brake fluid. In these cases, only silicone based fluid may be added to the system. Never mix DOT 3 and silicone fluids!

CAUTION: *Do not allow anyone to depress the brake pedal while the brake fluid reservoir cover is removed. Also, brake fluid will remove paint. If spilled, flush the area immediately with water.*

Power Steering Pump

FLUID LEVEL CHECK

The power steering hydraulic fluid reservoir level is checked in one of two manners. Some models use a dipstick attached to the underside of the reservoir cap, while others use a clear reservoir bottle with level gradations marked on the side. The fluid level can be checked with the fluid hot or cold, but the car should be parked on a level surface. Check the power steering fluid every 12 months or 7,500 miles, whichever comes first. If the fluid level is low, add power steering fluid until the level is correct. Be careful not to overfill and use ap-

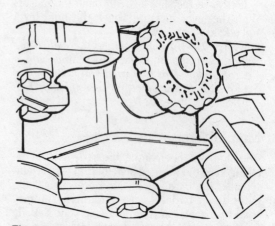

The power steering reservoir dipstick is attached to the cap; the four cylinder reservoir is right up front, behind the radiator

Chassis Lubrication

There are only two areas which require regular chassis greasing; the front suspension components and the steering linkage. These parts should be greased every 12 months or 7,500 miles with an EP grease meeting GM specification 6031M. If you choose to do this job yourself, you will need to purchase a hand-operated grease gun (if not already owned) and a flexible extension hose to reach the various grease fittings.

Press the end of the grease gun hose onto the grease fitting on the suspension or steering linkage component. Pump a few shots of grease into the fitting, until the rubber boot on the joint begins to expand, indicating that the joint is full. Remove the gun from the fitting. Be

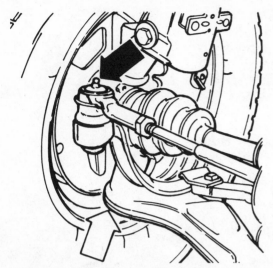

Grease the steering linkage at the knuckle (black arrow) and the ball joint at the lower arm (above the white arrow)

careful not to overfill the joints, which will rupture the rubber boots and allow the entry of dirt and water.

Every 12 months or 7,500 miles, the various linkages and hinges on the chassis and body should be lubricated as follows:

TRANSAXLE SHIFT LINKAGE

Lubricate the manual transaxle shift linkage contact points with EP grease used for chassis greasing (GM specification 6031M). The automatic transaxle linkage should be lubricated with clean engine oil.

HOOD LATCH AND HINGES

Clean the latch surfaces and apply clean engine oil to the latch pilot bolts and the spring anchor. Use engine oil to lubricate the hood hinges as well. Use a chassis grease to lubricate all the pivot points in the latch release mechanism.

DOOR HINGES

The gas tank filler door, car door and rear hatch or trunk lid hinges should be wiped clean and lubricated with clean engine oil. Silicone spray also works well on these parts, but must be applied more often. Use engine oil to lubricate the trunk or hatch lock mechanism and the lock bolt and striker. The door lock cylinders can be lubricated easily with a shot of silicone spray or one of the may dry penetrating lubricants commercially available.

PARKING BRAKE LINKAGE

Use chassis grease on the parking brake cable where it contacts the guides, links, levers and pulleys. The grease should be water resistant for durability in use under the car.

PUSHING AND TOWING

The N-Body cars may not be pushed or towed to start, since doing so may cause the catalytic converter to explode. If the battery is weak, the engine may be jump started using the procedure outlined in the following section.

Your N-Body may be towed on all four wheels at speeds less than 35 mph for distances up to 50 miles. The driveline and steering must be normally operable. If either one is damaged, the car may not be flat-towed. If the car is flat-towed (on all four wheels), the steering must be unlocked, the transaxle shifted into neutral and the parking brake released. Towing attachments must be made to the main structural members of the chassis, not to the bumpers or sheetmetal.

The car may be towed on its rear wheels by a wrecker; make sure that safety chains are used. N-Body cars with manual transaxles may be towed on their front wheels for short distances and at low speeds. Be sure the transaxle is in

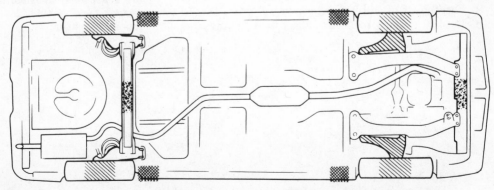

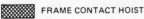 FRAME CONTACT HOIST   FLOOR JACK   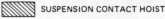 SUSPENSION CONTACT HOIST

Jacking and hoisting locations

JUMP STARTING A DEAD BATTERY

The chemical reaction in a battery produces explosive hydrogen gas. This is the safe way to jump start a dead battery, reducing the chances of an accidental spark that could cause an explosion.

Jump Starting Precautions

1. Be sure both batteries are of the same voltage.
2. Be sure both batteries are of the same polarity (have the same grounded terminal).
3. Be sure the vehicles are not touching.
4. Be sure the vent cap holes are not obstructed.
5. Do not smoke or allow sparks around the battery.
6. In cold weather, check for frozen electrolyte in the battery. Do not jump start a frozen battery.
7. Do not allow electrolyte on your skin or clothing.
8. Be sure the electrolyte is not frozen.
CAUTION: *Make certain that the ignition key, in the vehicle with the dead battery, is in the OFF position. Connecting cables to vehicles with on-board computers will result in computer destruction if the key is not in the OFF position.*

Jump Starting Procedure

1. Determine voltages of the two batteries; they must be the same.
2. Bring the starting vehicle close (they must not touch) so that the batteries can be reached easily.
3. Turn off all accessories and both engines. Put both cars in Neutral or Park and set the handbrake.
4. Cover the cell caps with a rag—do not cover terminals.
5. If the terminals on the run-down battery are heavily corroded, clean them.
6. Identify the positive and negative posts on both batteries and connect the cables in the order shown.
7. Start the engine of the starting vehicle and run it at fast idle. Try to start the car with the dead battery. Crank it for no more than 10 seconds at a time and let it cool off for 20 seconds in between tries.
8. If it doesn't start in 3 tries, there is something else wrong.
9. Disconnect the cables in the reverse order.
10. Replace the cell covers and dispose of the rags.

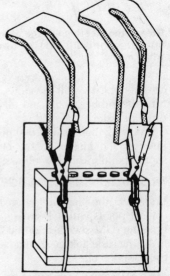

Side terminal batteries occasionally pose a problem when connecting jumper cables. There frequently isn't enough room to clamp the cables without touching sheet metal. Side terminal adaptors are available to alleviate this problem and should be removed after use.

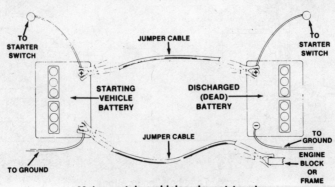

Make certain vehicles do not touch

This hook-up for negative ground cars only

Neutral. Cars with automatic transaxles should not be towed on their front wheels as transaxle damage may result. If it is impossible to tow the car on its rear wheels, place the front wheels on a dolly.

JACKING AND HOISTING

All N-Bodies are supplied with a jack for changing tires. This jack, although satisfactory for its intended purpose, is not meant to support the car while you go crawling around underneath it. Never crawl under the car while it is supported only by the bumper jack.

The car may also be jacked at the rear axle between the spring seats, or at the front end at the engine cradle crossbar or lower control arm. The car must never be lifted by the rear lower control arms. The car can be raised on a four point hoist which contacts the chassis at points just behind the front wheels and just ahead of the rear wheels. Make sure the lift pads do not contact the catalytic converter.

It is imperative that strict safety precautions be observed both while raising the car and in the subsequent support after the car is raised. If a jack is used to raise the car, the transaxle should be shifted to Park (automatic) or First gear (manual), the parking brake should be set and the opposite wheel should be blocked. Jacking should only be attempted on a hard, level surface.

CAUTION: *On front wheel drive vehicles, the center of gravity is further forward than on rear wheel drive vehicles. Whenever removing major components from the rear of the vehicle while it is supported on a hoist, take precautions to prevent the possibility of the vehicle tipping forward.*

Tune-Up and Performance Maintenance

T2

TUNE-UP PROCEDURES

In order to extract the full measure of performance and economy from your car's engine, it is essential that it be properly tuned at regular intervals. Although the recommended tune-up intervals for the N-Body are extended to 30,000 miles, a regular maintenance program is important for preventing the minor breakdowns and poor performance associated with an untuned engine. The tune-up intervals should be halved if the car is operated under severe conditions such as trailer towing, prolonged idling, continual stop-and-go driving or if starting and running problems are noticed.

An engine tune-up is a service designed to restore the maximum capability of power, performance, economy and reliability and, at the same time, assure the owner of a complete check and more lasting results in efficiency and trouble-free performance. Engine tune-up becomes increasingly important each year, to ensure that pollutant levels are in compliance with federal emissions standards. Routine mainte-

nance as described in the first chapter will have a definite effect on the results of a tune-up, especially in the area of emission control devices, filters and fluid levels.

It is advisable to follow a definite and thorough tune-up procedure. Tune-up consists of three separate steps:

1. Analysis—the process of determining whether normal wear is responsible for performance loss, and whether parts require replacement or service.

2. Parts Replacement or Service and Adjustment—where engine adjustments are returned to the original factory specifications. The extent of an engine tune-up is usually determined by the length of time since the previous service, although the type of driving and general mechanical conditioning of the engine must be considered. Specific maintenance should also be performed at regular intervals, depending on operating conditions.

3. Verification of Repair—the process of checking all work and adjustments to make sure everything was done correctly and within fac-

Tune-Up Specifications

(When analyzing compression test results, look for uniformity among cylinders rather than specific pressures.)

Year	Eng. V.I.N. Code	Eng. No. Cyl. Displacement (cu. in.)	Eng. Mfg.	hp	Spark Plugs Orig. Type	Gap (in.)	Ignition Timing (deg) Man. Trans.	Auto. Trans.	Valves Intake Opens (deg)	Fuel Pump Pressure (psi)	Idle Speed (rpm) Man. Trans.	Auto. Trans.
'85–'86	U	4-151	Pont.	54	R43TSX	.060	8B	8B	NA	NA	①	①
	L	6-183	Buick	125	R44LTS	.040	15B	15B	NA	NA	①	①

NOTE: The underhood specifications sticker often reflects tune-up specification changes made in production. Sticker figures must be used if they disagree with those in this chart.
B Before Top Dead Center
Part numbers in this chart are not recommendations by Chilton for any product by brand name
NA Not available at time of publication
① See underhood sticker

tory specifications. A persistent problem not remedied by the tune-up may require further troubleshooting and diagnosis to correct.

Troubleshooting is a logical sequence of procedures designed to lead the owner or technician to the particular cause of trouble. The Troubleshooting chapter of this manual is meant to be general in nature, yet specific enough to locate most common problems. Service usually comprises two areas; diagnosis and repair. While the apparent cause of trouble in many cases is worn or damaged parts, performance problems are less obvious. The first job is to locate the problem and cause. Once the problem has been isolated, refer to the appropriate section for repair, removal or adjustment procedures. It is advisable to read the entire chapter before beginning a tune-up.

Spark Plugs

A typical spark plug consists of a metal shell surrounding a ceramic insulator. A metal electrode extends downward through the center of the insulator and protrudes a small distance. Located at the end of the plug and attached to the side of the outer metal shell is the side electrode. The side electrode bends in at a 90° angle so that its tip is even with, and parallel to, the tip of the center electrode. The distance between these two electrodes (measured in thousandths of an inch) is called the spark plug gap. The spark plug in no way produces a spark but merely provides a gap across which the current can arc. The ignition coil produces anywhere from 20,000 to 40,000 volts which travels to the distributor where it is fed through the spark plug wires to the spark plugs. The current passes along the center electrode and jumps the gap to the side electrode and, in so doing, ignites the air/fuel mixture in the combustion chamber. The sequence in which the spark plugs ignite is called the firing order and is determined by the sequence in which the pistons reach Top Dead Center (TDC) of their compression stroke. The controlled explosion of the air/fuel mixture forces the piston down, turning the crankshaft and the rest of the power train in the process.

The average life of a spark plug in an N-Body car is 30,000 miles. Part of the reason for this is the exclusive use of unleaded fuel, which reduces the amount of deposits within the combustion chamber and on the spark plug electrode produced in the combustion process. An additional contribution to long life is made by the high energy ignition (HEI) system which fires the spark plugs with over 35,000 volts. However, the life of a spark plug is dependent on several factors, including the mechanical

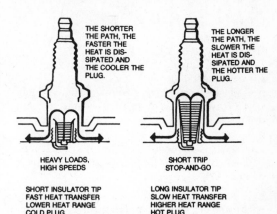

THE SHORTER THE PATH, THE FASTER THE HEAT IS DISSIPATED AND THE COOLER THE PLUG.

THE LONGER THE PATH, THE SLOWER THE HEAT IS DISSIPATED AND THE HOTTER THE PLUG.

HEAVY LOADS, HIGH SPEEDS

SHORT TRIP STOP-AND-GO

SHORT INSULATOR TIP
FAST HEAT TRANSFER
LOWER HEAT RANGE
COLD PLUG

LONG INSULATOR TIP
SLOW HEAT TRANSFER
HIGHER HEAT RANGE
HOT PLUG

Spark plug heat range

condition of the engine, driving conditions and the driver's habits. The quality and type of unleaded fuel used can also have an effect on the spark plug life.

When removing the plugs, check the condition of the electrodes; they are a good indication of the internal state of the engine. A small deposit of light tan or rust-red material on a plug that has been used for any period of time is to be considered normal. Any other color or abnormal amounts of wear or deposits indicates that there is something amiss with the engine or ignition system. The gap between the center electrode and side electrode can be expected to increase not more than 0.001 in. every 1000 miles under normal conditions.

When and if a plug fouls and begins to misfire, you will have to investigate and correct the cause of the fouling, then either clean or replace the spark plug. A lightly fouled plug may be cleaned and reused, but one with an excessive buildup of deposits should be replaced. A few of the most common reasons for plug fouling, and a description of the plug appearance, are listed in Chapter Nine and in the color insert in Chapter Four.

SPARK PLUG HEAT RANGE

Spark plug heat range is the ability of the plug to dissipate heat. The longer the insulator (or the farther it extends into the engine), the hotter the plug will operate; the shorter the insulator the cooler it will operate. A plug that absorbs little heat and remains too cool will quickly accumulate deposits of oil and carbon since it is not hot enough to burn them off. This leads to plug fouling and consequently to misfiring. A plug that absorbs too much heat will have no deposits, but, due to the excessive heat, the electrodes will burn away quickly and in some instances, preignition may result. Preignition takes place when plug tips get so hot that they glow sufficiently to ignite the fuel/air mixture before the actual spark occurs. This early ignition will usually cause a pinging during low speeds and heavy loads.

The general rule of thumb for choosing the correct heat range when picking a spark plug is: if most of your driving is long distance, high speed travel, use a colder plug; if most of your driving is stop and go, use a hotter plug. Original equipment plugs are compromise plugs, but most people never have occasion to change their plugs from the factory-recommended heat range.

REPLACING SPARK PLUGS

A set of spark plugs usually requires replacement after about 20,000 to 30,000 miles on cars with electronic ignition, depending on your style of driving. In normal operation, plug gap increases about 0.001 in. for every 1,000–2,500 miles. As the gap increases, the plug's voltage requirement also increases. It requires a greater voltage to jump the wider gap and about two or three times as much voltage to fire a plug at high speeds than at idle.

When you're removing spark plugs, you should work on one at a time. Don't start by removing the plug wires all at once, because unless you number them, they may become mixed up. Take a minute before you begin and number the wires with tape. The best location for numbering is near the cap.

1. Twist the spark plug boot and remove the boot and wire from the plug. Do not pull on the wire itself as this will ruin the wire.

2. If possible, use a brush or rag to clean the area around the spark plug. Make sure that all

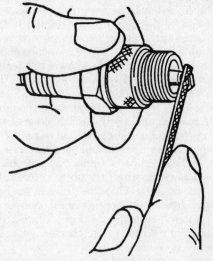

Plugs that are in good condition can be filed and reused

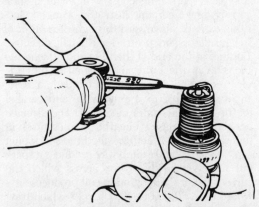

Always use a wire gauge to check the electrode gap

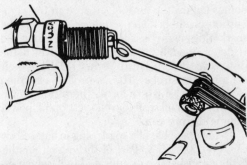

Adjust the electrode gap by bending the side electrode

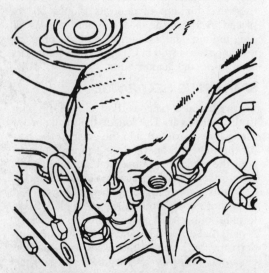

Twist and pull on the rubber boot to remove the spark plug wires; never pull on the wire itself

the dirt is removed so that none will enter the cylinder after the plug is removed.

3. Remove the spark plug using the proper size socket. Turn the socket counterclockwise

to remove the plug. Be sure to hold the socket straight on the plug to avoid breaking the plug, or rounding off the hex on the plug.

4. Once the plug is out, check it against the plugs shown in the color section to determine engine condition. This is crucial since plug readings are vital signs of engine condition.

5. Use a round wire feeler gauge to check the plug gap. The correct size gauge should pass through the electrode gap with a slight drag. If you're in doubt, try one size smaller and one larger. The smaller gauge should go through easily while the larger one shouldn't go through at all. If the gap is incorrect, use the electrode bending tool on the end of the gauge to adjust the gap. When adjusting the gap, always bend the side electrode. The center electrode is non-adjustable.

6. Squirt a drop of penetrating oil on the threads of the new plug and install it. Don't oil the threads too heavily. Turn the plug in clockwise by hand until it is snug.

7. When the plug is finger tight, tighten it with a wrench. Spark plugs whould be torqued to 14 ft. lbs.

8. Install the plug boot firmly over the plug. Proceed to the next plug.

CHECKING AND REPLACING SPARK PLUG CABLES

Visually inspect the spark plug cables for burns, cuts, or breaks in the insulation. Check the spark plug boots and the nipples on the distributor cap and coil. Replace any damaged wiring. If no physical damage is obvious, the wires can be checked with an ohmmeter for excessive resistance. Spark plug wires with excessive resistance will cause misfiring and may make the engine difficult to start in bad weather. Generally, the useful life of HEI cables is 45,000–60,000 miles.

To check resistance, remove the distributor cap with the ignition wires attached. Connect one lead of an ohmmeter to an electrode within the cap and the other lead to the corresponding spark plug wire terminal (remove it from the spark plug for this test). Replace any wire which shows any resistance over 30,000 ohms. The following chart gives resistance value as a function of length:

- 0–15 in.—3000–10,000 ohms
- 15–25 in.—4000–15,000 ohms
- 25–35 in.—6000–20,000 ohms
- Over 35 in.—25,000 ohms

When installing a new set of spark plug cables, replace the cables one at a time so there will be no mixup. Start by replacing the longest cable first. Install the boot firmly over the spark plug. Route the wire exactly the same as the original. Insert the nipple firmly into the tower on the distributor cap. Repeat the process for each cable.

FIRING ORDERS

NOTE: *To avoid confusion, always replace spark plug wires one at a time.*

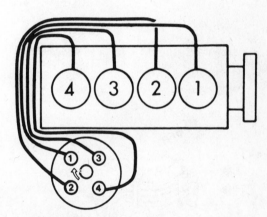

4 cyl firing order: 1-3-4-2

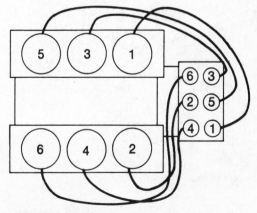

V6 with C3I igniton. Firing order: 1-6-5-4-3-2

INSERT SCREWDRIVER TO UNLOCK

RETAINER

DO NOT PULL ON WIRE WITH RETAINER LOCKED

Unlock the plastic retainers to replace the spark plug wires

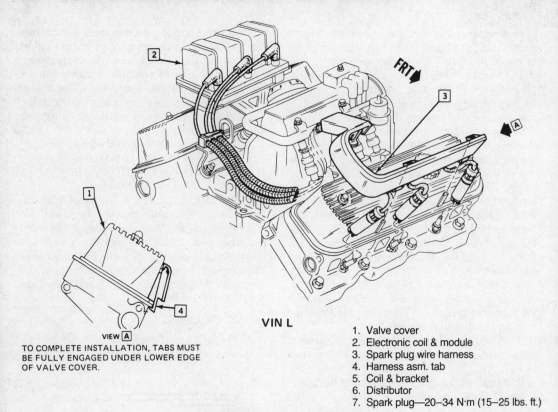

VIN L

TO COMPLETE INSTALLATION, TABS MUST
BE FULLY ENGAGED UNDER LOWER EDGE
OF VALVE COVER.

1. Valve cover
2. Electronic coil & module
3. Spark plug wire harness
4. Harness asm. tab
5. Coil & bracket
6. Distributor
7. Spark plug—20–34 N·m (15–25 lbs. ft.)

Spark plug wire routing on V6 engine

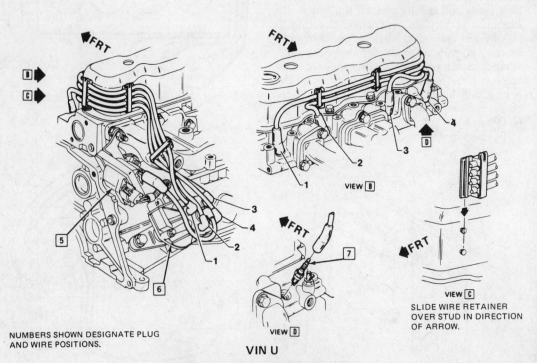

NUMBERS SHOWN DESIGNATE PLUG
AND WIRE POSITIONS.

SLIDE WIRE RETAINER
OVER STUD IN DIRECTION
OF ARROW.

VIN U

Spark plug wire routing on 4 cyl engine

Valve Adjustment

Both the 4 cylinder and V6 engines use hydraulic valve lifters which are non-adjustable. Hydraulic valve lifters keep all parts of the valve train in constant contact and adjust automatically to maintain zero lash under all conditions.

Idle Speed and Mixture Adjustment

On fuel injected engines, the idle speed and mixture are electronically controlled by the electronic control module (ECM). All adjustments are preset at the factory. The only time the idle speed should need adjustment is if fuel injection components are replaced. See Chapter 4 for more information.

Ignition Timing Adjustment

Timing specifications for each engine are listed in the Tune-Up Specifications Chart and on the underhood emission control label. The ignition timing marks are located on the engine front cover; a saw slot on the balancer indicates top dead center (TDC). On the 2.5L engine, the "Averaging Method" is used to set the ignition timing. This involves the use of BOTH the No. 1 and No. 4 spark plug wires to trigger the timing light. To set the timing on 2.5L engines:

1. See the underhood emission control label and follow all timing instructions given.

2. The engine should be at normal operating temperature, air cleaner installed, air conditioner off, electric cooling fan off and parking brake set firmly. Place the automatic transmission in Drive or the manual in Neutral.

3. Connect an inductive timing light pickup to the No. 1 plug wire and make sure the "Check Engine" light is not on.

4. Ground the ALCL connector under the dash by using a jumper wire to connect terminals A and B. The "Check Engine" light should begin flashing.

5. Using the timing light, check and record the position of the timing mark.

6. Repeat Step 3, but connect the timing light inductive pickup to the No. 4 spark plug wire. Take the total of the two recorded timing marks and divide by two to come up with an average timing. For example: No. 1 timing = 4° and No. 4 timing = 8°; 4 + 8 = 12 ÷ 2 = 6° average timing. If a change is necessary, subtract the average timing from the timing specification to determine the amount of timing change to No. 1 cylinder. For example: if the timing spec is 8° and the average timing is 6°, advance No. 1 cylinder 2° to set the timing.

7. Once the timing is properly set, remove the jumper wire from the ALCL connector. To clear the ECM memory, disconnect the ECM harness from the positive battery pigtail for 10 seconds with the key in the OFF position.

NOTE: *The ignition timing is not adjustable on the 3.0L engine with Computer Controlled Coil Ignition (C3I). For more information, see below.*

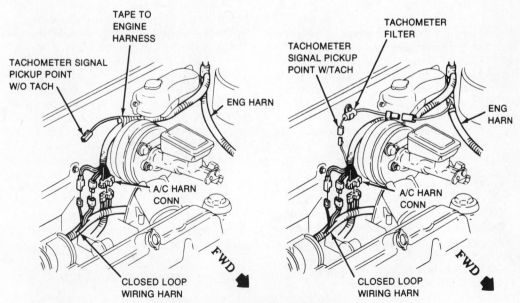

Tachometer hookup on the HEI distributor

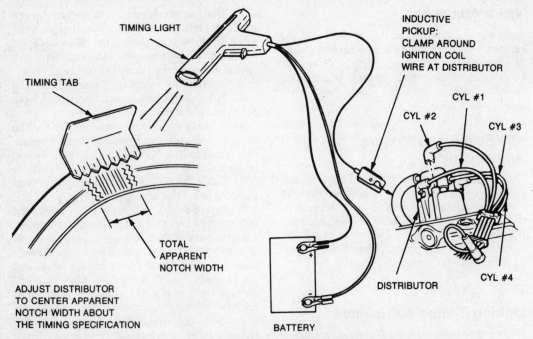

TIMING LIGHT

INDUCTIVE
PICKUP:
CLAMP AROUND
IGNITION COIL
WIRE AT DISTRIBUTOR

TIMING TAB

CYL #1

CYL #2

CYL #3

TOTAL
APPARENT
NOTCH WIDTH

ADJUST DISTRIBUTOR
TO CENTER APPARENT
NOTCH WIDTH ABOUT
THE TIMING SPECIFICATION

DISTRIBUTOR

CYL #4

BATTERY

Ignition timing is accomplished using the averaging method

ELECTRONIC IGNITION SYSTEMS

The solid state electronic ignition system has replaced the breaker point distributor on all current production automotive gasoline engines. By eliminating the breaker points, electronic ignition systems have become almost maintenance-free and performance doesn't deteriorate with mileage. In a typical system, the distributor contains an electronic control unit or module which replaces the breaker plate. Within the distributor body is a permanent magnet and a variable reluctance pick-up (or Hall Effect pick-up and rotating shutter). The electronic control module receives signals from the pick-up coil and in turn charges and fires the secondary ignition coil. A rotor then distributes the high voltage current to the proper spark plug through the distributor cap and wires. The only exception to this general description is the GM Computer Controlled Coil Ignition (C3I) system which eliminates the distributor altogether.

NOTE: *This book contains simple testing procedures for your N-Body's electronic ignition. More comprehensive testing on this system and other electronic control systems on your N-Body can be found in CHILTON'S GUIDE TO ELECTRONIC ENGINE CONTROLS, book part number 7535, available at most book stores and auto parts stores, or available directly from Chilton Co.*

All solid state ignition systems can be checked for proper operation by performing simple resistance tests, however some computer-based electronic ignition systems can be damaged by the use of incorrect test equipment. Before testing any primary ignition components, a secondary system inspection should be done to eliminate obvious problems such as loose or corroded connections, broken or shorted wires and damaged components. Intermittent problems can be caused by extremely high or low temperature operating conditions and any damage to the trigger wheel or Hall Effect pick-up (cracks, chips, etc.) will degrade ignition system performance. Service of solid state ignition systems involves testing and fault diagnosis of electronic components and circuits, using a volt-ohmmeter or digital multimeter. The control units, magnetic pick-ups and other solid state components are replaced as a unit so accurate troubleshooting is essential to avoid the needless replacement of expensive parts.

CAUTION: *Due to the dangerously high voltage levels present in any electronic ignition system, DO NOT touch any secondary ignition system components while the engine is running or the starter is being cranked. Use insulated tools to hold coil or spark plug wires when testing.*

GENERAL SERVICE PRECAUTIONS

• Always turn the ignition switch OFF when disconnecting or connecting any electrical connectors or components.

• Never reverse the battery polarity or disconnect the battery with the engine running.

• Do not pierce spark plug or wiring harness wires with test probes for any reason. Due to their more pliable construction, it is important to route spark plug wires properly to avoid chafing or cutting.

• Disconnect the ignition switch feed wire at the distributor when making compression tests to avoid arcing that may damage components, especially on computer-based ignition systems.

• Do not remove grease or dielectric compound from components or connectors when installing. Some manufacturers use grease to prevent corrosion and dielectric compound to dissipate heat generated during normal module operation.

• Check all replacement part numbers carefully. Installing the wrong component for a specific application can damage the system.

• All manufacturers instructions included with any testing equipment must be read carefully to insure proper capability and test results. Inaccurate readings and/or damage to ignition system components may result due to the use of improper test equipment.

High Energy Ignition (HEI) System

The HEI distributor with electronic spark timing (EST) combines all ignition components in one unit. The ignition coil is in the distributor cap and connects through a resistance brush to the rotor. The distributor has a magnetic pickup assembly located inside the distributor which contains a permanent magnet, pole piece with internal teeth and a pickup coil. When the teeth of the timer core, rotating inside the pole piece,

line up with the teeth of the pole piece, an induced voltage in the pickup coil signals the electronic module to trigger the coil primary circuit. The primary current decreases and a high voltage is induced in the ignition coil secondary winding which is directed through the rotor and spark plug wires to fire the spark plugs. The capacitor in the distributor is for radio noise suppression.

All spark timing changes are done electronically by the electronic control module (ECM), which monitors information from various engine sensors, computes the desired spark timing and signals the distributor to adjust the timing accordingly. A back-up spark advance system is incorporated to signal the ignition module in case of ECM failure. No vacuum or mechanical advance is used on the distributor.

An electronic spark control (ESC) system is used on 3.0L engines to retard the timing when detonation (spark knock) occurs. This retard mode is held for 20 seconds, after which the spark control again reverts to EST. The ESC sensor is mounted at the rear of the engine block and detects the presence (or absence) and intensity of detonation by the vibration characteristics of the engine. The sensor provides an electrical signal to the ESC controller, which processes this signal into a command to the distributor to modify the spark timing. The HEI distributor is modified so it can respond to the ESC controller signal.

GM Computer Controlled Coil Ignition (C3I) System

The C3I system eliminates the need for a distributor to control the flow of current between the battery and spark plugs. In its place, an electromagnetic sensor consisting of a Hall effect switch, magnet and interruptor ring. The gear on the shaft of this sensor is connected directly to the camshaft gear. At the heart of this system is an electronic coil module that replaces the distributor and coil used on previous electronic ignition systems. A microprocessor within the module receives and processes signals from the crankshaft and camshaft and, by way of three interconnecting coils, distributes high voltage current to the spark plugs.

Electromagnetic sensors take position readings from the crankshaft and camshaft, then transmit these readings to the electronics package. Using the information relayed from the electronic control module, the microprocessor then selects and sequentially triggers each of the three interconnecting coils to fire the spark plugs at the proper crankshaft position. An electronic spark control (ESC) is incorporated into the system to adjust the spark timing ac-

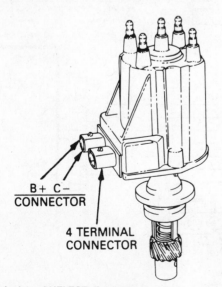

B+ C−
CONNECTOR

4 TERMINAL
CONNECTOR

Typical 4 cyl HEI/EST distributor

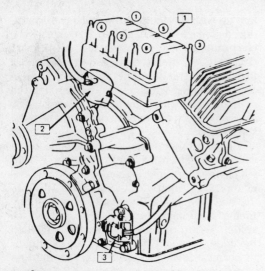

1. C³ ignition module and coil assembly
2. Cam sensor
3. Crankshaft sensor

C3I system components

cording to engine load and operating conditions. This closed loop system includes a piezoelectric sensor which transforms engine detonation vibrations into an electrical signal which is then fed to the electronic control module. The ECM uses this and other information on engine speed (rpm), intake air mass, coolant temperature and converter clutch operation to adjust the spark advance for the most efficient performance with the lowest emis-

sions. Because of this feature, there is no timing adjustment or regular maintenance required aside from periodic replacement of the spark plugs.

The C3I system uses a waste spark method of spark distribution. Companion cylinders are paired (1-4, 5-2, 3-6 on the V6 engine) and the spark occurs simultaneously in both cylinders. The cylinder on the exhaust stroke requires very little of the available voltage to arc, so the remaining high voltage is used by the cylinder in the firing position (TDC/compression). This same process is repeated when the companion cylinders reverse roles. There are three separate coils combined in the sealed coil/module assembly on the V6 engine. Spark distribution is synchronized by a signal from the crankshaft sensor which the ignition module uses to trigger each coil at the proper time.

NOTE: *The signal from the camshaft sensor is also used by the fuel injection electronic control module to trigger the fuel injectors, so a failed sensor can affect both the fuel and ignition system. A 7.5 amp ECM fuse is used to provide a low current source for the voltage to the sensors and internal circuitry; a 10 amp fuse provides voltage for the ignition coils.*

This system also incorporates an electronic spark timing (EST) system similar to other Delco distributor ignition systems. All connectors are lettered to make circuit identification easier. Terminal C (crankshaft sensor) provides the ECM with engine speed (rpm) and crankshaft

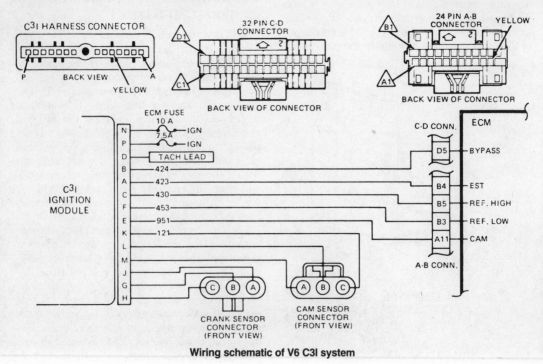

Wiring schematic of V6 C3I system

position information by passing a signal to the ignition module and then to ECM terminal B5. A plate with three vanes is mounted to the harmonic balancer and the vanes pass through slots in the crankshaft sensor. As the vanes pass through the slots, the Hall effect switch triggers and sends a voltage signal to the ECM. The signal from the Hall effect switch is either high or low and is used to trigger the ignition module for proper engine timing. Both the camshaft and crankshaft signal must be received by the ignition module in order for the ECM to take over spark timing control from the ignition module. An open or grounded circuit (terminal B) will set a trouble code 42 in the ECM memory and the engine will run in the bypass or "limp home" mode with the timing fixed at 10 degrees BTDC. The EST terminal A circuit triggers the HEI module by passing a reference signal which the ECM uses to advance or retard the timing according to the input from the crankshaft sensor. Cam terminal E is used by the ECM to determine when the No. 1 cylinder is on the compression stroke by a signal from the Hall effect camshaft position sensor. A loss of the cam signal will store a trouble code 41 if the engine is running and a loss of sensor signal during cranking will prevent the engine from starting.

The electronic control module uses information from the coolant sensor and mass air flow sensor in addition to engine speed to calculate the spark advance to allow more spark advance when the engine is cold or under minimum load. The ECM will retard the timing when the engine is hot or under a heavy load. When the system is running on the HEI module, it grounds the electronic spark timing signal. If the ECM detects voltage in the bypass circuit through a loss of ground for the EST signal, it sets a trouble code 42 and will not switch into the EST mode. When the engine reaches 400 rpm, the ECM applies 5 volts to the bypass circuit and the EST voltage will vary. If the bypass circuit is open, the ECM will store a trouble code 42.

TROUBLESHOOTING THE HEI SYSTEM

The symptoms of a defective component within the HEI system are exactly the same as those you would encounter in a conventional ignition system. Some of the symptoms are hard or no starting, rough idle, poor fuel economy or an engine miss under load or while accelerating.

If you suspect a problem in the ignition system, there are certain preliminary checks which should be carried out before testing the electronic portions of the system. First, it is extremely important to make sure the vehicle battery is in a good state of charge. A defective

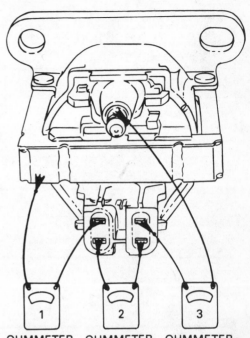

OHMMETER   OHMMETER   OHMMETER

Testing remote ignition coil. Ohmmeters 1 and 3 should read infinite (high scale); ohmmeter 2 should read very low or zero (low scale)

or poorly charged battery will cause the various components of the ignition system to read incorrectly when tested. Second, make sure all wiring connections are clean and tight at the

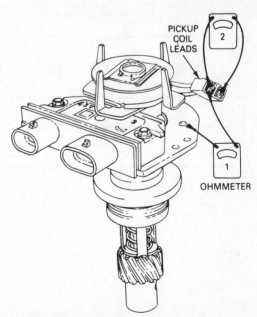

Testing pickup coil. Ohmmeter 1 should read infinite; ohmmeter 2 should read a steady value between 500–1500 ohms. Flex the leads to check for intermittent opens

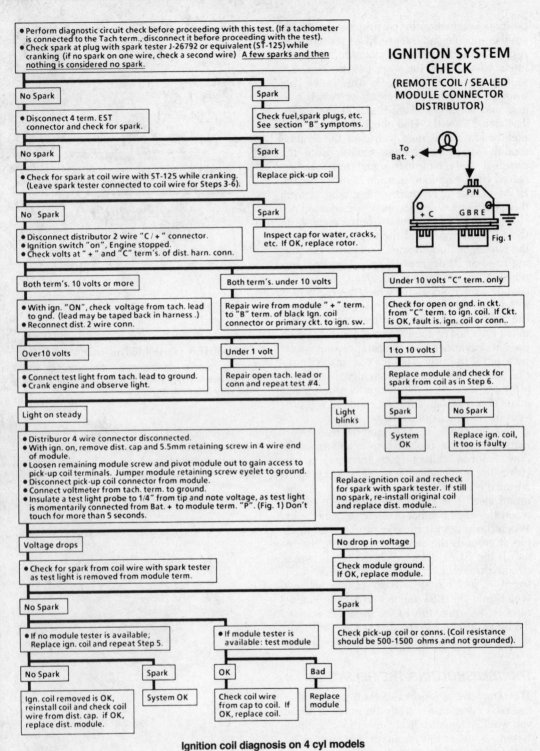

- Perform diagnostic circuit check before proceeding with this test. (If a tachometer is connected to the Tach term., disconnect it before proceeding with the test).
- Check spark at plug with spark tester J-26792 or equivalent (ST-125) while cranking (if no spark on one wire, check a second wire) A few sparks and then nothing is considered no spark.

IGNITION SYSTEM CHECK
(REMOTE COIL / SEALED MODULE CONNECTOR DISTRIBUTOR)

To Bat. +

P N
+ C   G B R E

Fig. 1

No Spark

- Disconnect 4 term. EST connector and check for spark.

Spark

Check fuel, spark plugs, etc. See section "B" symptoms.

No spark

- Check for spark at coil wire with ST-125 while cranking. (Leave spark tester connected to coil wire for Steps 3-6).

Spark

Replace pick-up coil

No Spark

- Disconnect distributor 2 wire "C / +" connector.
- Ignition switch "on", Engine stopped.
- Check volts at "+" and "C" term's. of dist. harn. conn.

Spark

Inspect cap for water, cracks, etc. If OK, replace rotor.

Both term's. 10 volts or more

- With ign. "ON", check voltage from tach. lead to gnd. (lead may be taped back in harness.)
- Reconnect dist. 2 wire conn.

Both term's. under 10 volts

Repair wire from module "+" term. to "B" term. of black Ign. coil connector or primary ckt. to ign. sw.

Under 10 volts "C" term. only

Check for open or gnd. in ckt. from "C" term. to ign. coil. If Ckt. is OK, fault is. ign. coil or conn..

Over 10 volts

- Connect test light from tach. lead to ground.
- Crank engine and observe light.

Under 1 volt

Repair open tach. lead or conn and repeat test #4.

1 to 10 volts

Replace module and check for spark from coil as in Step 6.

Light blinks

Spark

System OK

No Spark

Replace ign. coil, it too is faulty

Light on steady

- Distriburor 4 wire connector disconnected.
- With ign. on, remove dist. cap and 5.5mm retaining screw in 4 wire end of module.
- Loosen remaining module screw and pivot module out to gain access to pick-up coil terminals. Jumper module retaining screw eyelet to ground.
- Disconnect pick-up coil connector from module.
- Connect voltmeter from tach. term. to ground.
- Insulate a test light probe to 1/4" from tip and note voltage, as test light is momentarily connected from Bat. + to module term. "P". (Fig. 1) Don't touch for more than 5 seconds.

Replace ignition coil and recheck for spark with spark tester. If still no spark, re-install original coil and replace dist. module..

Voltage drops

- Check for spark from coil wire with spark tester as test light is removed from module term.

No drop in voltage

Check module ground. If OK, replace module.

No Spark

- If no module tester is available; Replace ign. coil and repeat Step 5.

Spark

- If module tester is available: test module

Check pick-up coil or conns. (Coil resistance should be 500-1500 ohms and not grounded).

No Spark

Ign. coil removed is OK, reinstall coil and check coil wire from dist. cap. if OK, replace dist. module.

Spark

System OK

OK

Check coil wire from cap to coil. If OK, replace coil.

Bad

Replace module

Ignition coil diagnosis on 4 cyl models

battery, distributor cap, ignition coil and electronic control module.

Since the only change between the HEI and a conventional ignition system is in the distributor component area, it is imperative to check the secondary ignition circuit first. If the secondary circuit checks out properly, the engine condition is probably not the fault of the ignition system. To check the secondary ignition circuit, perform a simple spark test. Remove one of the spark plug wires and insert an old spark plug with the electrode removed. Hold the plug with insulating pliers or a heavy rubber glove about ¼ in. away from the engine block and have an assistant crank the engine. If a normal spark occurs, then the problem is probably not in the ignition system; check for fuel system problems or fouled spark plugs. If there is no spark or a very weak spark, further ignition system testing is indicated.

TROUBLE DIAGNOSIS

NOTE: *For all removal and installation procedures on the HEI and C3I systems, see Chapter 3.*

Engine and Engine Overhaul

3

ENGINE ELECTRICAL

Alternator

All N-Body models use a Delco SI integral regulator charging system. Although several models of alternators are available with different idle and maximum outputs, their basic operating principles are the same.

A solid state regulator is mounted inside the alternator. All regulator components are mounted in a solid mold and this unit along with the brush holder assembly is attached to the slip ring end frame. The regulator voltage cannot be adjusted. If found to be defective, the regulator must be replaced as an assembly.

The alternator rotor bearings contain enough grease to eliminate the need for periodic lubrication. Two brushes carry current through two slip rings to the field coil mounted on the rotor. Stator windings are assembled inside a laminated core that forms part of the alternator frame. A rectifier bridge connected to the stator windings contains six diodes and electrically changes stator AC voltage to DC voltage, which is fed through the alternator output terminal. Alternator field current is supplied through a diode trio which is also connected to the stator windings. A capacitor or condenser mounted in the end frame protects the rectifier bridge and diode trio from high voltages and also suppresses radio noise. No periodic adjustment or maintenance of any kind is required on the entire alternator assembly.

ALTERNATOR PRECAUTIONS

To prevent damage to the alternator, regulator and on-board computer, the following precautions should be taken when working with the electrical system.

1. Never reverse the battery connections or attempt to disconnect or reconnect them with the ignition key ON. Take care not to let metal tools touch ground when disconnecting the positive battery cable.

2. Booster batteries for starting must be connected properly—positive-to-positive and negative-to-negative with the ignition turned OFF. Do not attempt to connect jumper cables from another vehicle while its engine is running.

3. Disconnect the battery cables before using a fast charger; the charger has a tendency to force current through the diodes in the opposite direction for which they were designed. This burns out the diodes.

4. Never use a fast charger as a booster for starting the vehicle.

5. Never disconnect the alternator connectors while the engine is running.

6. Do not short across or ground any of the terminals on the AC generator.

7. Never operate the alternator on an open circuit. Make sure that all connections within the circuit are clean and tight.

8. Disconnect the battery terminals when performing any service on the electrical system. This will eliminate the possibility of accidental reversal of polarity.

9. Disconnect the battery ground cable if arc welding is to be done on any part of the car.

REMOVAL AND INSTALLATION

1. Disconnect the negative battery cable.

2. Remove the two terminal plugs and battery leads on back of the alternator.

3. Loosen the adjusting bolts or adjuster and remove the drive belt.

4. Remove the alternator mounting bolts and lift the alternator clear.

5. Installation is the reverse of removal. On the 4 cylinder engine, adjust the drive belt tension to 70 lbs. on a used belt or 165 lbs. on a new belt. On the V6, adjust the drive belt ten-

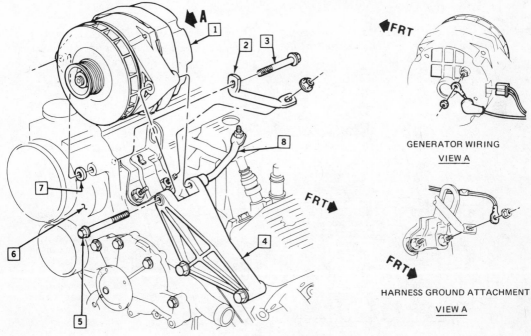

GENERATOR WIRING

VIEW A

HARNESS GROUND ATTACHMENT

VIEW A

1. Alternator
2. Alternator support
3. Bolt
4. Alternator support
5. Bolt
6. Tensioner bracket
7. Spacer
8. Support brace

V6 alternator mounting and wiring attachments

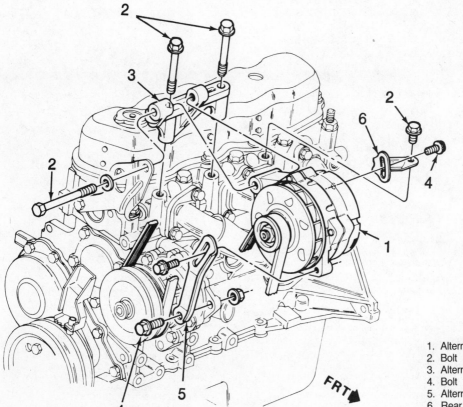

1. Alternator
2. Bolt
3. Alternator support
4. Bolt
5. Alternator brace
6. Rear brace

4 cyl alternator mounting

sion to 70 lbs. on a used belt or 145 lbs. on a new belt.

NOTE: *When adjusting belt tension, apply pressure at the center of the alternator, not against either end frame.*

Starter

The Delco 5MT starter is used on both 4 cylinder and V6 engines. Never operate the starter motor more than 30 seconds at a time without

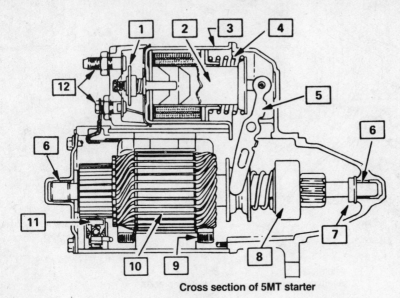

1. Contact disc
2. Plunger
3. Solenoid
4. Return spring
5. Shift lever
6. Bushing
7. Pinion stop
8. Clutch
9. Field coil
10. Armature
11. Brush
12. Terminals

Cross section of 5MT starter

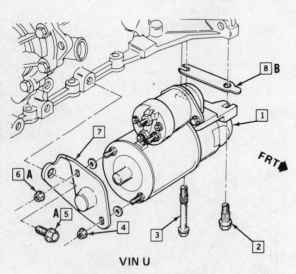

VIN U

1. STARTER MOTOR
2. BOLT/SCREW 36-50 N•m (27-37 LBS. FT.)
3. BOLT/SCREW 36-50 N•m (27-37 LBS. FT.)
4. NUT 2-4 N•m (18-36 LBS. IN.)
5. BOLT/SCREW 40-60 N•m (29-44 LBS. FT.)
6. NUT 2-4 N•m (18-36 LBS. IN.)
7. BRACKET
8. SHIM .38 - 1.14 MM (.015 - .045 IN.)
9. BOLT/SCREW 40-54 N•m (30-40 LBS. FT.)
10. BOLT/SCREW 40-54 N•m (30-40 LBS. FT.)
11. SHIM

A. TIGHTEN TO RECOMMENDED TORQUE AFTER STARTER MOTOR ATTACHING BOLTS HAVE BEEN TIGHTENED.
B. NOMINAL REQUIREMENTS TO BE 1.14 MM (.045 IN.). SHIMS TO BE USED TO CORRECT CENTER DISTANCE BY NOISE OBSERVATION.

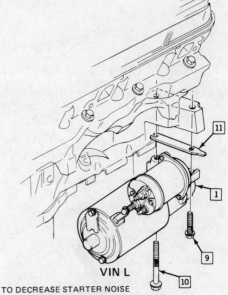

VIN L

TO DECREASE STARTER NOISE
1. GEAR LASH — REMOVE OUTBOARD MOUNTING BOLTS. LOOSEN REMAINING BOLT AND REMOVE SHIM. REPLACE AND RETIGHTEN MOUNTING BOLTS TO SPECIFIED TORQUE.

2. GEAR TOOTH INTERFERENCE — REMOVE OUTBOARD MOUNTING BOLT AND LOOSEN REMAINING BOLT. INSTALL ADDITIONAL SHIMS AS REQUIRED. (ACCUMULATED THICKNESS NOT TO EXCEED 1.2 MM [.047 IN.]). REPLACE AND RETIGHTEN MOUNTING BOLTS TO SPECIFIED TORQUE.

Typical starter mountings

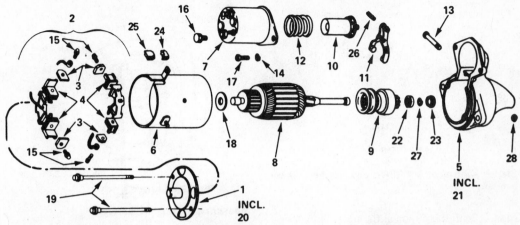

Exploded view of the 5MT starter motor

1. Commutator end frame
2. Brush and holder
3. Brush
4. Brush holder
5. Drive end housing
6. Frame and field assembly
7. Solenoid switch
8. Armature
9. Drive assembly
10. Plunger
11. Shift lever
12. Plunger return spring
13. Shift lever shaft
14. Lock washer
15. Brush attaching screw
16. Field lead to switch screw
17. Switch attaching screw
18. Brake washer
19. Through bolt
20. Commutator end bushing
21. Drive end bushing
22. Pinion stop collar
23. Thrust collar
24. Grommet
25. Grommet
26. Plunger pin
27. Pinion stop retainer ring
28. Lever shaft retaining ring

pausing to allow it to cool for at least two minutes.

REMOVAL AND INSTALLATION

1. Disconnect the negative battery cable.
2. Raise the car and support it safely.
3. Working beneath the car, remove the two starter mounting bolts and lower the starter. Be careful to note any shims during removal so they may be installed back in their original locations.
4. Remove the solenoid wires and battery cable, then remove the starter.
5. Installation is the reverse of removal.
CAUTION: *Be careful not to let the positive battery cable touch ground while it is removed from the starter.*

STARTER OVERHAUL

Drive Replacement

1. Disconnect the field coil straps from the solenoid.
2. Remove the thru-bolts and separate the commutator end frame, field frame assembly, drive housing and armature assembly from each other.
3. Slide the two piece thrust collar off the end of the armature shaft.
4. Slide a suitably sized metal cylinder (such as a standard half-inch pipe coupling or an old pinion) on the shaft so that the end of the cou-

pling or pinion butts up against the edge of the pinion retainer.

5. Support the lower end of the armature securely on a soft surface, such as a wooden block, and tap the end of the coupling or pinion, driving the retainer towards the armature end of the snap ring.

6. Remove the snap ring from the groove in the armature shaft with a pair of pliers, then slide the retainer and starter drive from the shaft.

7. To reassemble, lubricate the drive end of the armature shaft with silicone lubricant and then slide the starter drive onto the shaft with the pinion facing outward. Slide the retainer onto the shaft with the cupped surface facing outward.

8. Again support the armature on a soft

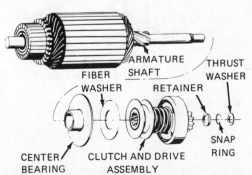

Removing drive assembly from the shaft

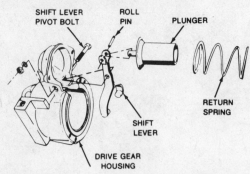

Starter shift lever and drive end housing disassembled

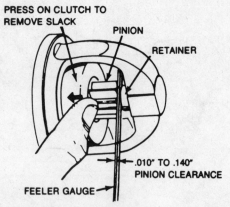

Measuring the pinion clearance

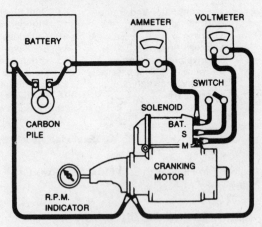

No-load test connections

surface, with the pinion at the upper end. Center the snap ring on the top of the shaft, using a new snap ring if the original was damaged during removal. Gently place a block of wood flat on top of the snap ring so as not to move it from a centered position. Tap the wooden block with a hammer in order to force the snap ring around the shaft, then slide the ring down into the snap ring groove.

9. Lay the armature down flat on the surface you're working on. Slide the retainer close up onto the shaft and position it and the thrust collar next to the snap ring. Using two pairs of pliers on opposite sides of the shaft, squeeze the thrust collar and the retainer together until the snap ring is forced into the retainer.

10. Lube the drive housing bushing with a silicone lubricant, then install the armature and clutch assembly into the drive housing, engaging the solenoid shift lever with the clutch and positioning the front end of the armature shaft into the bushing.

11. Apply a sealing compound approved for this application onto the drive housing, then position the field frame around the armature shaft and against the drive housing. Work slowly and carefully to prevent damaging the starter brushes.

12. Lubricate the bushing in the commuta-

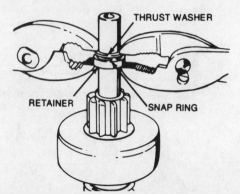

Starter drive retainer, thrust washer and snap ring installation

tor end frame with a silicone lubricant, place the leather brake washer onto the armature shaft, then slide the commutator end frame over the shaft and into position against the field frame. Line up the bolt holes, then install and tighten the thru-bolts.

13. Reconnect the field coil straps to the "motor" terminal of the solenoid.

NOTE: *If replacement of the starter drive fails to cure the improper engagement of the starter pinion to the flywheel, there are probably defective parts in the solenoid and/or shift lever. The best procedure would probably be to take the assembly to a shop where a pinion clearance check can be made by energizing the solenoid on a test bench. If the pinion clearance is incorrect, disassemble the solenoid and the shift lever and replace any worn parts.*

Brush Replacement

1. After removing the starter from the engine, disconnect the field coil from the motor solenoid terminal.

2. Remove the starter thru-bolts and remove the commutator end frame and washer.

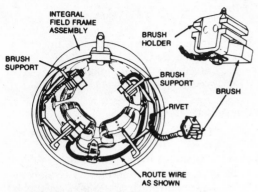

Starter brush replacement

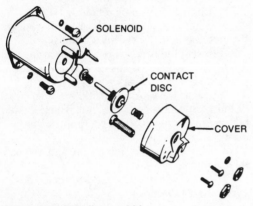

Solenoid switch disassembly

3. Remove the field frame and the armature assembly from the drive housing.

4. Remove the brush holder pivot pin which positions one insulated and one grounded brush.

5. Remove the brush springs.

6. Remove the brushes.

7. Installation is the reverse of removal.

HEI Distributor

REMOVAL AND INSTALLATION

2.5L Engine

1. Disconnect the ignition switch battery feed wire from the distributor.

2. Remove the distributor cap with the spark plug wires attached by releasing the two locking tabs and removing the coil wire. Move the cap out of the way.

3. Disconnect the 4-terminal ECM harness connector from the distributor. Release the locking tabs and remove the coil connector from the distributor.

4. Remove the distributor clamp screw and hold-down clamp.

5. Note the position of the rotor and scribe an alignment mark on the distributor base. Pull the distributor slowly up until the rotor stops

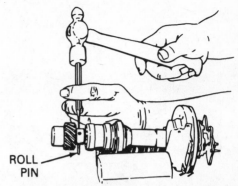

To disassemble the distributor, drive the roll pin from the gear and remove the shaft assembly. Mark the gear and shaft for correct reassembly

turning counterclockwise and again scribe an alignment mark on the distributor base.

6. Installation is the reverse of removal. Set the rotor at the second alignment mark and lower the distributor into the engine. The rotor should rotate clockwise to the first alignment mark when the distributor is installed.

NOTE: *The engine should not be rotated while the distributor is removed. If the engine was accidentally cranked with the distributor out, proceed as follows.*

7. Remove the No. 1 spark plug.

8. Place your finger over the No. 1 spark plug hole and rotate the engine slowly in the normal direction or rotation until compression is felt.

9. Align the timing mark on the pulley to TDC (0) on the engine timing indicator.

10. Turn the distributor rotor so it points between the No. 1 and No. 3 spark plug towers.

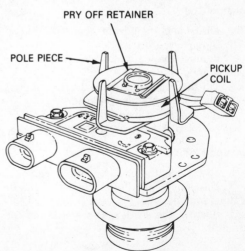

To remove the pickup coil, pry off the retainer then lift the coil assembly straight up

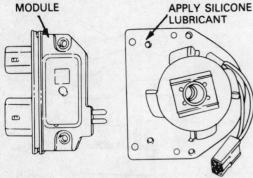

MODULE   APPLY SILICONE LUBRICANT

Apply silicone lubricant between the module and base for heat dissipation when installing

11. Install the distributor and connect all wiring, then install the distributor cap.

12. Start the engine and check the timing as outlined in Chapter 2.

Ignition Coil

REMOVAL AND INSTALLATION

1. Disconnect the negative battery cable.

2. Remove the bolt securing the radio capacitor to the ignition coil and then remove the capacitor.

3. Disconnect the electrical connector and the coil high tension lead.

4. Remove the remaining three coil mounting bolts and remove the coil.

5. Installation is the reverse of removal.

Computer Controlled Coil Ignition (C3I)

COMPONENT REMOVAL

Ignition Coil

1. Disconnect the negative battery cable.

2. Remove the spark plug wires.

3. Remove the screws holding the coil to the ignition module.

4. Tilt the coil assembly to the rear and remove the coil to module connectors.

5. Remove the coil assembly.

6. Installation is the reverse of removal.

Ignition Module

1. Disconnect the negative battery cable.

2. Disconnect the 14-pin connector at the ignition module.

3. Remove the spark plug wires at the coil assembly.

4. Remove the nuts and washers securing the ignition module assembly to the mounting bracket.

5. Remove the screws securing the ignition module to the coil.

6. Tilt the coil and disconnect the coil to module connectors.

7. Separate the coil and module.

8. Installation is the reverse of removal.

Crankshaft Sensor

NOTE: *It is not necessary to remove the sensor bracket.*

1. Disconnect the negative battery cable.

2. Disconnect the sensor 3-way connector.

3. Raise the vehicle and support it safely.

4. Rotate the harmonic balancer so the slot in the disc is aligned with the sensor.

5. Loosen the sensor retaining bolt.

6. Slide the sensor outboard and remove through the notch in the sensor housing.

7. Install the new sensor in the housing and rotate the harmonic balancer so that the disc is positioned in the sensor.

8. Adjust the sensor so that there is an equal distance on each side of the disc. There should be approximately .030 in. (.76mm) clearance between the disc and the sensor.

9. Tighten the retaining bolt and recheck the clearance.

10. Install remaining components in the reverse order of removal.

Camshaft Position Sensor

NOTE: *If only the camshaft sensor is being replaced, it is not necessary to remove the entire assembly. The sensor is replaceable separately.*

1. Disconnect the negative battery cable.

2. Disconnect the ignition module 14-pin connector.

3. Remove the spark plug wires at the coil assembly.

4. Remove the ignition module bracket assembly.

5. Disconnect the sensor 3-way connector.

6. Remove the sensor mounting screws, then remove the sensor.

7. Installation is the reverse of removal.

Camshaft Position Sensor Drive Assembly

1. Follow steps 1–6 of the cam sensor removal procedure. Note the position of the slot in the rotating vane.

2. Remove the bolt securing the drive assembly to the engine.

3. Remove the drive assembly.

4. Install the drive assembly with the slot in the vane. Install mounting bolt.

5. Install the camshaft sensor.

6. Rotate the engine to set the No. 1 cylinder at TDC/compression.

7. Mark the harmonic balancer and rotate the engine to 25 degrees after top dead center.

8. Remove the plug wires from the coil assembly.

9. Using weatherpack removal tool J-28742-A, or equivalent, remove terminal B of the sensor 3-way connector on the module side.

10. Probe terminal B by installing a jumper and reconnecting the wire removed to the jumper wire.

11. Connect a voltmeter between the jumper wire and ground.

12. With the key ON and the engine stopped, rotate the camshaft sensor counterclockwise until the sensor switch just closes. This is indicated by the voltage reading going from a high 5–12 volts to a low 0–2 volts. The low voltage indicates the switch is closed.

13. Tighten the retaining bolt and reinstall the wire into terminal B.

14. Install remaining components.

ENGINE MECHANICAL

Engine Overhaul Tips

Most engine overhaul procedures are fairly standard. In addition to specific parts replacement procedures and complete specifications for your individual engine, this chapter also is a guide to accept rebuilding procedures. Examples of standard rebuilding practice are shown

and should be used along with specific details concerning your particular engine.

Competent and accurate machine shop services will ensure maximum performance, reliability and engine life. In most instances it is more profitable for the do-it-yourself mechanic to remove, clean and inspect the component, buy the necessary parts and deliver these to a shop for actual machine work. On the other hand, much of the rebuilding work (crankshaft, block, bearings, piston rods, and other components) is well within the scope of the do-it-yourself mechanic.

TOOLS

The tools required for an engine overhaul or parts replacement will depend on the depth of your involvement. With a few exceptions, they will be the tools found in a mechanic's tool kit (see Chapter 1). More in-depth work will require any or all of the following:

- a dial indicator (reading in thousandths) mounted on a universal base
- micrometers and telescope gauges
- jaw and screw-type pullers
- scraper
- valve spring compressor
- ring groove cleaner
- piston ring expander and compressor
- ridge reamer
- cylinder hone or glaze breaker
- Plastigage®
- engine stand

The use of most of these tools is illustrated in

General Engine Specifications

Year	Engine No. Cyl. Displ. Cu. In.	Engine V.I.N. Code	Fuel Delivery System	Engine Mfg.	Horsepower @ rpm	Torque @ rpm (ft. lbs.)	Bore x Stroke	Compression Ratio	Oil Pressure @ rpm
'85–'86	4-151	U	TBI	Pont.	92 @ 4500	138 @ 2400	4.00 x 3.00	9.0:1	36–41 @ 2000
	6-183	L	MFI	Buick	125 @ 4900	150 @ 2400	3.80 x 2.66	8.45:1	37 @ 2400

Valve Specifications

Year	Eng. V.I.N. Code	Engine No. Cyl. Displacement (cu. in.)	Eng. Mfg.	Seat Angle (deg)	Face Angle (deg)	Spring Test Pressure (lbs. @ In.)	Spring Installed Height (in.)	Stem to Guide Clearance (in.) Intake	Stem to Guide Clearance (in.) Exhaust	Stem Diameter (in.) Intake	Stem Diameter (in.) Exhaust
'85–'86	U	4-151	Pont.	46	45	78–86 @ 1.66	1.69	0.0010– 0.0027	0.0010– 0.0027 ①	0.342– 0.343	0.342– 0.343
	L	6-183	Buick	45	45	210–230 @ 1.340	1.727	0.0015– 0.0035	0.0015– 0.0032	0.3401– 0.3412	0.3405– 0.3412

① The exhaust valve stem is tapered. The clearance at the top of the guide is shown. The clearance at the bottom of the guide is 0.0020–0.0037

Camshaft Specifications
(All measurements in inches)

Year	Eng. V.I.N. Code	Engine	Eng. Mfg.	Journal Diameter					Bearing Clearance	Lobe Lift		Camshaft End Play
				1	2	3	4	5		Intake	Exhaust	
'85–'86	U	4-151	Pont.	——1.869——					.0007–.0027	.398	.398	.0015–.0050
	L	6-183	Buick	——1.785–1.786——					.0005–.0025	.358	.384	—

Crankshaft and Connecting Rod Specifications
(All measurements are given in inches)

Year	Eng. V.I.N. Code	Engine No. Cyl. Displacement (cu. in.)	Eng. Mfg.	Crankshaft				Connecting Rod		
				Main Brg. Journal Dia.	Main Brg. Oil Clearance	Shaft End-Play	Thrust on No.	Journal Diameter	Oil Clearance	Side Clearance
'85–'86	U	4-151	Pont.	2.30	.0005–.0022	.0035–.0085	5	2.00	.0005–.0022	.006–.022
	L	6-183	Buick	2.4995	.0003–.0018	.0030–.0150	2	2.487	.0005–.0026	.003–.015

Piston and Ring Specifications
(All measurements are given in inches.)

Year	Eng. V.I.N. Code	Engine No. Cyl. Disp. (cu in)	Eng. Mfg.	Piston-to-Bore Clearance	Ring Gap			Ring Side Clearance		
					Top Compression	Bottom Compression	Oil Control	Top Compression	Bottom Compression	Oil Control
'85–'86	U	4-151	Pont.	.0014–.0022 ①	.010–.020	.010–.020	.020–.060	.002–.003	.001–.003	.015–.055
	L	6-183	Buick	.0008–.0020	.010–.020	.010–.020	.015–.055	.010–.020	.010–.020	.015–.055

① Measured 1.8 inches from piston top
② Measured at the top of the skirt

Torque Specifications
(All readings in ft. lbs.)

Year	V.I.N. Code	Engine No. Cyl. Displacement (cu. in.)	Eng. Mfg.	Cylinder Head Bolts	Rod Bearing Bolts	Main Bearing Bolts	Crankshaft Bolt	Flywheel to Crankshaft Bolts	Manifold	
									Intake	Exhaust
'85–'86	U	4-151	Pont.	92	32	70	200	44	29	44
	L	6-183	Buick	80	40	100	200	60	47	25

this chapter. Many can be rented for a one-time use from a local parts jobber or tool supply house specializing in automotive work. Occasionally, the use of special tools is called for. See the information on Special Tools and Safety Notice in the front of this book before substituting another tool.

INSPECTION TECHNIQUES

Procedures and specifications are given in this chapter for inspecting, cleaning and assessing the wear limits of most major components. Other procedures such as Magnaflux® and Zyglo® can be used to locate material flaws and

Standard Torque Specifications and Fastener Markings

In the absence of specific torques, the following chart can be used as a guide to the maximum safe torque of a particular size/grade of fastener.

- There is no torque difference for fine or coarse threads.
- Torque values are based on clean, dry threads. Reduce the value by 10% if threads are oiled prior to assembly.
- The torque required for aluminum components or fasteners is considerably less.

U.S. Bolts

SAE Grade Number	1 or 2			5			6 or 7		
Number of lines always 2 less than the grade number.									
Bolt Size (Inches)—(Thread)	Maximum Torque			Maximum Torque			Maximum Torque		
	Ft./Lbs.	Kgm	Nm	Ft./Lbs.	Kgm	Nm	Ft./Lbs.	Kgm	Nm
¼ — 20	5	0.7	6.8	8	1.1	10.8	10	1.4	13.5
— 28	6	0.8	8.1	10	1.4	13.6			
5/16 — 18	11	1.5	14.9	17	2.3	23.0	19	2.6	25.8
— 24	13	1.8	17.6	19	2.6	25.7			
3/8 — 16	18	2.5	24.4	31	4.3	42.0	34	4.7	46.0
— 24	20	2.75	27.1	35	4.8	47.5			
7/16 — 14	28	3.8	37.0	49	6.8	66.4	55	7.6	74.5
— 20	30	4.2	40.7	55	7.6	74.5			
½ — 13	39	5.4	52.8	75	10.4	101.7	85	11.75	115.2
— 20	41	5.7	55.6	85	11.7	115.2			
9/16 — 12	51	7.0	69.2	110	15.2	149.1	120	16.6	162.7
— 18	55	7.6	74.5	120	16.6	162.7			
5/8 — 11	83	11.5	112.5	150	20.7	203.3	167	23.0	226.5
— 18	95	13.1	128.8	170	23.5	230.5			
¾ — 10	105	14.5	142.3	270	37.3	366.0	280	38.7	379.6
— 16	115	15.9	155.9	295	40.8	400.0			
7/8 — 9	160	22.1	216.9	395	54.6	535.5	440	60.9	596.5
— 14	175	24.2	237.2	435	60.1	589.7			
1 — 8	236	32.5	318.6	590	81.6	799.9	660	91.3	894.8
— 14	250	34.6	338.9	660	91.3	849.8			

Metric Bolts

Relative Strength Marking	4.6, 4.8			8.8		
Bolt Markings						
Bolt Size Thread Size x Pitch (mm)	Maximum Torque			Maximum Torque		
	Ft./Lbs.	Kgm	Nm	Ft./Lbs.	Kgm	Nm
6 x 1.0	2–3	.2–.4	3–4	3–6	.4–.8	5–8
8 x 1.25	6–8	.8–1	8–12	9–14	1.2–1.9	13–19
10 x 1.25	12–17	1.5–2.3	16–23	20–29	2.7–4.0	27–39
12 x 1.25	21–32	2.9–4.4	29–43	35–53	4.8–7.3	47–72
14 x 1.5	35–52	4.8–7.1	48–70	57–85	7.8–11.7	77–110
16 x 1.5	51–77	7.0–10.6	67–100	90–120	12.4–16.5	130–160
18 x 1.5	74–110	10.2–15.1	100–150	130–170	17.9–23.4	180–230
20 x 1.5	110–140	15.1–19.3	150–190	190–240	26.2–46.9	160–320
22 x 1.5	150–190	22.0–26.2	200–260	250–320	34.5–44.1	340–430
24 x 1.5	190–240	26.2–46.9	260–320	310–410	42.7–56.5	420–550

stress cracks. Magnaflux® is a magnetic process applicable only to ferrous materials. The Zyglo® process coats the material with a flourescent dye penetrant and can be used on any material. Check for suspected surface cracks can be more readily made using spot check dye. The dye is sprayed onto the suspected area, wiped off and the area sprayed with a developer. Cracks will show up brightly.

OVERHAUL NOTES

Aluminum has become extremely popular for use in engines, due to its low weight. Observe the following precautions when handling aluminum parts:

• Never hot tank aluminum parts; the caustic hot-tank solution will eat the aluminum.

• Remove all aluminum parts (identification tag, etc.) from engine parts prior to the tanking.

• Always coat threads lightly with engine oil or anti-seize compounds before installation, to prevent seizure.

• Never over-torque bolts or spark plugs, especially in aluminum threads.

When assembling the engine, any parts that will be in frictional contact must be prelubed to provide lubrication at initial start-up. Any product specifically formulated for this purpose can be used, but engine oil is not recommended as a prelube.

When semi-permanent (locked, but removable) installation of bolts or nuts is desired, threads should be cleaned and coated with Loctite® or other similar, commercial nonhardening sealant.

REPAIRING DAMAGED THREADS

Several methods of repairing damaged threads are available. Heli-Coil® (shown here), Keenserts® and Microdot® are among the most widely used. All involve basically the same principle

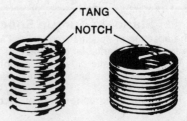

Standard thread repair insert (left) and spark plug thread insert (right)

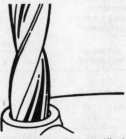

Drill out the damaged threads with specified drill. Drill completely through the hole or to the bottom of a blind hole

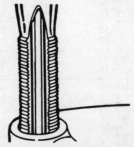

With the tap supplied, tap the hole to receive the thread insert. Keep the tap well oiled and back it out frequently to avoid clogging the threads

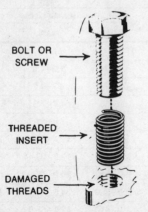

Damaged bolt holes can be repaired with thread repair inserts

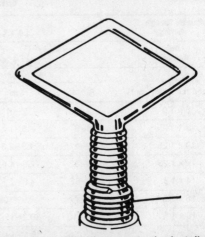

Screw the threaded insert onto the installation tool until the tang engages the slot. Screw the insert into the tapped hole until it is ¼–½ turn below the top surface, After installation break off the tang with a hammer and punch

(drilling out stripped threads, tapping the hole and installing a prewound insert), making welding, plugging and oversize fasteners unnecessary.

Two types of thread repair inserts are usually supplied; a standard type for most Inch Coarse, Inch Fine, Metric Course and Metric Fine thread sizes and a spark lug type to fit most spark plug port sizes. Consult the individual manufacturer's catalog to determine exact applications. Typical thread repair kits will contain a selection of prewound threaded inserts, a tap (corresponding to the outside diameter threads of the insert) and an installation tool. Spark plug inserts usually differ because they require a tap equipped with pilot threads and a combined reamer/tap section. Most manufacturers also supply blister-packed thread repair inserts separately in addition to a master kit containing a variety of taps and inserts plus installation tools.

Before effecting a repair to a threaded hole, remove any snapped, broken or damaged bolts or studs. Penetrating oil can be used to free frozen threads; the offending item can be removed with locking pliers or with a screw or stud extractor. After the hole is clear, the thread can be repaired.

CHECKING ENGINE COMPRESSION

A noticeable lack of engine power, excessive oil consumption and/or poor fuel mileage measured over an extended period are all indicators of internal engine wear. Worn piston rings, scored or worn cylinder bores, blown head gaskets, sticking or burnt valves and worn valve seats are all possible culprits here. A check of each cylinder's compression will help you locate the problems.

As mentioned in the "Tools and Equipment" section of Chapter 1, a screw-in type compression gauge is more accurate that the type you simply hold against the spark plug hole, although it takes slightly longer to use. It's worth

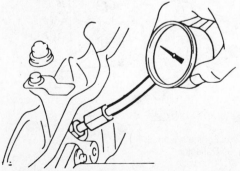

The screw-in type compression gauge is more accurate

it to obtain a more accurate reading. Follow the procedures below.

1. Warm up the engine to normal operating temperature.

2. Remove all spark plugs.

3. Disconnect the high-tension lead from the ignition coil.

4. Disconnect all fuel injector electrical connections.

5. Screw the compression gauge into the No. 1 spark plug hole until the fitting is snug.

NOTE: *Be careful not to crossthread the plug hole. On aluminum cylinder heads use extra care, as the threads in these heads are easily ruined.*

6. Have an assistant depress the accelerator pedal fully. Then, while you read the compression gauge, ask the assistant to crank the engine two or three times in short bursts using the ignition switch.

7. Read the compression gauge at the end of each series of cranks, and record the highest of these readings. Repeat this procedure for each of the engine's cylinders. Maximum compression should be 175–185 psi. A cylinder's compression pressure is usually acceptable if it is not less than 80% of maximum. The difference between each cylinder should be no more than 12–14 psi.

8. If a cylinder is unusually low, pour a tablespoon of clean engine oil into the cylinder through the spark plug hole and repeat the compression test. If the compression comes up after adding the oil, it appears that the cylinder's piston rings or bore are damaged or worn. If the pressure remains low, the valves may not be seating properly (a valve job is needed), or the head gasket may be blown near that cylinder. If compression in any two adjacent cylinders is low, and if the addition of oil doesn't help the compression, there is leakage past the head gasket. Oil and coolant water in the combustion chamber can result from this problem. There may be evidence of water droplets on the engine dipstick when a head gasket has blown.

Engine
REMOVAL AND INSTALLATION
2.5L Engine

NOTE: *Fuel system pressure must be relieved before attempting this procedure. See Chapter 4 for details.*

1. Disconnect both battery cables.

2. Drain the cooling system.

CAUTION: *When draining the coolant, keep in mind that cats and dogs are attracted by the ethelyne glycol antifreeze, and are quite*

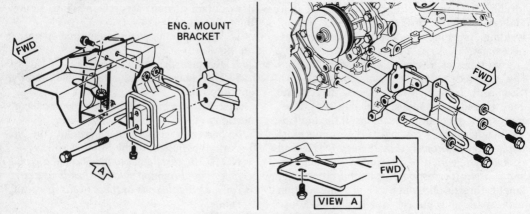

2.5L forward engine mount

likely to drink any that is left in an uncovered container or in puddles on the ground. This will prove fatal in sufficient quantity. Always drain the coolant into a sealable container. Coolant should be reused unless it is contaminated or several years old.

3. Remove the air cleaner assembly.

4. Disconnect the ECM harness from the computer and feed the harness through the bulkhead. Lay the harness across the engine.

5. Disconnect the engine wiring harness and lay it across the engine.

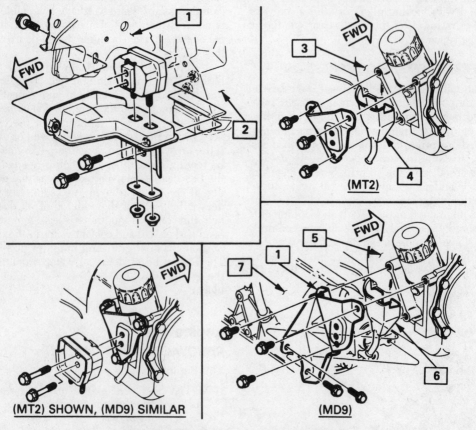

1. Right hand rail assembly
2. Cowl assembly
3. Engine assembly
4. Deflector
5. Engine assembly
6. Deflector
7. Transaxle assembly

2.5L rear engine mounts

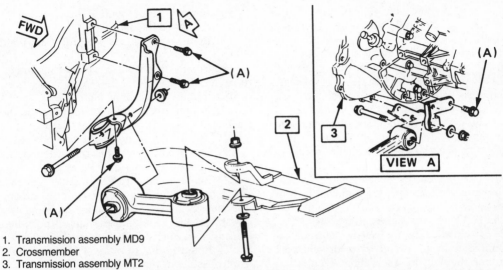

1. Transmission assembly MD9
2. Crossmember
3. Transmission assembly MT2

2.5L forward transaxle strut. Bolts marked (A) must be replaced whenever they are removed

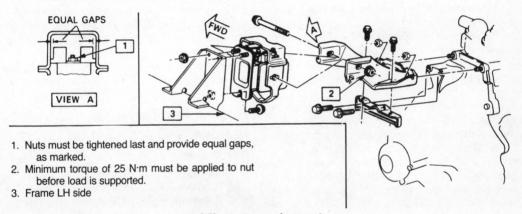

1. Nuts must be tightened last and provide equal gaps, as marked.
2. Minimum torque of 25 N·m must be applied to nut before load is supported.
3. Frame LH side

2.5L rear transaxle mount

6. Tag and disconnect all engine vacuum hoses.

7. Remove the radiator and heater hoses.

8. Remove the air conditioning compressor from its mounting bracket without disconnecting any refrigerant lines and tie it to the chassis out of the way. Do not let the compressor hang by the refrigerant lines.

9. Remove the power steering pump from its mounting bracket without disconnecting any hoses and tie it to the chassis out of the way. Do not let the power steering pump hang by its hoses.

10. Disconnect the front transaxle strut.

11. Disconnect the fuel lines at the throttle body (TBI) or at the fuel rail (Port Injection). If the fuel pressure was not relieved before starting this procedure, wrap a clean rag around the fuel fitting while loosening to catch any fuel spray.

12. Disconnect the transaxle cooler lines and the shift linkage on automatic models, or the clutch linkage on manual transaxles.

13. Disconnect the downshift cable and throttle cable at the throttle body.

14. Disconnect the redundant ground cable and multi relay bracket.

15. Raise the vehicle and support it safely.

16. Disconnect the power steering line bracket from the engine.

17. Remove both front wheels.

18. Remove the front brake calipers and wire them to the springs. Do not let the calipers hang by their brake hoses.

19. Remove the brake rotors.

20. Remove the knuckle-to-strut bolts (two per side).

21. Remove the exhaust pipe at the manifold and hangers and swing it aside.

22. Remove the body to cradle bolts (two each side) at the lower control arm.

23. Loosen the remaining eight body-to-

cradle bolts at the ends. Remove one bolt at each end of each cradle side, leaving one bolt per corner.

24. Place a dolly under the engine and transaxle assembly, then lower the vehicle and allow the engine and transaxle to rest on the dolly. Use wood blocks to maintain the engine/transaxle position on the dolly.

25. Remove the engine mount bolts and right front bracket.

26. Remove the remaining four cradle-to-body bolts.

27. Slowly raise the vehicle enough to allow the engine and transaxle to be moved forward from under the car on the dolly.

28. Separate the engine and transaxle.

29. Installation is the reverse of removal. Assemble the engine and transaxle and position it on the dolly for installation as a unit.

3.0L Engine

1. Disconnect both battery cables and place fender covers on the vehicle.

2. Scribe marks around the hood hinges and remove the hood.

3. Raise the vehicle and support it safely.

4. Tag and disconnect the starter wiring and remove the starter.

5. Remove the flexplate cover and scribe a matchmark on the torque converter and flex plate. Remove the three torque converter bolts.

6. Disconnect the air conditioning compressor from its mounting bracket with the refrigerant hoses intact and lay it aside. Disconnect the wiring connector to the compressor before moving it aside.

7. Drain the cooling system.

CAUTION: *When draining the coolant, keep in mind that cats and dogs are attracted by the ethelyne glycol antifreeze, and are quite likely to drink any that is left in an uncovered container or in puddles on the ground. This will prove fatal in sufficient quantity. Always drain the coolant into a sealable container. Coolant should be reused unless it is contaminated or several years old.*

8. Disconnect the lower radiator hose.

9. Disconnect the right front motor mount bolts.

10. Remove the right inner fender splash shield.

11. Remove the transaxle to engine mount bolt located between the transaxle and the cylinder block.

12. Remove the two right rear motor mount nuts.

13. Remove the exhaust pipe from the manifold.

14. Remove the heater hoses.

15. Lower the vehicle.

16. Remove the serpentine drive belt, alternator wiring and the alternator.

17. Remove the power steering pump and fluid lines.

18. Remove the mass air flow sensor and intake duct.

19. Remove the cooling fan.

20. Remove the upper radiator hose and the radiator.

21. Attach a lifting device to the engine.

22. Remove the left upper transaxle mount.

23. Remove the master cylinder.

24. Remove the fuel lines at the fuel rail. See Chapter 4 for procedure on depressurizing the fuel system before loosening any fuel lines. Wrap a clean rag around the fuel fitting when loosening to catch any fuel spray.

25. Remove the throttle, T.V. and cruise control cables at the throttle body.

26. Remove the remaining engine to transaxle mounting bolts while lightly loading the lifting device to take the weight off the bolts.

27. Carefully lift the engine clear with the lifting device.

28. Installation is the reverse of removal. Bleed the brake system after installing the master cylinder. Refill the cooling system.

Rocker Arm Cover

REMOVAL AND INSTALLATION

2.5L Engine

1. Remove the air cleaner.

2. Disconnect the PCV valve and hose.

3. Disconnect the EGR valve.

4. Remove the rocker arm cover bolts.

5. Remove the spark plug wires from the spark plugs and clips.

6. Tap the rocker arm cover gently with a

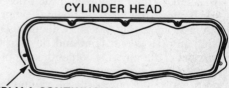

CYLINDER HEAD

APPLY A CONTINUOUS 3/16″ DIAMETER BEAD OF RTV AS SHOWN

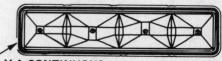

PUSH ROD COVER

APPLY A CONTINUOUS 3/16″ DIAMETER BEAD OF RTV AS SHOWN

Apply sealer as shown when installing pushrod cover

rubber mallet to break the gasket loose then remove the cover. Do not pry on the cover or damage to the sealing surfaces may result.

7. Clean the sealing surfaces of all old gasket material.

8. Installation is the reverse of removal. Apply a continuous ³/₁₆ in. bead of RTV sealant around the cylinder head sealing surface inboard at the bolt holes. Keep sealant out of the bolt holes. Torque the rocker arm cover mounting bolts to 6 ft.lb. (8 Nm).

3.0L V6

FRONT ROCKER ARM COVER

1. Disconnect the negative battery cable.
2. Remove the crankcase ventilation hose.
3. Remove the spark plug wire harness cover.
4. Tag and disconnect the spark plug wires at the plugs.
5. Remove the rocker cover nuts, washers and seals.
6. Remove the rocker cover and gasket. Clean all sealing surfaces of old gasket material.
7. Installation is the reverse of removal. Torque the mounting nuts to 7 ft.lb. (10 Nm).

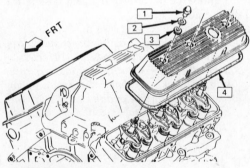

1. Nut 10 N·m (88 lb. in.)
2. Washer
3. Rubber grommet
4. Formed rubber gasket

V6 rocker arm cover and gasket

REAR ROCKER COVER

1. Disconnect the negative battery cable.
2. Remove the C3I ignition coil module with the spark plug wires attached.
3. Disconnect the EGR solenoid wiring and vacuum hoses after tagging them for installation.
4. Disconnect the serpentine drive belt.
5. Tag and disconnect the alternator wiring.
6. Remove the rear alternator mounting bolt and rotate the alternator toward the front of the vehicle.
7. Disconnect the power steering pump from

the belt tensioner and remove the belt tensioner assembly.

8. Remove the engine lifting bracket and the rear alternator brace.

9. Drain the engine coolant below the heater hose level, then remove the throttle body heater hoses.

CAUTION: *When draining the coolant, keep in mind that cats and dogs are attracted by the ethelyne glycol antifreeze, and are quite likely to drink any that is left in an uncovered container or in puddles on the ground. This will prove fatal in sufficient quantity. Always drain the coolant into a sealable container. Coolant should be reused unless it is contaminated or several years old.*

10. Remove the rocker cover nuts, washers and seals.

11. Remove the rocker cover and gasket. Clean all mating surfaces of old gasket material.

12. Installation is the reverse of removal. Torque the mounting nuts to 7 ft.lb. (10 Nm).

Rocker Arm Assembly

REMOVAL AND INSTALLATION

2.5L Engine

1. Remove the rocker arm cover.
2. Remove the rocker arm bolt and ball. If

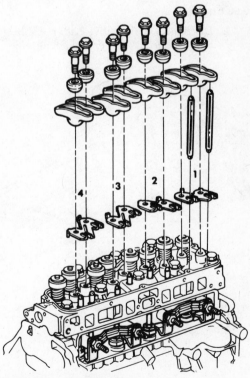

2.5L rocker arm assembly

replacing the pushrod only, loosen the rocker arm bolt and swing the arm clear of the pushrod.

3. Remove the rocker arm, pushrod and guide. Store all components in order so they can be reassembled in their original location. Pushrod guides are different and must be reassembled in the previous location.

4. Installation is the reverse of removal. When new rocker arms or balls are used, coat the bearing surfaces with Molykote® or equivalent. Torque the rocker arm bolt to 20 ft.lb. (27 Nm).

3.0L V6

1. Remove the rocker arm cover as previously described.

2. Remove the rocker arm pedestal retaining bolts.

3. Remove the rocker arm and pedestal assembly. Note the position of the double ended bolts for reassembly. Store all components on a clean surface in order so they may be installed in their original locations.

4. Installation is the reverse of removal. Torque the rocker arm pedestal bolts to 45 ft.lb. (60 Nm). Replace any components that show signs of unusual wear.

Intake Manifold

REMOVAL AND INSTALLATION

2.5L Engine

1. Disconnect the negative battery cable.
2. Remove the air cleaner and hot air pipe.

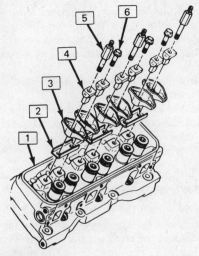

1. Cylinder head
2. Pedestal retainer
3. Rocker arm
4. Pedestal
5. Double ended bolt
   60 N·m (45 ft. lbs.)
6. 60 N·m (45 ft. lbs.)

V6 rocker arm assembly

3. Remove the PCV valve and hose at the TBI assembly.

4. Drain the cooling system.

CAUTION: *When draining the coolant, keep in mind that cats and dogs are attracted by the ethelyne glycol antifreeze, and are quite likely to drink any that is left in an uncovered container or in puddles on the ground. This will prove fatal in sufficient quantity.*

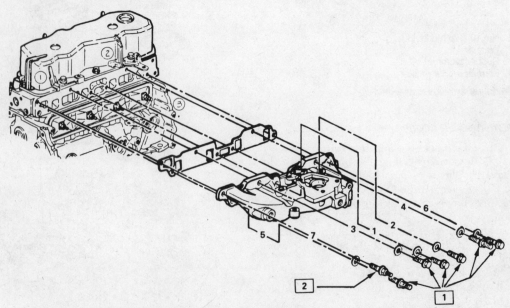

2.5L intake manifold. Torque all bolts in sequence shown to 25 ft. lbs. (1) or 37 ft. lbs. (2)

Always drain the coolant into a sealable container. Coolant should be reused unless it is contaminated or several years old.

5. Depressurize the fuel system as described in Chapter 4 and remove the fuel lines.

6. Tag and remove the vacuum hoses.

7. Tag and remove the wiring and throttle linkage from the TBI assembly.

8. Remove the transaxle downshift linkage.

9. Remove the cruise control and linkage if installed.

10. Remove the throttle linkage and bell-crank and lay aside for clearance.

11. Disconnect the heater hose.

12. Remove the upper power steering pump bracket.

13. Remove the ignition coil.

14. Remove the retaining bolts and lift off the intake manifold. Clean all gasket mating surfaces on the intake manifold and cylinder head.

15. Installation is the reverse of removal. Torque the intake manifold retaining bolts to 25 ft.lb. (34 Nm) in the sequence illustrated. Note that the No. 7 bolt is torqued to 37 ft.lb. (50 Nm).

3.0L V6

NOTE: *A special bolt wrench J-24394 or equivalent is required for this procedure.*

1. Disconnect the negative battery cable.

2. Remove the mass air flow sensor and air intake duct.

3. Remove the serpentine accessory drive belt, alternator and bracket.

4. Remove the C3I ignition module with the spark plug cables attached. Tag all wiring connectors before disconnecting.

5. Tag and disconnect all vacuum lines and wiring connectors as necessary to gain clearance to remove the manifold.

6. Remove the throttle, cruise control and T.V. cables from the throttle body.

7. Drain the cooling system.

CAUTION: *When draining the coolant, keep in mind that cats and dogs are attracted by the ethelyne glycol antifreeze, and are quite likely to drink any that is left in an uncovered container or in puddles on the ground. This will prove fatal in sufficient quantity. Always drain the coolant into a sealable container. Coolant should be reused unless it is contaminated or several years old.*

8. Remove the heater hoses from the throttle body.

9. Remove the upper radiator hose.

10. Depressurize the fuel system as described in Chapter 4, then remove the fuel lines, fuel rail and injectors.

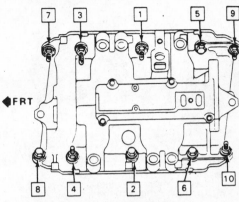

V6 intake manifold bolt torque sequence

11. Remove the intake manifold bolts. Loosen in reverse of the torque sequence to prevent manifold warping. Remove the intake manifold and gasket.

12. Installation is the reverse of removal. Clean all gasket mating surfaces and apply sealer No. 1050026 or equivalent if a steel gasket is used. Torque all manifold bolts in sequence to 32 ft.lb. (44 Nm).

Exhaust Manifold

REMOVAL AND INSTALLATION

2.5L Engine

1. Disconnect the air cleaner and hot air tube.

2. Disconnect the alternator top mounts and swing it aside.

3. Disconnect the oxygen sensor connector.

4. Raise the vehicle and support it safely.

5. Disconnect the exhaust pipe from the manifold.

6. Lower the vehicle.

7. Remove the exhaust manifold retaining bolts, then remove the exhaust manifold and gasket.

8. Clean all gasket mating surfaces on the cylinder head and manifold.

9. Installation is the reverse of removal. Torque all exhaust manifold mounting bolts to 44 ft.lb. (60 Nm) in sequence.

3.0L V6

1. Disconnect the negative battery cable.

2. Raise and support the vehicle safely.

3. Remove the bolts attaching the exhaust pipe to the manifold.

4. Lower the vehicle.

5. Disconnect the oxygen sensor connector.

6. Remove the spark plug wires. Tag them for installation.

7. Remove the two nuts retaining the crossover pipe to the manifold.

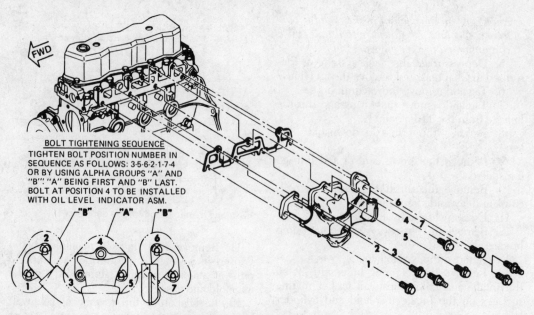

BOLT TIGHTENING SEQUENCE
TIGHTEN BOLT POSITION NUMBER IN
SEQUENCE AS FOLLOWS: 3-5-6-2-1-7-4
OR BY USING ALPHA GROUPS "A" AND
"B": "A" BEING FIRST AND "B" LAST.
BOLT AT POSITION 4 TO BE INSTALLED
WITH OIL LEVEL INDICATOR ASM.

2.5L exhaust manifold bolt torque sequence

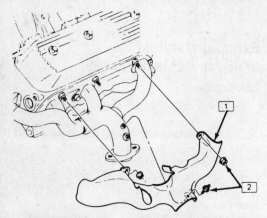

1. Exhaust manifold
   shield
2. 15 N·m (11 ft. lbs.)

V6 exhaust manifold heat shield-right side

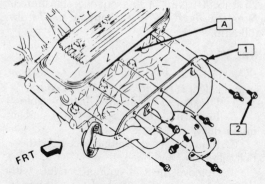

1. Manifold
2. Bolts 50 N·m (37 lb. ft.)
A. Apply sealant between manifold
   and cylinder head

V6 exhaust manifold-right side

1. Heat shield
2. Washer
3. Nut 17 N·m (150 lb. in.)

V6 exhaust manifold heat shield-left side

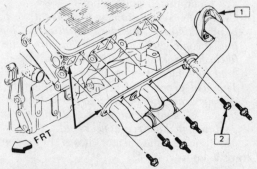

1. Manifold
2. Bolts 50 N·m (37 ft. lb.)
A. Apply sealant between manifold and cyl. head

V6 exhaust manifold-left side

8. Remove the bolts attaching the exhaust manifold and remove the exhaust manifold from the engine.

9. Installation is the reverse of removal. Clean all gasket mating surfaces and torque the exhaust manifold bolts to 37 ft.lb. (50 Nm).

Cylinder Head

REMOVAL AND INSTALLATION

2.5L Engine

1. Drain the cooling system.

CAUTION: *When draining the coolant, keep in mind that cats and dogs are attracted by the ethelyne glycol antifreeze, and are quite likely to drink any that is left in an uncovered container or in puddles on the ground. This will prove fatal in sufficient quantity. Always drain the coolant into a sealable container. Coolant should be reused unless it is contaminated or several years old.*

2. Raise the vehicle and support it safely.

3. Disconnect the exhaust pipe.

4. Lower the vehicle.

5. Disconnect the negative battery cable.

6. Remove the dipstick tube.

7. Remove the air cleaner.

8. Tag and disconnect the wiring and throttle linkage from the TBI assembly.

9. Depressurize the fuel system as described in Chapter 4 and remove the fuel line.

10. Disconnect the heater hose from the intake manifold.

11. Remove the ignition coil.

12. Tag and disconnect all wiring connections from the intake manifold and cylinder head.

13. If top-mounted, disconnect the air conditioning compressor with the lines attached and swing it aside.

14. Disconnect the alternator brackets and lay it aside.

15. Disconnect the power steering pump upper bracket if top-mounted.

16. Disconnect the radiator hoses.

17. Remove the rocker arm cover.

18. Loosen the rocker arms and remove the

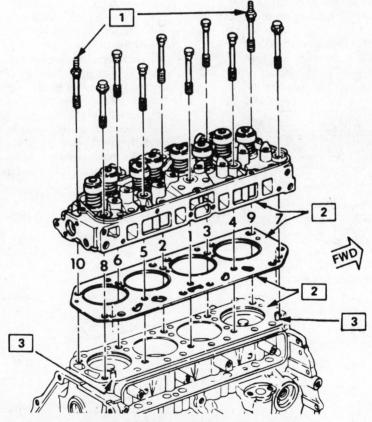

1. Apply sealing compound to threads of the bolts shown
2. Mounting surfaces of block, head and both sides of gasket must be free of dirt and oil
3. Locating pins

2.5L cylinder head bolt torque sequence

pushrods. Keep all components in order so they may be installed in their original locations.

19. Loosen the cylinder head bolts in reverse of the torque sequence and remove them. Lift off the cylinder head with the manifolds attached and continue disassembly on the bench.

20. Installation is the reverse of removal. Clean all gasket mating surfaces and torque the cylinder head bolts in sequence to 92 ft.lb. (125 Nm) with a suitable sealer coating the threads.

3.0L V6

NOTE: *Depressurize the fuel system before starting this procedure.*

1. Disconnect the negative battery cable.
2. Drain the cooling system.

CAUTION: *When draining the coolant, keep in mind that cats and dogs are attracted by the ethelyne glycol antifreeze, and are quite likely to drink any that is left in an uncovered container or in puddles on the ground. This will prove fatal in sufficient quantity. Always drain the coolant into a sealable container. Coolant should be reused unless it is contaminated or several years old.*

3. Remove the mass air flow sensor and air intake duct.
4. Disconnect the serpentine drive belt.
5. Remove the alternator and bracket.
6. Remove the C3I ignition module and wiring. Tag all connectors for assembly.

7. Tag and disconnect all vacuum lines and wiring connectors as necessary to gain working clearance.

8. Disconnect the throttle, cruise control and T.V. linkage from the throttle body.

9. Disconnect the fuel lines and fuel rail. See Chapter 4 for the procedure on depressurizing the fuel system before removing any fuel lines.

10. Disconnect the heater and radiator hoses from the throttle body and intake manifold.

11. Remove the spark plug wires from the engine after tagging them for assembly.

12. Remove the intake manifold. Loosen the bolts in reverse of the torque sequence.

13. Remove the valve covers.

14. Remove the radiator and cooling fan.

15. Disconnect both exhaust manifolds. It may be easier to raise the vehicle and disconnect the exhaust pipe, then remove the right exhaust manifold with the cylinder head.

16. Remove the rocker arms, pedestals and pushrods. Keep all parts in order so they may be assembled in their original locations.

17. Disconnect the power steering pump and lay it aside with the lines connected.

18. Remove the dipstick tube.

19. Loosen the cylinder head bolts in reverse of the torque sequence. Lift the cylinder head clear and continue disassembly on the bench. Do not pry against the mating surfaces to loosen the cylinder head. Tapping lightly with a hammer should break the gasket free.

20. Installation is the reverse of removal. Torque all bolts in sequence to specifications. For all overhaul procedures, see below.

NOTE: *New cylinder head bolts are required whenever the head is removed for service.*

CLEANING AND INSPECTION

1. Remove all traces of carbon from the head, using a decarbon-type wire brush mounted in

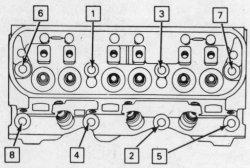

V6 head bolt torque sequence

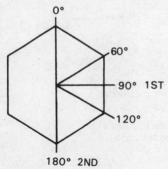

Tightening steps for V6 head bolts

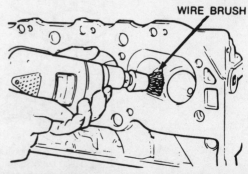

Use a wire brush and electric drill to remove carbon from the combustion chambers and exhaust ports

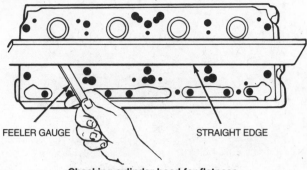

Checking cylinder head for flatness

an electric drill. Do not use a motorized brush on any gasket mating surface.

2. Lay a straight edge across the cylinder head face and check between the straight edge and the head with feeler gauges. Make the check at six points minimum. Cylinder head flatness should be within .003–.006 inch. These surfaces may be reconditioned by parallel grinding. If more than 10% must be removed, the head should be replaced.

Valves

REMOVAL AND INSPECTION

1. Remove the cylinder head(s) from the vehicle as previously outlined.

2. Using a suitable valve spring compres-

J-5892

ENGAGE AT LEAST 3 THREADS

Compressing the valve spring—typical

sor, compress the valve spring and remove the valve keys using a magnetic retrieval tool.

3. Slowly release the compressor and remove the valve spring caps (or rotors) and the valve springs.

4. Fabricate a valve arrangement board to use when you remove the valves, which will indicate the port in which each valve was originally installed (and which cylinder head on V6 models). Also note that the valve keys, rotators, caps, etc. should be arranged in a manner which will allow you to install them on the valve on which they were originally used.

5. Remove and discard the valve seals. On models using the umbrella type seals, note the location of the large and small seals for assembly purposes.

6. Thoroughly clean the valves on the wire wheel of a bench grinder, then clean the cylinder head mating surface with a soft wire wheel, a soft wire brush, or a wooden scraper. Avoid using a metallic scraper, since this can cause damage to the cylinder head mating surface, especially on models with aluminum heads.

7. Using a valve guide cleaner chucked into a drill, clean all of the valve guides.

8. Install each valve into its respective port (guide) of the cylinder head.

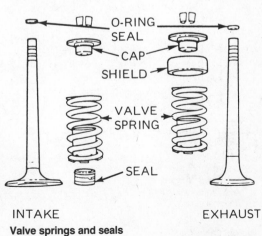

O-RING SEAL
CAP
SHIELD
VALVE SPRING
SEAL

INTAKE EXHAUST

Valve springs and seals

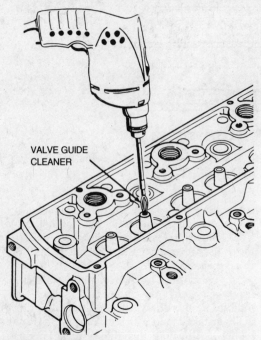

VALVE GUIDE
CLEANER

Cleaning valve guides

1. Proper tip pattern (rotator
   functioning properly)
2. No rotation pattern (replace
   rotator & check rotation)
3. Partial rotation tip pattern
   (replace rotator & check rotation)

Typical valve stem wear patterns

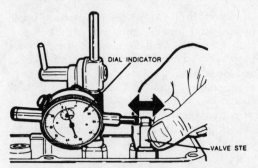

DIAL INDICATOR

VALVE STE

Checking the valve stem-to-guide clearance

9. Mount a dial indicator so that the stem is at 90° to the valve stem, as close to the valve guide as possible.

10. Move the valve off its seat, and measure the valve guide-to-stem clearance by rocking

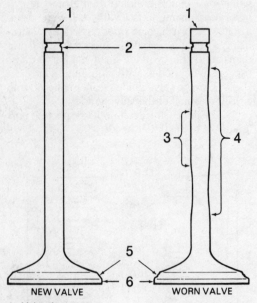

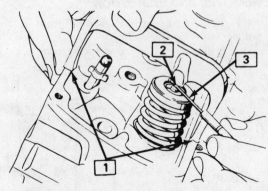

1. This area must be clean and smooth
2. .015 in. minimum clearance
3. Measuring gauge

Measuring valve stem height with special gauging tool

NEW VALVE   WORN VALVE

1. Valve tip
2. Keeper groove
3. Least worn valve stem
4. Most worn valve stem
5. Valve face
6. Margin

Typical valve wear

the stem back and forth to actuate the dial indicator.

11. Measure the valve stems using a micrometer, and compare to specifications, to determine whether stem or guide wear is responsible for excessive clearance. Consult the Specifications tables earlier in this chapter.

REFACING

NOTE: *All machine work should be performed by a competent, professional machine shop. Valve face angle is not always identical to valve seat angle.*

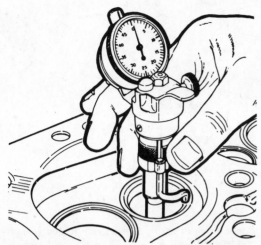

Have the valve seat concentricity checked at a machine shop

Home-made valve lapping tool

A minimum margin of $\frac{1}{32}$ in. should remain after grinding the valve. The valve stem top should also be squared and resurfaced, by placing the stem in the V-block of the grinder, and turning it while pressing lightly against the grinding wheel. Be sure to chamfer the edge of the tip so that the squared edges don't dig into the rocker arm.

LAPPING

This procedure should be performed after the valves and seats have been machined, to insure that each valve mates to each seat precisely.

1. Invert the cylinder head, lightly lubricate the valve stems, and install the valves in the head as numbered.
2. Coat valve seats with fine grinding compound, and attach the lapping tool suction cup to a valve head. Moisten the suction cup.
3. Rotate the tool between your palms, changing position and lifting the tool often to prevent grooving.
4. Lap the valve until a smooth, polished seat is evident.
5. Remove the valve and tool, and rinse away all traces of grinding compound.

Valve Guide Service

The valve guides used in these engines are integral with the cylinder head, that is, they cannot be replaced. Refer to the previous "Valves—Removal and Installation" to check the valve guides for wear.

Valve guides are most accurately repaired using the bronze wall rebuilding method. In this operation, "threads" are cut into the bore of the valve guide and bronze wire is turned into the threads. The bronze "wall" is then reamed to the proper diameter. This method

Lapping the valves by hand

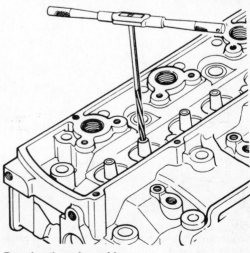

Reaming the valve guides

is well received for a number of reasons: it is relatively inexpensive, it offers better valve lubrication (the wire forms channels which retain oil), it offers less valve friction, and it preserves the original valve guide-to-seat relationship.

Another popular method of repairing valve guides is to have the guides "knurled." Knurling entails cutting into the bore of the valve guide with a special tool The cutting action "raises" metal off of the guide bore which actually narrows the inner diameter of the bore, thereby reducing the clearance between the valve guide bore and the valve stem. This method offers the same advantages as the bronze wall method, but will generally wear faster.

Either of the above services must be performed by a professional machine shop which has the specialized knowledge and tools necessary to perform the service.

Valve Seat Service

The valve seats are integral with the cylinder head on all engines. On all engines the seats are machined into the cylinder head casting itself.

VALVE SPRING TESTING

Place the spring on a flat surface next to a square. Measure the height of the spring, and rotate it against the edge of the square to measure distortion. If spring height varies (by comparison) by more than 1/16 in. or if distortion exceeds 1/16 in., replace the spring.

In addition to evaluating the spring as above, test the spring pressure at the installed and compressed (installed height minus valve lift) height using a valve spring tester. Spring pressure should be ± 1 lb. of all other springs in either position.

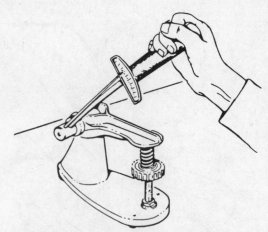

Checking valve spring tension with torque wrench and tension tool

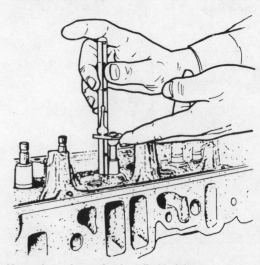

Measuring valve spring installed height

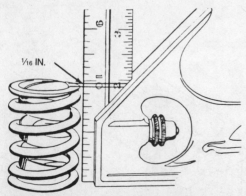

1/16 IN.

Checking valve spring for squareness. There should be no more than 1/16 in. variance in height while rotating springs

VALVE AND SPRING INSTALLATION

NOTE: *Be sure that all traces of lapping compound have been cleaned off before the valves are installed.*

1. Lubricate all of the valve stems with a light coating of engine oil, then install the valves into the proper ports/guides.

2. If umbrella-type valve seals are used, install them at this time. Be sure to use a seal protector to prevent damage to the seals as they are pushed over the valve keeper grooves. If O-ring seals are used, don't install them yet.

3. Install the valve springs and the spring retainers (or rotators), and using the valve compressing tool, compress the springs.

4. If umbrella-type seals are used, just install the valve keepers (white grease may be used to hold them in place) and release the pressure on the compressing tool. If O-ring type seals are used, carefully work the seals into the

second groove of the valve (closest to the head), install the valve keepers and release the pressure on the tool.

NOTE: *If the O-ring seals are installed BEFORE the springs and retainers are compressed, the seal will be destroyed.*

5. After all of the valves are installed and retained, tap each valve spring retainer with a rubber mallet to seat the keepers in the retainer.

Timing Gear Cover

REMOVAL AND INSTALLATION

2.5L Engine

1. Remove the drive belt(s).
2. Remove the right front inner fender splash shield.
3. Remove the crankshaft pulley bolt and remove the crankshaft pulley.

NOTE: *If only the timing cover crankshaft oil seal is to be replaced, it is not necessary to remove the timing cover.*

4. Remove the alternator lower bracket.
5. Remove the front engine mounts.

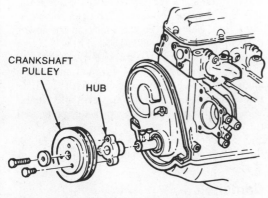

Removing the crankshaft pulley and hub

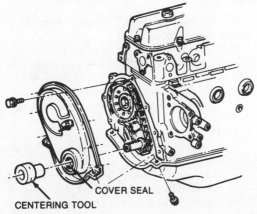

Front cover installation; a centering tool can aid in positioning

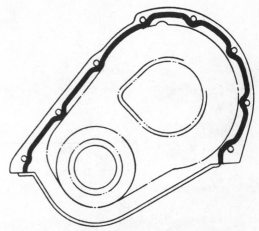

Apply sealer to timing gear cover as shown

6. Using a floor jack and a block of wood, raise the engine slightly to gain working clearance.
7. Remove the engine mount bracket-to-cylinder block bolts and remove the bracket and mount as an assembly.
8. Remove the oil pan to front cover bolts.
9. Remove the front cover to block bolts.
10. Pull the cover slightly forward just enough to allow cutting of the oil pan front seal flush with the block on both sides.
11. Remove the front cover and attached portion of the oil pan seal.
12. Clean all gasket surfaces thoroughly on both the timing gear cover and cylinder block. Using a suitable installing tool, replace the crankshaft oil seal.
13. Apply a ⅜ in. wide by 3/16 in. bead of RTV sealer to the joint at the oil pan and timing gear cover.
14. Apply a ¼ in. wide by ⅛ in. thick bead of RTV sealer to the timing gear cover at the block mating surfaces.
15. Align the front cover seal with a centering tool (J-34995 or equivalent) and install the front cover. Tighten two opposing cover screws with the centering tool in place, then remove the tool.
16. Torque the timing cover mounting screws to 7.5 ft.lb. (10 Nm) in alternating sequence.
17. The remainder of the installation is the reverse of the removal procedure. Torque the harmonic balancer center bolt to 200 ft.lb. (260 Nm).

3.0L V6

1. Disconnect the negative battery cable.
2. Loosen, but do not remove, the water pump pulley bolts.
3. Remove the serpentine drive belt.

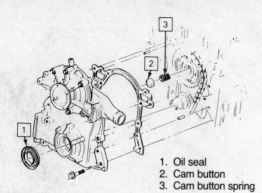

1. Oil seal
2. Cam button
3. Cam button spring

V6 front cover and seal

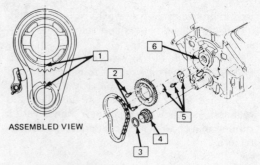

ASSEMBLED VIEW

1. Timing marks aligned
2. 22 ft. lbs. (30 Nm)
3. Seal
4. Crankshaft gear
5. Dampner assembly
6. Camshaft

V6 timing chain and sprockets

4. Remove the water pump pulley and bolts.

5. Raise the vehicle and support it safely.

6. Remove the right tire and wheel assembly.

7. Remove the right inner fender splash shield.

8. Drain the cooling system.

CAUTION: *When draining the coolant, keep in mind that cats and dogs are attracted by the ethelyne glycol antifreeze, and are quite likely to drink any that is left in an uncovered container or in puddles on the ground. This will prove fatal in sufficient quantity. Always drain the coolant into a sealable container. Coolant should be reused unless it is contaminated or several years old.*

9. Remove the crankshaft balancer.

10. Drain the crankcase and remove the oil filter.

11. Remove the radiator and heater hoses.

12. Remove the crankshaft sensor.

13. Remove the oil pan and gasket.

14. Remove the water pump.

15. Remove the front cover bolts, then remove the front cover and gasket.

16. Clean all gasket mating surfaces on the front cover and oil pan.

17. Installation is the reverse of removal. Make sure the oil pump drive gear is properly engaged to the crankshaft drive gear. Apply thread sealer/lubricant to all front cover and water pump bolts. Torque the front cover bolts to 22 ft.lb. (30 Nm); oil pan bolts to 7 ft.lb. (10 Nm); and water pump bolts to 7.5 ft.lb. (11 Nm). Tighten the crankshaft balancer center bolt to 200 ft.lb. (270 Nm) and the water pump pulley bolts to 7 ft.lb. (10 Nm).

Timing Chain or Gear

REMOVAL AND INSTALLATION

2.5L Engine

The camshaft gear must be pressed from the camshaft using an arbor press. See the following section on camshaft removal procedures.

3.0L V6

1. Remove the timing chain cover as previously described.

2. Place the No. 1 piston at TDC with the marks on the camshaft and crankshaft sprocket aligned.

3. Remove the camshaft sprocket bolts and remove the sprocket and chain together. If the sprocket does not slide from the camshaft easily, a light blow with a soft mallet at the lower edge of the sprocket will dislodge it.

4. To install, hold the sprocket vertically with the chain hanging down. Align the marks, then align the dowel in the camshaft with the hole in the sprocket. Install the sprocket and chain.

5. Install the camshaft sprocket bolts and torque to 31 ft.lb. (42 Nm). Lubricate the chain and sprocket with clean engine oil and install the timing cover as outlined previously.

Camshaft

REMOVAL AND INSTALLATION

2.5L Engine

1. Remove the engine from the vehicle as previously outlined.

2. Remove the rocker cover, loosen the rocker arms and pivot them aside. Remove the pushrods and valve lifters, keeping them in order so they may be installed in their original locations. A lifter removal tool is necessary.

3. Remove the distributor.

4. Remove the oil pump drive shaft.

5. Remove the front pulley and crankshaft hub.

6. Remove the timing gear cover.

7. Remove the camshaft thrust plate screws.

8. Carefully remove the camshaft and gear through the front of the block.

9. Use an arbor press and adapter J791 mandrel or equivalent to separate the gear from

Removing camshaft thrust plate screws on 4 cyl

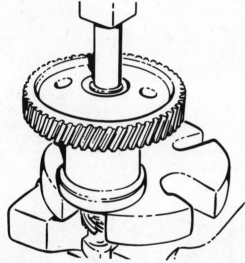

Removing camshaft timing gear with an arbor press

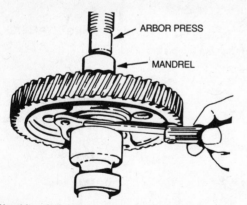

Checking timing gear and thrust plate end clearance

ity engine oil supplement and align the timing marks with the No. 1 cylinder at TDC. Torque the camshaft thrust plate to block screws to 7.5 ft.lb. (10 Nm) and the front pulley and hub center bolt to 160 ft.lb. (212 Nm).

3.0L V6

1. Remove the engine as previously outlined.
2. Mount the engine on a suitable work stand.
3. Remove the intake manifold.
4. Remove the rocker arm covers.
5. Remove the rocker arm assemblies, pushrods and valve lifters, keeping all parts in order so they may be assembled in their original locations. A lifter removal tool is available to make this job easier.
6. Remove the crankshaft pulley and harmonic balancer assembly. Do not attempt to separate the pulley from the hub.
7. Remove the timing chain cover.
8. Align the timing marks to avoid burring the camshaft journals during removal.
9. Remove the timing chain and sprockets.
10. Remove the camshaft thrust plate screws and carefully slide the camshaft forward out of the engine block. Be careful not to scratch any camshaft bearing surfaces with the cam lobes during removal or installation.
11. Installation is the reverse of removal. Coat the camshaft with clean engine oil or suitable high quality oil additive before installing. Torque all bolts to specifications.

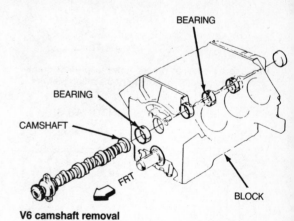

V6 camshaft removal

the camshaft. Support the camshaft when installing or removing the gear and position the thrust plate to avoid damage by interference with the woodruff key as the gear is removed. Thrust plate end clearance should be .0015–.0050 in. If less, replace the spacer ring; if more, replace the thrust plate.

10. Installation is the reverse of removal. Lubricate the camshaft journals with high qual-

Pistons and Connecting Rod Assemblies

REMOVAL

1. Remove the engine assembly from the vehicle.
2. Remove the intake manifold, cylinder head or heads.

3. Remove the oil pan.

4. Remove the oil pump assembly.

5. Stamp the cylinder number on the machine surfaces of the bolt bosses of the connecting rod and cap for identification when reinstalling. If the pistons are to be removed from the connecting rod, mark the cylinder number on the piston with a silver pencil or quick drying paint for proper cylinder indentification and cap-to-rod location. Engines are numbered oddly on the right bank; evenly on the left.

6. Examine the cylinder bore above the ring travel. If a ridge exists, remove the ridge with a ridge reamer before attempting to remove the piston and rod assembly.

7. Remove the rod bearing cap and bearing.

8. Install a guide hose over threads of rod bolts. This is to prevent damage to bearing journal and rod bolt threads.

9. Remove the rod and piston assembly through the top of the cylinder bore.

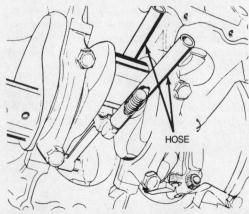

Use short pieces of rubber hose to protect crankshaft journals when removing or installing pistons

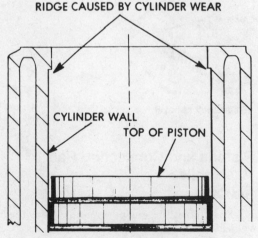

Ridge formed by piston rings at the top of their travel

10. Remove the other rod and piston assemblies in the same manner.

PISTON PIN REMOVAL AND INSTALLATION

Use care at all times when handling and servicing connecting rods and pistons. To prevent possible damage to these units, do not clamp the rod or piston in a vise since they may become distorted. Do not allow the pistons to strike against one another, against hard objects or bench surfaces, since distortion of the piston contour or nicks in the soft aluminum material may result.

1. Remove the piston rings using a suitable piston ring remover.

2. Remove the piston pin lockring, if used. Install the guide bushing of the piston pin removing and installing tool.

3. Install the piston and connecting rod assembly on a support, and place the assembly in an arbor press. Press the pin out of the connecting rod, using the appropriate piston pin tool.

4. Assembly is the reverse of disassembly. Use new lockrings where needed.

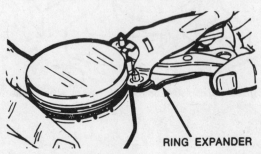

Removing the piston rings

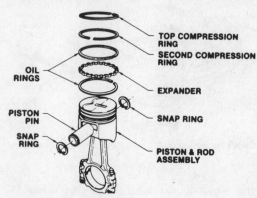

Piston rings and wrist pin

CLEANING AND INSPECTION
Connecting Rods

Wash connecting rods in cleaning solvent and dry with compressed air. Check for twisted or bent rods and inspect for nicks or cracks. Replace connecting rods that are damaged.

Pistons

Clean varnish from piston skirts and pins with a cleaning solvent. DO NOT WIRE BRUSH ANY PART OF THE PISTON. Clean the ring grooves with a groove cleaner and make sure oil ring holes and slots are clean.

Inspect the piston for cracked ring lands, skirts or pin bosses, wavy or worn ring lands, scuffed or damaged skirts, eroded areas at the top of the piston. Replace pistons that are damaged or show signs of excessive wear. Inspect the grooves for nicks or burrs that might cause the rings to hang up. Measure piston skirt (across center line of piston pin) and check piston clearance.

MEASURING THE OLD PISTONS

Check used piston-to-cylinder bore clearance as follows:

1. Measure the cylinder bore diameter with a telescope gauge.

2. Measure the piston diameter. When measuring the pistons for size or taper, measurements must be made with the piston pin removed.

3. Subtract the piston diameter from the

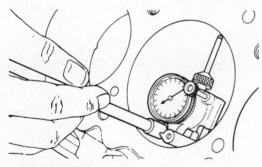

Measuring cylinder bore

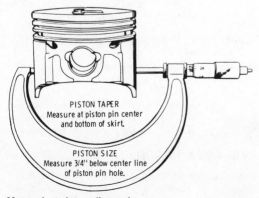

PISTON TAPER
Measure at piston pin center
and bottom of skirt.

PISTON SIZE
Measure 3/4'' below center line
of piston pin hole.

Measuring piston dimensions

cylinder bore diameter to determine piston-to-bore clearance.

4. Compare the piston-to-bore clearances obtained with those clearances recommended. Determine if the piston-to-bore clearance is in the acceptable range.

5. When measuring taper, the largest reading must be at the bottom of the piston skirt.

SELECTING NEW PISTONS

1. If the used piston is not acceptable, check the service piston size and determine if a new piston can be selected. Service pistons are available in standard, high limit and standard 0.254mm (0.010 in.) oversize.

2. If the cylinder bore must be reconditioned, measure the new piston diameter, then hone the cylinder bore to obtain the prefered clearance.

3. Select a new piston and mark the piston to identify the cylinder for which it was fitted. On some cars, oversize pistons may be found. These pistons will be 0.254mm (0.010 in.) oversize.

CYLINDER HONING

1. When cylinders are being honed, follow the manufacturer's recommendations for the use of the hone.

2. Occasionally during the honing operation, the cylinder bore should be thoroughly cleaned and the selected piston checked for correct fit.

3. When finish-honing a cylinder bore, the hone should be moved up and down at a sufficient speed to obtain a very fine uniform surface finish in a cross-hatch pattern of approximately 45–65 degrees included angle. The finish marks should be clean but not sharp, free from imbedded particles and torn or folded metal.

4. Permanently mark the piston for the cylinder to which it has been fitted and proceed to hone the remaining cylinders.

NOTE: *Handle pistons with care. Do not attempt to force pistons through cylinders until the cylinders have been honed to correct size. Pistons can be distorted through careless handling.*

5. Thoroughly clean the bores with hot water and detergent. Scrub well with a stiff bristle brush and rinse thoroughly with hot water. It is extremely essential that a good cleaning operation be performed. If any of the abrasive material is allowed to remain in the cylinder bores, it will rapidly wear the new rings and cylinder bores. The bores should be swabbed several times with light engine oil and a clean cloth and then wiped with a clean dry cloth. CYLINDERS SHOULD NOT BE CLEANED WITH KEROSENE OR GASOLINE. Clean

the remainder of the cylinder block to remove the excess material spread during the honing operation.

CHECKING CYLINDER BORE

Cylinder bore size can be measured with inside micrometers or a cylinder gauge. The most wear will occur at the top of the ring travel. Reconditioned cylinder bores should be held to not more than 0.025mm (0.001 in.) taper.

If the cylinder bores are smooth, the cylinder walls should not be deglazed. If the cylinder walls are scored, the walls may have to be honed before installing new rings. It is important that reconditioned cylinder bores be thoroughly washed with a soap and water solution to remove all traces of abrasive material to eliminate premature wear.

Piston Rings

The pistons have three rings (two compression rings and one oil ring). The oil ring consists of two rails and an expander. Pistons do not have oil drain holes behind the rings.

RING TOLERANCES

When installing new rings, ring gap and side clearance should be checked as follows:

Piston Ring and Rail Gap

Each ring and rail gap must be measured with the ring or rail positioned squarely and at the bottom of the ring-travel area of the bore.

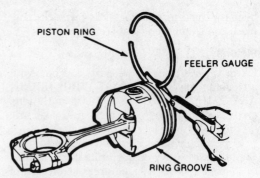

Checking ring side clearance

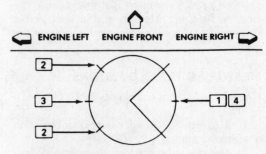

1. Oil ring spacer gap
   (tang in hole or slot with ARC)
2. Oil ring rail gaps
3. 2nd compression ring gap
4. Top compression ring cap

Piston ring gap locations

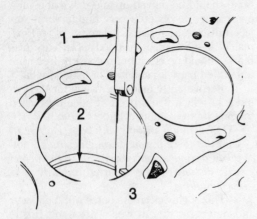

1. Feeler gauge
2. Piston pin
3. Measure clearance with ring at bottom of travel

Measuring piston ring gap

Side Clearance

Each ring must be checked for side clearance in its respective piston groove by inserting a feeler gauge between the ring and its upper land. The piston grooves must be cleaned be-

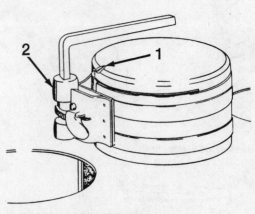

1. Notch toward front of engine
2. Ring compressor

Installing piston into cylinder bore

fore checking the ring for side clearance specifications. To check oil ring side clearance, the oil rings must be installed on the piston.

RING INSTALLATION

For service ring specifications and detailed installation productions, refer to the instructions furnished with the parts package.

Connecting Rod Bearings

If you have already removed the connecting rod and piston assemblies from the engine, follow only Steps 3–7 of the following procedure.

REMOVAL, INSPECTION AND INSTALLATION

The connecting rod bearings are designed to have a slight projection above the rod and cap faces to insure a positive contact. The bearings can be replaced without removing the rod and piston assemblies from the engine.

1. Remove the oil pan. See the Oil Pan procedures, below. It may be necessary to remove the oil pump to provide access to rear connecting rod bearings.

2. With the the connecting rod journal at the bottom, stamp the cylinder number on the machined surfaces of the connecting rod and cap for identification when installing, then remove the caps.

3. Inspect journals for roughness and wear. Slight roughness may be removed with a fine grit polishing cloth saturated with engine oil. Burrs may be removed with a fine oil stone by moving the stone on the journal circumference. Do not move the stone back and forth across the journal. If the journals are scored or ridged, the crankshaft must be replaced.

4. The connecting rod journals should be checked for out-of-round and correct size with a micrometer.

NOTE: *Crankshaft rod journals will normally be standard size. If any undersized bearings are used, all will be 0.254mm undersize and 0.254mm will be stamped on the number 4 counterweight.*

If plastic gauging material is to be used:

5. Clean oil from the journal bearing cap, connecting rod and outer and inner surfaces of the bearing inserts. Position the insert so that the tang is properly aligned with the notch in the rod and cap.

6. Place a piece of plastic gauging material in the center of lower bearing shell.

7. Remove the bearing cap and determine the bearing clearances by comparing the width of the flattened plastic gauging material at its widest point with the graduation on the container. The number within the graduation on the envelope indicates the clearance in thousandths of an inch or millimeters. If this clearance is excessive, replace the bearing and recheck the clearance with the plastic gauging material. Lubricate the bearing with engine oil before installation. Repeat Steps 2–7 on the remaining connecting rod bearings. All rods must be connected to their journals when rotating the crankshaft, to prevent engine damage.

Piston and Connecting Rod

INSTALLATION

1. Install some lengths of rubber tubing over the connecting rod bolts to prevent damage to the journals.

2. Apply engine oil to the rings and piston, then install a piston ring compressing tool on the piston.

3. Install the assembly in its respective cylinder bore.

4. Lubricate the crankshaft journal with engine oil and install the connecting rod bearing and cap, with the bearing index tang in rod and cap on same side.

NOTE: *When more than one rod and piston assembly is being installed, the connecting rod cap attaching nuts should be tightened only enough to keep each rod in position until all have been installed. This will aid installation of the remaining piston assemblies.*

5. Torque the rod bolt nuts to specification. Using a feeler gauge and small prybar, check connecting rod side clearance.

6. Install all other parts in reverse order of removal.

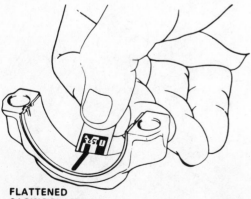

FLATTENED
GAGING PLASTIC

Checking rod bearing clearance with Plastigage® or equivalent

RING COMPRESSOR

Using a wooden hammer handle, tap the piston down through the ring compressor and into the cylinder

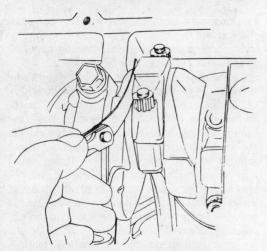

Measuring side clearance on single rod journal

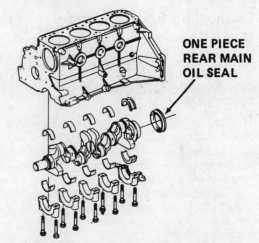

ONE PIECE
REAR MAIN
OIL SEAL

Exploded view of 4 cyl crankshaft and bearings

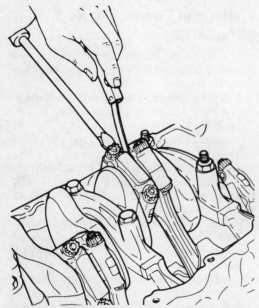

Checking connecting rod side clearance with a feeler gauge. Use a small pry bar to carefully spread the connecting rods

7. Install the engine in the car. See Engine Removal and Installation.

Crankshaft
REMOVAL

1. Remove the engine assembly as previously outlined.
2. Remove the engine front cover.
3. Remove the timing chain and sprockets.
4. Remove the oil pan.
5. Remove the oil pump.
6. Stamp the cylinder number on the machined surfaces of the bolt boses of the con-

necting rods and caps for identification when installing. If the pistons are to be removed from the connecting rod, mark the cylinder number on each piston with an indelible marker, silver pencil or quick drying paint for proper cylinder identification and cap to rod location.

7. Remove the connecting rod caps and store them so that they can be installed in their original positions.

8. Remove all the main bearing caps.

9. Note the position of the keyway in the crankshaft so it can be installed in the same position.

10. Lift the crankshaft out of the block. The rods will pivot to the center of the engine when the crankshaft is removed.

11. Remove both halves of the rear main oil seal. 2.5L engines use a one-piece seal.

INSPECTION AND INSTALLATION

1. Using a dial indicator, check the crankshaft journal runout. Measure the crankshaft

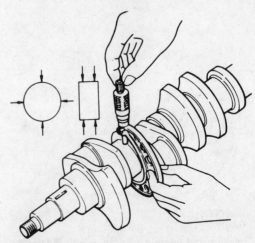

Checking main bearing journal diameter

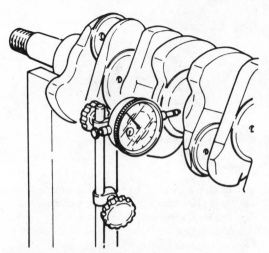

Checking crankshaft journal runout

journals with a micrometer to determine the correct size rod and main bearings to be used. Whenever a new or reconditioned crankshaft is installed, new connecting rod bearings and main bearings should be installed. See Main Bearings and Rod Bearings.

2. Clean all oil passages in the block and crankshaft if it is being reused.

NOTE: *A new rear main seal should be installed anytime the crankshaft is removed or replaced.*

3. Install sufficient oil pan bolts in the block to align with the connecting rod bolts. Use rubber bands between the bolts to position the connecting rods as required. Connecting rod position can be adjusted by increasing the tension on the rubber bands with additional turns around the pan bolts or thread protectors.

4. Position the upper half of main bearings in the block and lubricate them with engine oil.

5. Position crankshaft keyway in the same position as removed and lower it into block. The connecting rods will follow the crank pins into the correct position as the crankshaft is lowered.

6. Lubricate the thrust flanges with 10501609 Lubricant or equivalent. Install caps with the lower half of the bearings lubricated with engine oil. Lubricate the cap bolts with engine oil and install, but do not tighten.

7. With a block of wood, bump the shaft in each direction to align the thrust flanges of the main bearing. After bumping the shaft in each direction, wedge the shaft to the front and hold it while torquing the thrust bearing cap bolts.

NOTE: *In order to prevent the possibility of cylinder block and/or main bearing cap damage, the main bearing caps are to be tapped into their cylinder block cavity using a wood or rubber mallet before the bolts are*

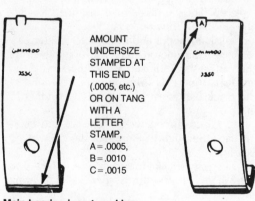

AMOUNT UNDERSIZE STAMPED AT THIS END (.0005, etc.) OR ON TANG WITH A LETTER STAMP, A = .0005, B = .0010 C = .0015

Main bearing insert markings

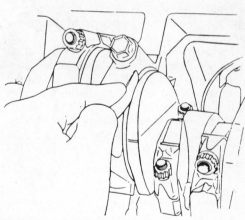

Measuring crankshaft end play

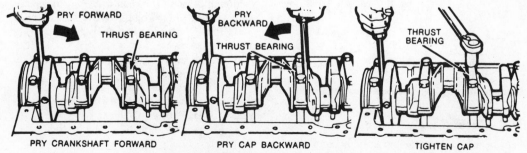

PRY FORWARD — THRUST BEARING

PRY BACKWARD — THRUST BEARING

THRUST BEARING

PRY CRANKSHAFT FORWARD   PRY CAP BACKWARD   TIGHTEN CAP

Aligning the crankshaft thrust bearing

installed. Do not use attaching bolts to pull the main bearing caps into their seats. Failure to observe this information may damage the cylinder block or a bearing cap.

8. Torque all main bearing caps to specification. Check crankshaft endplay, using a flat feeler gauge.

9. Remove the connecting rod bolt thread protectors and lubricate the connecting rod bearings with engine oil.

10. Install the connecting rod bearing caps in their original position. Torque the nuts to specification.

11. Complete the installation by reversing the removal steps.

Main Bearings

CHECKING BEARING CLEARANCE

1. Remove the bearing cap and wipe the oil from the crankshaft journal and the outer and inner surfaces of the bearing shell.

2. Place a piece of plastic gauging material in the center of the bearing.

3. Use a floor jack or other means to hold the crankshaft against the upper bearing shell. This is necessary to obtain accurate clearance readings when using plastic gauging material.

4. Install the bearing cap and bearing. Place engine oil on the cap bolts and install. Torque the bolts to specification.

5. Remove the bearing cap and determine the bearing clearance by comparing the width of the flattened plastic gauging material at its widest point with the graduations on the gauging material container. The number within the graduation on the envelope indicates the clearance in millimeters or thousandths of an inch. If the clearance is greater than allowed, REPLACE BOTH BEARING SHELLS AS A SET. Recheck the clearance after replacing the shells.

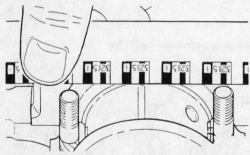

Measuring bearing clearance with gauging material

REPLACEMENT

Main bearing clearances must be corrected by the use of selective upper and lower shells.

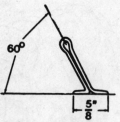

Home-made bearing roll-out pin

UNDER NO CIRCUMSTANCES should the use of shims behind the shells to compensate for wear be attempted. To install the main bearing shells, proceed as follows:

1. Remove the oil pan as outlined below. On some models, the oil pump may also have to be removed.

2. Loosen all main bearing caps.

3. Remove the bearing cap and remove the lower shell.

4. Insert a flattened cotter pin or roll pin in the oil passage hole in the crankshaft, then rotate the crankshaft in the direction opposite to cranking rotation. The pin will contact the upper shell and roll it out.

5. The main bearing journals should be checked for roughness and wear. Slight roughness may be removed with a fine grit polishing cloth saturated with engine oil. Burrs may be removed with a fine oil stone. If the journals are scored or ridged, the crankshaft must be replaced. The journals can be measured for out-of-round with the crankshaft installed by using a crankshaft caliper and inside micrometer or a main bearing micrometer. The upper bearing shell must be removed when measuring the crankshaft journals. Maximum out-of-round of the crankshaft journals must not exceed 0.0015 in. (0.037mm).

6. Clean the crankshaft journals and bearing caps thoroughly before installing new main bearings.

7. Apply special lubricant, No. 1050169 or equivalent, to the thrust flanges of bearing shells.

8. Place a new upper shell on the crankshaft journal with locating tang in the correct position and rotate the shaft to turn it into place using a cotter pin or roll pin as during removal.

9. Place a new bearing shell in the bearing cap.

10. Install a new oil seal in the rear main bearing cap and block.

11. Lubricate the main bearings with engine oil. Lubricate the thrust surface with lubricant 1050169 or equivalent.

12. Lubricate the main bearing cap bolts with engine oil.

NOTE: *In order to prevent the possibility of*

cylinder block and/or main bearing cap damage, the main bearing caps are to be tapped into their cylinder block cavity using a wood or rubber mallet before the attaching bolts are installed. Do not use attaching bolts to pull the main bearing caps into their seats. Failure to observe this information may damage the cylinder block or a bearing cap.

13. Torque the main bearing cap bolts to specifications.

Oil Pan

REMOVAL AND INSTALLATION

2.5L Engine

1. Disconnect both battery cables.
2. Raise the vehicle and support it safely.
3. Drain the crankcase.
4. Disconnect the exhaust pipe at the manifold and hangers and swing it out of the way.
5. Remove the starter and flywheel covers.
6. Remove the starter.
7. Remove the oil pan bolts and remove the oil pan.
8. Installation is the reverse of removal. Clean all gasket mating surfaces. Tighten the oil pan bolts to 4.5 ft.lb. (6 Nm).

3.0L V6

1. Disconnect the negative battery cable.
2. Raise and support the vehicle safely.
3. Drain the crankcase.
4. Remove the oil filter.
5. Remove the flywheel cover.
6. Remove the oil pan bolts and oil pan tensioner spring located behind the oil filter adapter.
7. Remove the oil pan.
8. Installation is the reverse of removal. Clean

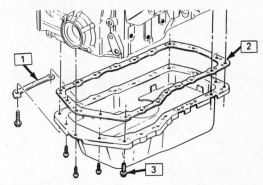

1. Tension spring
2. Rubber gasket
3. Bolt

V6 oil pan installation. Do not overtighten pan bolts

all gasket mating surfaces and torque the oil pan bolts to 7.5 ft.lb. (10 Nm). Do not overtighten.

Oil Pump

REMOVAL, OVERHAUL AND INSTALLATION

2.5L Engine

1. Remove the oil pan as outlined above.
2. Remove the two flange mounting bolts from the main bearing cap bolt.
3. Remove the oil pump and screen as an assembly.
4. Drain the oil from the pump.
5. Remove the suction pipe and screen assembly.
6. Remove the oil pump cover.
7. Remove the pump gears.
8. Remove the cotter pin or unscrew the plug from the pressure regulator valve bore,

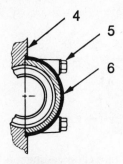

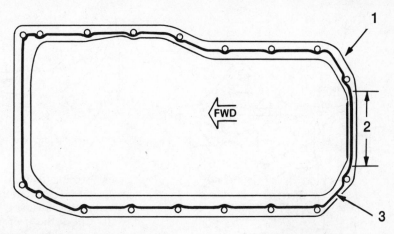

1. Oil pan
2. Apply sealer
3. Apply sealer
4. Engine block
5. Rear bearing
6. Bearing cap groove

2.5L oil pan sealer application

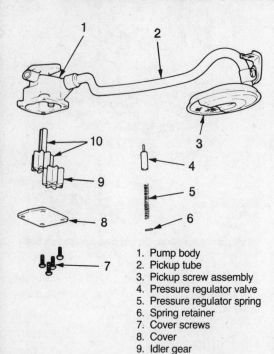

1. Pump body
2. Pickup tube
3. Pickup screw assembly
4. Pressure regulator valve
5. Pressure regulator spring
6. Spring retainer
7. Cover screws
8. Cover
9. Idler gear
10. Drive gear and shaft

2.5L oil pump assembly

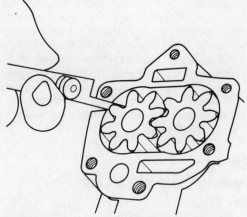

Measuring oil pump gear side clearance on 2.5L

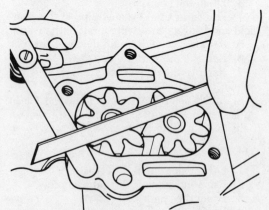

Measuring oil pump end clearance on 2.5L

then remove the spring and pressure regulator valve. If the valve is stuck, soak the pump housing in carburetor cleaning solvent to free up the valve.

CAUTION: *The pressure regulator valve spring is under tension. Exercise caution when removing the cotter pin or unscrewing the plug to disassemble the pressure regulator or bodily injury may result.*

9. Clean all oil pump parts of sludge, oil and varnish by soaking the parts in carburetor cleaning solvent. Check the pump housing for

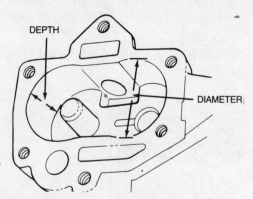

Measuring oil pump gear pocket on 2.5L

cracks, scoring, damaged threads or casting imperfections. If any problems are noted, replace the oil pump housing.

10. Check the pressure regulator valve for scoring or sticking. Burrs may be removed with a fine oil stone. Check the regulator valve spring for loss of tension and bending; if in doubt, replace the spring.

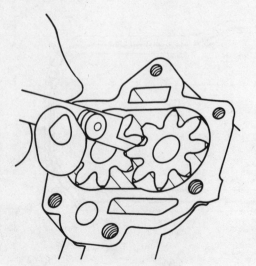

Measuring oil pump gear lash on 2.5L

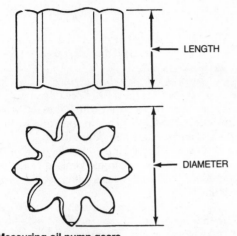

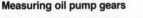

Measuring oil pump gears

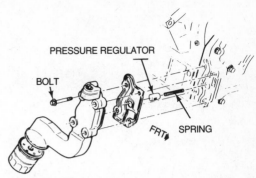

V6 oil filter adapter

11. Check the oil pump gears for chipping, galling or wear and replace as necessary.

12. Install the gears into the pump housing and check clearances as follows:

a. Backlash—0.009–0.015 in. (0.23–0.38mm)

b. Gear Pocket Depth—0.995–0.998 in. (25.27–25.35mm)

c. Gear Pocket Diameter—1.503–1.506 in. (38.18–38.25mm)

d. Gear Pocket Length—0.999–1.002 in. (25.37–25.45mm)

e. Drive Gear Diameter—1.496–1.500 in. (38.05–38.10mm)

f. Gear Side Clearance—0.004 in. max (0.10mm)

g. End Clearance—0.002–0.005 in. (0.05–0.13mm)

h. Valve-to-Bore Clearance—0.0015–0.0035 in. (0.038–0.089mm)

13. Lubricate all oil pump parts with clean engine oil during assembly and pack all pump cavities with petroleum jelly before final assembly of the gears to insure oil pump priming.

CAUTION: *It is essential to pack the oil pump properly with petroleum jelly to avoid possible engine damage from oil starvation when the engine is started after an oil pump overhaul.*

14. The remainder of the oil pump installation is the reverse of removal. Use original equipment gaskets when assembling the oil pump as the gasket thickness is critical to proper pump operation. Torque the pump cover bolts to 10 ft.lb. (14 Nm) and the suction tube bolts to 7.5 ft.lb. (10 Nm). If used, torque the pressure regulator valve plug to 15 ft.lb. (20 Nm).

3.0L V6

1. Remove the timing chain cover from the engine as previously described.

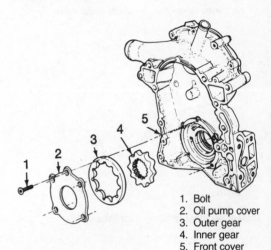

1. Bolt
2. Oil pump cover
3. Outer gear
4. Inner gear
5. Front cover

V6 oil pump assembly

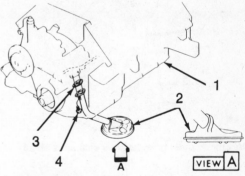

1. Engine block
2. Oil pump pipe and screen
3. Gasket
4. Bolt

V6 oil pump pipe and screen assembly

2. Remove the oil filter adapter.

3. Remove the pressure regulator valve and valve spring. Exercise caution when removing the valve spring; it is under tension.

4. Remove the oil pump cover attaching screws and remove the cover.

5. Remove the pump gears. Clean all parts in solvent to remove varnish, sludge and dirt.

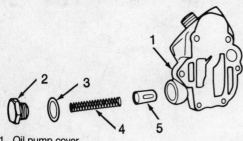

1. Oil pump cover
2. Plug
3. Washer
4. Spring
5. Relief valve

V6 oil pump cover and pressure relief valve

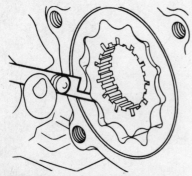

Measuring inner gear tip clearance on V6

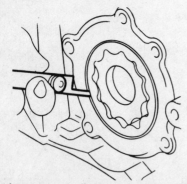

Measuring outer gear diameter clearance on V6

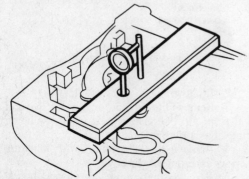

Measuring gear end clearance on V6

Remove all old gasket material from all mating surfaces.

6. Inspect the front cover and housing for cracks, scoring, damaged threads, excessive wear or a damaged casing.

7. Inspect the pressure regulator valve for scoring, sticking in the valve bore or burrs. Minor burrs may be removed with a fine oil stone. Check the regulator spring for bending or tension loss and replace if in doubt.

8. Inspect the pump gears for chipping, galling or excessive wear and replace as necessary. Measure the clearances with a feeler gauge as follows:

    a. Inner Gear Tip Clearance—0.006 in. (0.152mm)

    b. Outer Gear Diameter Clearance— 0.008–0.015 in. (0.203–0.381mm)

    c. Gear End Clearance—0.001–0.0035 in. (0.025–0.089mm)

9. Lubricate the gears with clean engine oil and assemble into the housing.

10. Pack all pump cavities with petroleum jelly. This is extremely important to avoid oil starvation when the engine is started after overhauling the pump.

11. Install the pump cover and tighten the bolts to 8 ft.lb. (11 Nm).

12. Install the pressure regulator valve spring and valve, then install the oil filter adapter using a new gasket. Tighten the oil filter adapter to 30 ft.lb. (41 Nm).

13. Install the front cover on the engine and refill the crankcase with clean engine oil. Replace the filter.

Rear Main Oil Seal

REMOVAL AND INSTALLATION

2.5L Engine

NOTE: *The rear main bearing oil seal is a one piece unit and can be replaced without removal of the oil pan or crankshaft.*

1. Remove the transaxle assembly as described in Chapter 6.

2. If equipped with manual transmission, remove the pressure plate and clutch disc.

3. Remove the retaining bolts and the flywheel.

4. Pry out the rear main seal with a suitable small prybar.

5. Clean the block and crankshaft-to-seal mating surfaces.

6. Using installer tool J-34924 or equivalent, lubricate the outside of the seal and press it evenly into the block.

7. Install the remaining components in the reverse of the removal procedure. Torque the flywheel bolts to 44 ft.lb. (60 Nm).

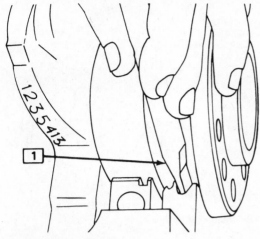

1. Packing tool J-21526-2

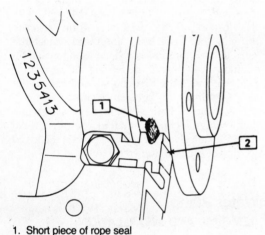

1. Short piece of rope seal
2. Guide tool J-21526-1 installed

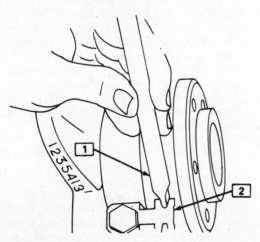

1. Packing tool
2. Guide tool

Rear main seal installation on V6

3.0L V6

Braided fabric seals are pressed into grooves formed in the crankcase and rear bearing cap to seal against the leakage of oil around the crankshaft. A new braided fabric seal can be installed in the crankcase only when crankshaft is removed, but it can be repaired while the crankshaft is installed. The seal can be replaced in the bearing cap whenever the cap is removed. Remove the old cap seal and place a new seal in the groove with both ends projecting above the parting surface of the cap. Force the seal into the groove by rubbing down with a hammer handle or smooth stick until the seal projects above the groove not more than $1/16$ in. Cut ends off flush with the mating surface of the cap, using a sharp knife or razor blade.

NOTE: *The engine must be operated at a slow speed when first started after a new braided seal is installed.*

Neoprene composition seals are placed in grooves in the sides of bearing cap to seal against leakage in the joints between cap and crankcase. The neoprene composition swells in the presence of oil and heat. The seals are undersize when newly installed and may even leak for a short time until the seals have had time to swell and seal the opening. The neoprene seals are slightly longer than the grooves in the bearing cap but must not be cut to length. Before installing the seals, soak them for two minutes in light oil or kerosene. After installation of the bearing cap in the crankcase, install the seal in

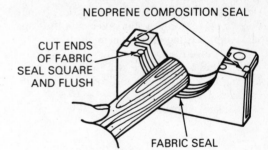

NEOPRENE COMPOSITION SEAL
CUT ENDS OF FABRIC SEAL SQUARE AND FLUSH
FABRIC SEAL

Installing rear main bearing cap oil seal on V6

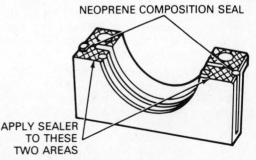

NEOPRENE COMPOSITION SEAL
APPLY SEALER TO THESE TWO AREAS

Applying sealer to bearing cap on V6

the bearing cap. After the seal is installed, force it up into the cap with a blunt instrument to be sure of a seal at the upper parting line between the cap and case.

NOTE: *To help eliminate oil leakage at the joint where the cap meets the crankcase, apply silicone sealer or equivalent to the rear main bearing cap split line. When applying sealer, use only a thin coat as an over abundance will not allow the cap to seat properly.*

REAR MAIN BEARING UPPER OIL SEAL REPAIR

1. Remove oil pan.
2. Insert packing tool (J-21526-2) against one end of the seal in the cylinder block. Drive the old seal gently into the groove until it is packed tight. This varies from ¼–¾ in. depending on the amount of pack required.
3. Repeat Step 2 on the other end of the seal in the cylinder block.
4. Measure the amount the seal was driven up on one side and add ¹⁄₁₆ in. Using a single edge razor blade, cut that length from the old seal removed from the rear main bearing cap. Repeat the procedure for the other side. Use the rear main bearing cap as a holding fixture when cutting the seal.
5. Install Guide Tool (J-21526-1) onto cylinder block.
6. Using packing tool, work the short pieces cut in Step 4 into the guide tool and then pack into cylinder block. The guide tool and packing tool have been machined to provide a built-in stop. Use this procedure for both sides. It may help to use oil on the short pieces of the rope seal when packing into the cylinder block.
7. Remove the guide tool.
8. Install a new fabric seal in the rear main bearing cap. Install cap and torque to specifications.
9. Install oil pan.

Flywheel and Ring Gear
REMOVAL AND INSTALLATION

On all engines, the flywheel and ring gear (or flexplate) is removed in basically the same manner. Remove the transaxle and clutch assembly (if equipped with manual transmission), then match mark the flywheel position with paint. Loosen the attaching bolts in a criss-cross pattern and lift the flywheel clear. When tightening the attaching bolts, torque them in a criss-cross pattern.

Flexplate imbalance can be corrected by the use of balance weights clipped to the flexplate. Mark the flywheel in four locations 90° apart,

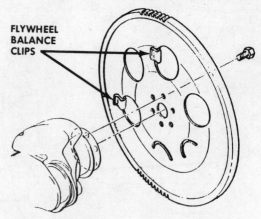

Balancing the flywheel

then install one clip at one of the marked locations. Install the transaxle, then start the engine and, with the transaxle in Neutral, note the vibration. If the vibration is worse, relocate the clip 180° from its position and repeat the test. If the vibration has decreased, install an additional clip next to the first one. If no change is noted, move the first clip 90° and repeat the test. Continue this procedure until the vibration is reduced. Fine adjustments may be made by moving the clips in small increments. Make sure the clips are properly secured to avoid shifting at high engine rpm.

Water Pump
REMOVAL AND INSTALLATION
2.5L Engine

1. Disconnect the negative battery cable.
2. Drain the cooling system.
CAUTION: *When draining the coolant, keep in mind that cats and dogs are attracted by the ethelyne glycol antifreeze, and are quite likely to drink any that is left in an uncovered container or in puddles on the ground. This will prove fatal in sufficient quantity. Always drain the coolant into a sealable container. Coolant should be reused unless it is contaminated or several years old.*
3. Remove the accessory drive belts.
4. Disconnect the hose from the water pump.
5. Remove the water pump attaching bolts and remove the water pump.
6. Installation is the reverse of removal. Clean all gasket mating surfaces and torque the water pump bolts to 25 ft.lb. (34 Nm). If installing a new pump, the pulley must be removed from the old water pump using a suitable puller. Water pump bolts should be coated with RTV sealer to avoid coolant leaks.

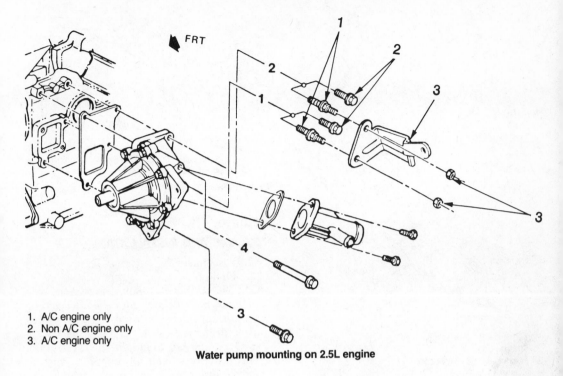

FRT

1. A/C engine only
2. Non A/C engine only
3. A/C engine only

Water pump mounting on 2.5L engine

3.0L V6

1. Disconnect the negative battery cable.
2. Drain the cooling system.

CAUTION: *When draining the coolant, keep in mind that cats and dogs are attracted by the ethelyne glycol antifreeze, and are quite likely to drink any that is left in an uncovered container or in puddles on the ground. This will prove fatal in sufficient quantity. Always drain the coolant into a sealable container. Coolant should be reused unless it is contaminated or several years old.*

3. Remove the serpentine drive belt.
4. Disconnect the coolant hoses at the water pump.
5. Remove the water pump pulley bolts. The long bolt is removed through the access hole provided in the body side rail.

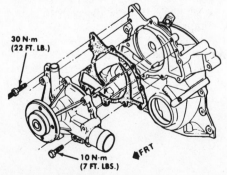

30 N·m
(22 FT. LB.)

10 N·m
(7 FT. LBS.)

FRT

Water pump mounting on V6 engine

6. Remove the pulley.
7. Remove the water pump mounting bolts and remove the water pump.
8. Installation is the reverse of removal. Clean all gasket mating surfaces before installing the pump. Torque the water pump mounting bolts to 22 ft.lb. (30 Nm).

Thermostat

REMOVAL AND INSTALLATION

2.5L Engine

On the four cylinder engine, the thermostat is easily replaced by simply draining the coolant below the level of the thermostat housing, removing the housing cap, then grasping the thermostat handle and lifting the thermostat out of the housing.

CAUTION: *When draining the coolant, keep in mind that cats and dogs are attracted by the ethelyne glycol antifreeze, and are quite likely to drink any that is left in an uncovered container or in puddles on the ground. This will prove fatal in sufficient quantity. Always drain the coolant into a sealable container. Coolant should be reused unless it is contaminated or several years old.*

The engine should be cold for this procedure. Install the new thermostat into the housing and replace the cap, then refill the cooling system.

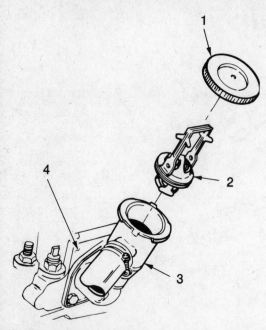

1. Thermostat housing cap
2. Thermostat
3. Thermostat housing assembly
4. Cylinder head

4 cyl thermostat housing

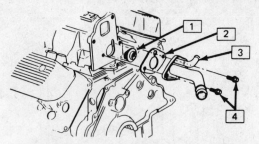

1. Thermostat   3. Thermostat housing
2. Gasket   4. Bolt

V6 thermostat housing

3.0L V6

1. Disconnect the negative battery cable.
2. Drain the engine coolant below the level of the thermostat housing located at the rear of the intake manifold.

CAUTION: *When draining the coolant, keep in mind that cats and dogs are attracted by the ethelyne glycol antifreeze, and are quite likely to drink any that is left in an uncovered container or in puddles on the ground. This will prove fatal in sufficient quantity. Always drain the coolant into a sealable container. Coolant should be reused unless it is contaminated or several years old.*

3. Remove the thermostat housing mounting bolts.
4. Remove the thermostat housing and lift out the thermostat.
5. Installation is the reverse of removal. Clean all gasket mating surfaces and run a ⅛ in. bead of RTV sealer around the thermostat housing. Torque the housing bolts to 21 ft.lb. (28 Nm).

Radiator

REMOVAL AND INSTALLATION

1. Disconnect the negative battery cable.
2. Drain the cooling system.

CAUTION: *When draining the coolant, keep in mind that cats and dogs are attracted by the ethelyne glycol antifreeze, and are quite likely to drink any that is left in an uncovered container or in puddles on the ground. This will prove fatal in sufficient quantity. Always drain the coolant into a sealable container. Coolant should be reused unless it is contaminated or several years old.*

3. Disconnect the engine forward strut bracket at the radiator support (if equipped), then swing the strut rearward. To prevent shearing of the rubber bushing, loosen the bolt before swinging the strut.
4. Disconnect the forward lamp harness from the frame and unplug the fan connector.
5. Remove the fan mounting bolts.
6. Scribe a mark around the hood latch, then remove the hood latch from the radiator support.
7. Remove the coolant hoses from the radiator.
8. Disconnect the transaxle fluid cooler lines from the radiator.
9. Remove the radiator mounting bolts and remove the radiator by lifting it upward. If equipped with air conditioning, it may be necessary to raise the right hand (driver) side of the radiator first to allow the neck to clear the A/C compressor.
10. Installation is the reverse of removal. Torque the radiator mounting bolts to 7.5 ft.lb. (10 Nm); transaxle cooler lines to 20 ft.lb. (27 Nm); and hood latch bolts to 18 ft.lb. (25 Nm).

Emission Controls and Fuel Systems

4

EMISSION CONTROLS

There are three sources of automotive pollutants: crankcase fumes, exhaust gases and gasoline vapors. The pollutants formed from these substances fall into three categories: unburnt hydrocarbons (HC), carbon monoxide (CO) and oxides of nitrogen (NOx). Devices used to limit these pollutants are referred to as emission control equipment, such as a PCV valve or catalytic converter, but in fact the entire fuel delivery system with its on-board computer control unit plays a part in limiting unwanted emissions from the engine. It is important to understand that all of the components in any emission control system are designed to operate together. A malfunction in one component may affect the entire system operation. When diagnosing or servicing emission control-related problems it is important to keep this in mind and make sure all components such as vacuum lines or electrical harness connectors are installed properly if disconnected for testing.

Crankcase Emission Controls

POSITIVE CRANKCASE VENTILATION (PCV) SYSTEM

All N-Body cars are equipped with a PCV system to control crankcase blowby vapors. When the engine is running, a small portion of the

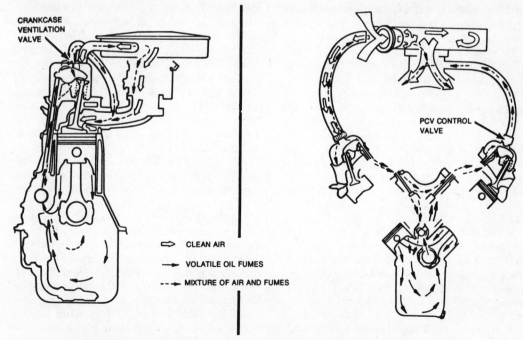

CRANKCASE VENTILATION VALVE

PCV CONTROL VALVE

⇨ CLEAN AIR

→ VOLATILE OIL FUMES

⇢ MIXTURE OF AIR AND FUMES

Cross-section schematics of the four cylinder (left) and V6 (right) PCV systems

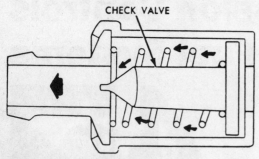

CHECK VALVE

Cross section of a PCV valve

gases which are formed in the combustion chamber leak by the piston rings and enter the crankcase. Since these gases are under pressure, they tend to escape from the crankcase and enter the atmosphere. If these gases are allowed to remain in the crankcase for any period of time, they contaminate the engine oil and cause sludge to build up in the crankcase. If allowed to escape into the atmosphere, they pollute the air with unburned hydrocarbons. The crankcase emission control system recycles these gases back into the combustion chambers where they are burned in the normal combustion process.

The crankcase blowby gases are recycled in the following manner. As the engine is running, clean filtered air is drawn through the air filter and into the crankcase. As the air passes through the crankcase, it picks up the combustion gases and carries them out of the crankcase, through the oil separator, through the PCV valve and into the induction system. As they enter the intake manifold, they are drawn into the combustion chamber where they are reburned.

The most critical component in the system is the PCV valve. This valve controls the amount of gases which are recycled into the combustion chamber. At low engine speeds, the valve is partially closed, limiting the flow of gases into the intake manifold. As engine speed increases, the valve opens to admit greater quantities of gases into the intake manifold. If the valve should become blocked or plugged, the gases will be prevented from escaping from the crankcase by the normal route. Since these gases are under pressure, they will find their own way out of the crankcase. This alternate route is usually through a weak oil seal or gasket in the engine, which causes an oil leak. Besides oil leaks, a clogged PCV valve also allows these gases to remain in the crankcase for an extended period of time, promoting the formation of sludge and diluting the oil with unburned gasoline. It should be noted that the PCV system is totally mechanical and the only emission control system that is not controlled by the on-board computer; however a malfunction in this system could cause engine operating problems that may affect the idle and performance.

PCV SYSTEM SERVICE

Every 30,000 miles, the PCV system should be inspected for damage, deterioration and proper operation. Inspect the PCV system hose connections and replace any deteriorated hoses. Check the PCV valve operation. To maintain idle quality, the PCV valve restricts the flow when intake manifold vacuum is high. A plugged valve or hose could cause a rough idle, stalling or slow idle speed, oil leaks, oil in the air cleaner or sludge in the engine. A leaking valve would cause a rough idle, stalling or an unusually high idle speed. To check the valve:

1. Remove the PCV valve from the rocker arm cover or intake manifold with the vacuum line to the intake attached.

2. Start the engine and allow it to idle.

3. Place your thumb over the end of the PCV valve to check for vacuum. If there is no vacuum at the valve, check for plugged hoses or manifold port or a clogged PCV valve.

4. Turn the engine OFF and remove the PCV valve. Shake the valve and listen for a rattle. If the valve does not rattle, replace it. Do not attempt to clean the PCV valve in solvent. If a problem is suspected, replace the valve.

Evaporative Emission Control System (EECS)

The basic Evaporative Emission Control System (EECS) used on all N-Body vehicles is the carbon canister storage method. This method transfers fuel vapors to an activated charcoal storage device which absorbs and stores the vapor that is emitted from the engine induction system and fuel tank when the engine is not running. When the engine is running, the stored vapor is purged from the charcoal canister by the intake air flow and then burned in the normal combustion process. As the manifold vacuum reaches a certain point, it opens a purge control valve mounted on top of the storage canister, allowing air to be drawn into the canister and forcing existing fuel vapors back into the engine to be burned normally. Air enters the canister through the bottom filter which should be checked and replaced periodically.

On the 3.0L V6 engine, the electronic control module (ECM) operates a solenoid valve which controls vacuum to the purge valve in the charcoal canister. Under cold engine or idle conditions, the solenoid is turned on by the ECM, which closes the valve and blocks vacuum to the canister purge valve. The ECM

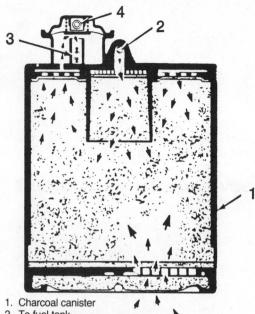

1. Charcoal canister
2. To fuel tank
3. Purge valve (ported vacuum)
4. Control valve (manifold vacuum)

Charcoal canister used on 4 cyl engine

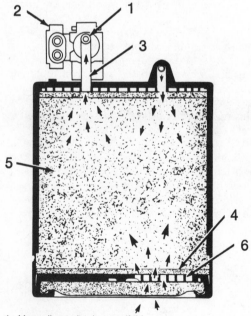

1. Vapor line to intake manifold
2. Solenoid
3. Vapor from fuel tank
4. Filter
5. Carbon
6. Grid

Charcoal canister used on V6 engine

turns off the solenoid valve and allows purge when the engine is warm, after it has been running for a preset time, above a programmed road speed or above a programmed throttle

opening. If the solenoid is open or is not receiving power, the canister can purge to the intake manifold at all times, allowing extra fuel at idle or during warmup which can cause rough or unstable idle, or too rich operation during warmup.

TESTING EECS SYSTEM

Attach a short length of hose to the lower tube or purge valve and attempt to blow air through it. Little or no air should pass into the canister. A small amount of air will pass if the canister has a constant purge hole. Using a hand vacuum pump, apply 15 in. Hg through the control valve tube (upper tube). If the diaphragm does not hold vacuum for at least 20 seconds, the diaphragm is leaking and the canister must be replaced. If the diaphragm holds vacuum, again try to blow through the hose connected to the lower tube while vacuum is still being applied. An increased flow of air should be observed. If not, the canister or control valve must be replaced. Tag all hoses for installation before removing the canister from the vehicle.

Check the canister for cracks or damage, fuel leaking from the bottom, the condition of the filter and all hoses leading to and away from the canister for cracks or deterioration. Replace any components found to be defective.

Exhaust Emission Controls

Exhaust emission control systems constitute the largest body of emission control devices installed on the N-Body engine. Included in this category are catalytic converter, exhaust gas recirculation (EGR), thermostatic air cleaner, air management and the Computer Command Control (CCC) system. It should be noted that the on-board computer controls most emission control functions in one way or another and has a built-in self-diagnostic system to aid in troubleshooting. This troubleshooting feature is explained in greater detail later on in this chapter.

Catalytic Converter

The catalytic converter is a muffler-like container built into the exhaust system to aid in the reduction of exhaust emissions, specifically hydrocarbons (HC), carbon monoxide (CO) and oxides of nitrogen (NOx) formed in the normal process of combustion. The N-Bodies all utilize a three-way catalytic converter.

The three-way converter is capable of reducing HC, CO and NOx emissions all at the same time. It can do this, however, only if the amount of oxygen present in the exhaust gas is precisely controlled. This is accomplished by means

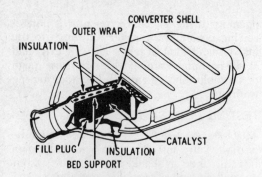

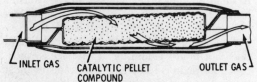

Bead type catalytic converter

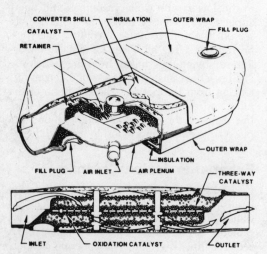

Dual bed type catalytic converter

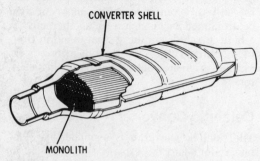

Single bed monolith catalytic converter

fuel, the catalytic converter has no maintenance requirements. Under normal conditions, it should last the life of the car unless contaminated with leaded fuel or physically damaged in some way. The converter body should be periodically inspected for dents or other indications of internal damage and replaced if the damage is excessive. Impact damage can shatter the catalyst bed and in extreme cases plug the catalyst and exhaust system completely.

Exhaust Gas Recirculation (EGR) System

All engines are equipped with an exhaust gas recirculation (EGR) system to lower the oxides of nitrogen (NOx) emissions caused by high combustion temperatures. It accomplishes this by reby high combustion temperatures. It accomplishes this by recirculating inert exhaust gases that mix with the intake recirculating inert exhaust gases that mix with the intake fuel charge and lower the combustion chamber temperatures. The main element of this system is the EGR valve, which regulates the amount of exhaust gas recycled into the intake manifold.

The EGR valve is opened by either ported manifold or full manifold vacuum to let exhaust gas flow into the intake manifold. The exhaust gas then moves with the air/fuel mixture into the combustion chambers. If too much exhaust gas enters, combustion will not occur and for this reason, very little exhaust gas is allowed to pass through the valve, especially at idle. The EGR valve is usually open during warm engine operation and above idle speed. The amount of exhaust gas recirculated is controlled by variations in vacuum and, in some cases, exhaust back pressure. Two sources of vacuum are used; the four cylinder takes its vacuum signal from a port above the throttle valve and the V6 uses

of an oxygen sensor installed in the exhaust manifold that continuously monitors the level of oxygen in the exhaust and transmits an electrical signal to the on-board computer. This oxygen sensor system is explained in detail later in this chapter.

Aside from the need to use only unleaded

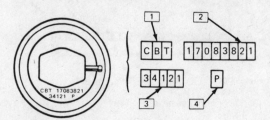

1. Assembly plant code
2. Part number
3. Date built
4. Lock here for letter
    P = positive back pressure
    N = negative back pressure
    blank = ported valve

EGR valve identification

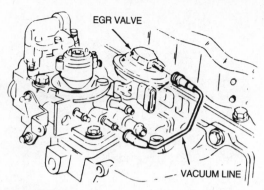

2.5L EGR valve

full manifold vacuum from an intake manifold port.

There are three types of EGR valve used on GM engines; ported, positive backpressure and negative backpressure. The positive backpressure valve has an air bleed located inside the EGR valve assembly which acts as a vacuum regulator. This bleed valve controls the amount of vacuum in the vacuum chamber by bleeding vacuum to the atmosphere during the open phase of the cycle. When the bleed valve receives sufficient backpressure through the hollow shaft, it closes the bleed. At this point, maximum available vacuum is applied to the diaphragm and the EGR valve opens. If there is little or no vacuum in the vacuum chamber such as at idle or wide open throttle, or if there is little or no pressure in the exhaust manifold, the EGR valve will not open. This type of valve will not open if vacuum is applied to it with the engine stopped or idling.

The negative backpressure EGR valve is similar to the positive backpressure valve except that the bleed valve spring is moved from above the valve to below, and the valve is normally closed. The negative backpressure valve

varies the amount of exhaust gas flow into the manifold depending on manifold vacuum and variations in exhaust backpressure. The diaphragm on this valve has an internal air bleed hole which is held closed by a small spring when there is no exhaust backpressure. Engine vacuum opens the EGR valve against the pressure of a large spring. When manifold vacuum combines with negative exhaust backpressure, the vacuum bleed hole opens and the EGR valve closes.

The port EGR valve is controlled by a flexible diaphragm which is spring loaded to hold the valve closed. Ported vacuum applied to the top side of the diaphragm overcomes the spring pressure and opens the valve in the exhaust gas port. This allows the exhaust gas to be drawn into the intake manifold and enter the engine combustion chambers.

Positive backpressure EGR valves will have a "P" stamped on the top side of the valve after the part number. Negative backpressure valves will have an "N" stamped on the top side of the valve after the part number. Port EGR valves have no identification stamped after the part number.

On V6 engines, a solenoid controlled by the electronic control module (ECM) regulates vacuum flow to the EGR valve. The ECM uses information from the coolant temperature sensor, throttle position sensor and mass air flow sensor to regulate the solenoid operation. The solenoid uses "pulse width modulation" which

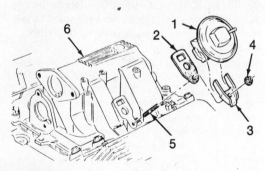

1. EGR valve
2. Gasket
3. Clamp
4. Nut
5. Stud
6. Intake manifold

V6 EGR valve

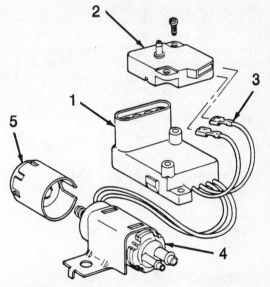

1. Vacuum control assembly base
2. Vauum diagnostic control switch
3. Diagnostic switch connectors
4. EGR solenoid
5. Filter

EGR vacuum control assembly on V6 engine

turns the solenoid on and off many times a second and varies the amount of "on time" (pulse width) to vary the amount of EGR delivered to the engine. A diagnostic switch is part of the control and monitors vacuum to the EGR valve. This switch will trigger the "CHECK ENGINE" or "SERVICE ENGINE SOON" light and set a trouble code (usually 32) in the event of a vacuum circuit failure.

Too much EGR flow tends to weaken combustion, causing the engine to run roughly or to stall. With too much EGR flow at idle, cruise or cold operation, any of the following conditions may occur:

- Engine stalls after cold start
- Engine stalls at idle after deceleration
- Engine surges during cruise
- Engine idles roughly

If the EGR valve should stay open all of the time, the engine may not idle. Too little or no EGR flow allows combustion temperatures to get too high during acceleration and load conditions, causing a spark knock (ping), overheating or an emission test failure due to the high amount of NOx present in the exhaust gas.

REMOVAL AND INSTALLATION

1. Remove the air cleaner.
2. Disconnect the EGR vacuum hose at the valve.
3. Remove the EGR valve mounting bolts.
4. Remove the EGR valve and gasket. Clean all gasket mating surfaces.
5. If the EGR passages in the intake manifold show an excessive buildup of carbon, the passages should be cleaned. Care should be taken that all loose particles are completely removed to prevent them from clogging the EGR valve or being ingested into the engine. Buff the deposits from all mounting surfaces with a wire wheel and look for deposits in the valve outlet. Remove deposits with a small scraping tool or bristle bore brush.
6. Installation is the reverse of removal. Use a new EGR gasket and tighten the mounting bolts to 14 ft.lb. (18 Nm).

NOTE: *On V6 engines, an EGR filter on the vacuum solenoid should be replaced every 30,000 miles. Grasp and pull the filter off with a rocking motion, then push on the new filter, making sure the cutout for the wires is properly aligned.*

Thermostatic Air Cleaner (THERMAC)

A heated intake air system is used to give good driveability under various climatic conditions. By maintaining uniform intake air temperatures, the fuel system can be calibrated to re-

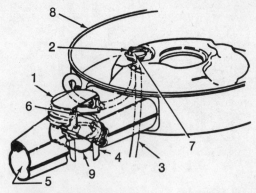

1. Vacuum diaphragm motor
2. Temperature sensor
3. Hose to manifold vacuum
4. Heat stove duct
5. Snorkel
6. Linkage
7. Air bleed valve
8. Air cleaner assembly
9. Damper door

Typical thermostatic air cleaner

duce exhaust emissions and to eliminate throttle valve icing. The THERMAC air cleaner operates by heated air and manifold vacuum. Air enters the air cleaner either from outside the engine compartment or from a heat stove built around the exhaust manifold.

When the temperature is below 86°F (30°C), the sensor allows vacuum to the motor and the damper door will be up, shutting off outside air and allowing only heated air from the exhaust manifold to enter the air cleaner. When the temperature is above 131°F (55°C), the damper door drops down and only outside air enters the air cleaner. Between the temperature ranges, the damper door allows both heated air and outside air to enter the air cleaner.

The most common problems associated with the THERMAC system are hesitation during warmup or sluggish operation when the engine is warm. Hesitation can be caused by a disconnected heat stove tube, inoperative diaphragm motor, lack of manifold vacuum (disconnected vacuum hose), a stuck damper door, any missing seal such as the air cleaner to TBI gasket, loose top cover or loose air cleaner assembly. Lack of power when warm can be caused by a damper door that does not open to admit outside air or a temperature sensor that fails to bleed off vacuum.

THERMAC TESTING

1. Inspect the system to make sure all hoses and the heat stove tube are connected. Check for kinked, plugged or deteriorated hoses.
2. Check the air cleaner to TBI gasket and

top cover seal for breaks, leaks or deterioration.

3. Make sure the damper door is open to outside air with the air cleaner installed and the engine off.

4. Start the engine and watch the damper door in the air cleaner snorkel. A small hand mirror and a flashlight makes this check easier. When the engine is first started, the damper door should move and close off outside air. As the engine warms up, the damper door should gradually drop down to admit outside air to the air cleaner.

5. If the air cleaner fails to operate as described, continue with the vacuum motor test. If it operates, but a driveability problem is still noted, the door may not be moving at the right temperature. Perform the sensor check.

VACUUM MOTOR TEST

1. With the engine off, disconnect the vacuum hose at the vacuum diaphragm motor.

2. Apply at least 7 in. Hg of vacuum to the vacuum diaphragm motor using a hand vacuum pump. The damper door should completely block off outside air when vacuum is applied. If not, check to see if the linkage is hooked up correctly.

3. With vacuum still applied, trap vacuum in the vacuum diaphragm motor by kinking the hose. The damper door should remain closed. If not, replace the vacuum diaphragm motor assembly.

NOTE: *Failure of the vacuum diaphragm motor assembly is more likely to be caused from binding linkage or a corroded snorkel than from a failed diaphragm. Check this before replacing the diaphragm.*

4. If the vacuum motor checks OK, inspect the vacuum hoses and connections. If no problem is found, continue with the temperature sensor test.

TEMPERATURE SENSOR TEST

1. Begin the test with the air cleaner temperature below 86°F (30°C). If the engine has been run recently, remove the air cleaner cover and place a thermometer as close as possible to the sensor. Let the air cleaner cool until the thermometer reads below 86°F, then install the air cleaner cover with the thermometer left in place.

2. Start the engine and allow it to idle. The damper door should move to close off outside air immediately if the engine is cool enough. When the damper door starts to open the snorkel passage, remove the air cleaner cover and read the thermometer. It should read about 131°F (55°C).

3. If the damper door is not open to outside

air at the temperature indicated, the temperature sensor is malfunctioning and must be replaced.

VACUUM DIAPHRAGM MOTOR REPLACEMENT

1. Remove the air cleaner.

2. Disconnect the vacuum hose from the motor.

3. Drill out the two spot welds with a ⅟₁₆ in. (1.6mm) drill, then enlarge as required to remove the retaining strap. Be careful not to damage the snorkel tube.

4. Remove the motor retaining strap.

5. Lift the motor upward, cocking it to one side to disconnect the motor linkage at the control damper assembly.

6. To install the new motor, drill a ⁷⁄₆₄ in. (2.8mm) hole in the snorkel tube at the center of the vacuum motor retaining strap.

7. Connect the vacuum motor linkage into the control damper assembly.

8. Use the motor retaining strap and sheet metal screw provided in the motor service package to secure the motor to the snorkel tube. Make sure the screw does not interfere with the operation of the damper assembly. Shorten the screw if required.

9. Install the vacuum hose to the new motor and install the air cleaner.

TEMPERATURE SENSOR REPLACEMENT

1. Remove the air cleaner.

2. Disconnect the vacuum hoses at the sensor. Tag them for installation.

3. Pry up on the tabs on the sensor retaining clip, then remove the clip and the sensor from the air cleaner. Note the position of the sensor for installation.

4. Install the new gasket and sensor assembly into the original position.

5. Install the retainer clip on the hose connections, then connect the vacuum hoses, making sure they are installed properly.

6. Install the air cleaner on the engine.

Computer Command Control (CCC) System

The Computer Command Control system is used on all N-Body cars. It monitors up to 15 various engine/vehicle operating conditions, then uses this information to control as many as 9 engine related systems. The CCC system makes constant adjustments to the air/fuel mixture and ignition timing to maintain good vehicle performance under all driving conditions, while at the same time allowing the catalytic converter to effectively control the emissions of HC, CO and NOx. In addition, the CCC sys-

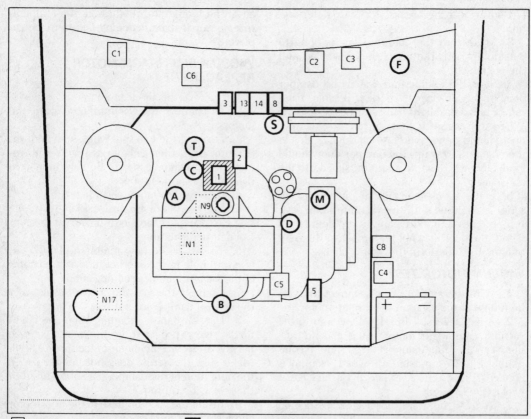

COMPUTER HARNESS
- C1 Electronic Control Module (ECM)
- C2 ALCL diagnostic connector
- C3 "CHECK ENG./SERV ENG SOON" light
- C4 ECM power
- C5 ECM harness ground
- C6 Fuse panel
- C8 Fuel pump test connector

NOT ECM CONNECTED
- N1 Crankcase vent valve (PCV)
- N9 Exhaust Gas Recirculation valve
- N17 Fuel vapor canister

CONTROLLED DEVICES
- 1 Fuel injector solenoid
- 2 Idle air control valve
- 3 Fuel pump relay
- 5 Trans. Converter Clutch connector
- 8 Engine cooling fan relay
- 13 A/C compressor relay
- 14 A/C fan relay

Exhaust Gas Recirculation valve

INFORMATION SENSORS
- A Manifold differential pressure
- B Exhaust oxygen
- C Throttle position
- D Coolant temperature
- F Vehicle speed buffer amplifier
- M P/N switch
- S P/S pressure switch
- T Trans axle speed sensor

Computer Command Control component locations on 4 cyl engine

tem has a built-in self-diagnosis feature that recognizes and identifies operational problems and alerts the driver through a "CHECK EN-GINE" or "SERVICE ENGINE SOON" light on the instrument panel. By grounding a test lead under the dash board, the light will flash a trouble code to indicate the problem area that should be checked.

The heart of the CCC system is the electronic control module (ECM) which is basically a computer in a metal box, usually mounted behind the right (passenger) side kick panel under the dash board. The ECM contains a calibration unit called a PROM (Programmable Read-Only Memory), which tailors the on-board

computer to the specific vehicle, engine and transmission. The ECM controls the fuel injection system, spark timing, idle air control (idle speed), EGR operation, charcoal canister purging, cooling fan, transmission converter clutch (automatic only) and air conditioner. The ECM contains a fail-safe device that allows the vehicle to be driven in the event of a computer failure. This device is called a CALPAK and is located inside the ECM body, next to the PROM. The CALPAK will allow the engine to start and run (albeit poorly) so the vehicle may be driven for short distances to the nearest service facility. This feature is often referred to as the "limp home mode." One can better under-

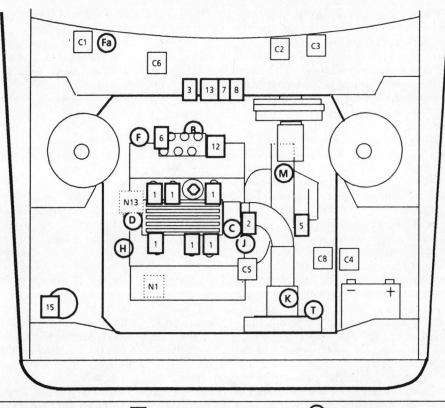

COMPUTER HARNESS

C1 Electronic Control Module (ECM)
C2 ALCL diagnostic connector
C3 "CHECK ENG/SERV ENG SOON" light
C4 ECM power
C5 ECM harness ground
C6 Fuse panel
C8 Fuel pump test connector

NOT ECM CONNECTED

N 1 Crankcase vent valve (PCV)
N13 Coolant fan temp. override switch

CONTROLLED DEVICES

1 Fuel injector
2 Idle air control motor
3 Fuel pump relay
5 Trans. Converter Clutch connector
6 Computer Controlled Coil Ignition(C^3I)
7 Electronic Spark Control module (ESC)
8 Engine coolant fan relay
12 Exh. Gas Recirc. vacuum solenoid
13 A/C compressor relay
15 Fuel vapor canister solenoid

◇ Exhaust Gas Recirculation valve

INFORMATION SENSORS

B Exhaust oxygen
C Throttle position (TPS)
D Coolant temperature
F Vehicle speed
Fa Vehicle speed sensor buffer
H Crkshft pos. Reference/RPM (C^3I)
J ESC knock
K Mass air flow
M P/N switch
T Air temperature (ATS)

Computer Command Control component locations on V6 engine

stand the operation of the CCC system by examining the various engine sensors the computer uses to perform various functions.

The coolant temperature sensor is a thermistor (a resistor which changes its value according to temperature) mounted in the engine coolant stream, usually on the block or intake manifold. Low coolant temperature produces a high resistance, while high temperature produces low resistance. The ECM supplies a five volt signal to the coolant sensor through a resistor in the ECM and measures the voltage. The voltage will be high when the engine is cold and low when the engine is hot. By measuring this voltage, the ECM knows the engine coolant temperature and this affects most sys-

tems the ECM controls. A failure in the coolant sensor circuit should set either a Code 14 or 15 in the ECM trouble diagnosis memory.

The manifold absolute pressure (MAP) sensor measures changes in the intake manifold pressure which result from engine load and speed changes and converts these changes into a voltage output to the ECM. A closed throttle on engine coastdown would produce a relatively low MAP output, while a wide open throttle would produce a high output. This high output is produced because the pressure inside the manifold is the same as outside the manifold, so you measure 100% of outside air pressure. Manifold absolute pressure is the opposite of what you would measure on a vacuum gauge. When manifold pressure is high, vacuum is low. The MAP sensor is also used to measure barometric pressure under certain conditions, which allows the ECM to automatically adjust for different altitudes. The ECM sends a five volt reference signal to the MAP sensor. As the manifold pressure changes, the electrical resistance of the sensor also changes. By monitoring the sensor output, the ECM knows the manifold pressure and adjusts the fuel mixture accordingly. A high pressure (low vacuum) requires more fuel, while a low pressue (high vacuum) requires less fuel. The ECM uses the MAP sensor signal to control fuel delivery and ignition timing. A failure in the MAP sensor circuit will set a trouble code 33 or 34.

The exhaust oxygen sensor is mounted in the exhaust system (usually in the exhaust manifold) where it can monitor the oxygen content of the exhaust gas stream. The oxygen content in the exhaust gases reacts with the oxygen sensor to produce a voltage output. This voltage ranges from approximately 0.1 volts (high O_2-lean mixture) to 0.9 volts (low O_2-rich mixture). By monitoring the voltage output of the oxygen sensor, the ECM will know what fuel mixture command to give the injector. For example, a lean mixture (low voltage) causes a rich command, and vice versa. This fuel mixture control is referred to as "closed loop" and the ECM will only go into the closed loop mode of operation when it receives a signal from the oxygen sensor. If the oxygen sensor fails, the CCC system will operate in the open loop mode, which uses preprogrammed mixture and timing values that are not adjusted as the engine operates. A failed oxygen sensor will set a trouble code 13; a shorted sensor circuit should set a code 44 and high voltage in the circuit will set a code 45.

The throttle position sensor (TPS) is connected to the throttle shaft on the throttle body. It is a potentiometer with one end connected to five volts from the ECM and the other to ground. A third wire is connected to the ECM to measure the voltage from the TPS. As the throttle valve angle is changed when the accelerator is depressed, the output of the TPS changes. At a closed throttle position, the output of the TPS is low (about 0.5 volts); as the throttle valve opens, the output increases so that at wide open throttle the output voltage should be about five volts. By monitoring the output voltage from the TPS, the ECM can determine fuel delivery based on throttle valve angle (driver demand). If the sensor circuit is open, the ECM will set a trouble code 22. If the circuit is shorted, the ECM will think that the engine is at wide open throttle (WOT) and a trouble code 21 will be set. A broken or loose TPS can cause intermittent bursts of fuel from the injector(s) and an unstable idle because the ECM thinks the throttle is moving. Once a trouble code is set, the ECM will use an artificial value for TPS and some vehicle performance will return (the limp home mode mentioned earlier). On all engines, the TPS is not adjustable. The ECM uses the reading at idle for the zero reading, so no adjustment is necessary.

On models equipped with an automatic transaxle, a park/neutral switch tells the ECM when the transmission is in Park or Neutral. This information is used for the transmission converter clutch (TCC) and idle air control (IAC) valve operation. The ECM also looks at the starter solenoid to tell when the engine is cranking (start mode). If this signal is not available, the car may be hard to start in extremely cold weather. In addition, when the air conditioning switch is turned ON, the ECM uses the switch signal to adjust the idle speed to compensate for the increased engine load.

The vehicle speed sensor (VSS) sends a pulsing voltage signal to the ECM which the ECM converts to miles per hour. This sensor mainly controls the operation of the torque converter clutch (TCC) system. The distributor also sends a signal to the ECM to tell it both engine rpm and crankshaft position. The ECM uses this information to operate the electronic spark timing (EST) system, adjusting the ignition timing for maximum performance and economy with minimum emissions.

TROUBLESHOOTING THE CCC SYSTEM

One of the most important checks that must be done as part of any diagnosis procedure is a careful visual/physical inspection. This can often lead to fixing a problem without further testing by simply reconnecting a loose wiring connector or vacuum line. Inspect all vacuum hoses for correct routing, pinches, cuts or looseness; be sure to check hoses that are difficult to get to beneath the air cleaner, etc. Check all wiring in the engine compartment for tight connections, corrosion, burned or chaffed spots, pinched wires or contact with sharp edges or hot exhaust manifolds.

Before attempting to diagnose any computerized engine control system, some basic knowledge is required. You should understand the basic theory of electricity and know the meaning of voltage, amps and ohms. You should understand what happens in a circuit with an open or shorted wire and should be able to read and understand a wiring diagram. You should know how to use a test light, how to connect and use a tachometer and how to use jumper wires to bypass components to test circuits. Fi-

CHILTON'S
FUEL ECONOMY & TUNE-UP TIPS

Tune-up • Spark Plug Diagnosis • Emission Controls

Fuel System • Cooling System • Tires and Wheels

General Maintenance

55 WAYS TO IMPROVE FUEL ECONOMY

CHILTON'S FUEL ECONOMY & TUNE-UP TIPS

Fuel economy is important to everyone, no matter what kind of vehicle you drive. The maintenance-minded motorist can save both money and fuel using these tips and the periodic maintenance and tune-up procedures in this Repair and Tune-Up Guide.

There are more than 130,000,000 cars and trucks registered for private use in the United States. Each travels an average of 10-12,000 miles per year, and, and in total they consume close to 70 billion gallons of fuel each year. This represents nearly ⅔ of the oil imported by the United States each year. The Federal government's goal is to reduce consumption 10% by 1985. A variety of methods are either already in use or under serious consideration, and they all affect you driving and the cars you will drive. In addition to "down-sizing", the auto industry is using or investigating the use of electronic fuel delivery, electronic engine controls and alternative engines for use in smaller and lighter vehicles, among other alternatives to meet the federally mandated Corporate Average Fuel Economy (CAFE) of 27.5 mpg by 1985. The government, for its part, is considering rationing, mandatory driving curtailments and tax increases on motor vehicle fuel in an effort to reduce consumption. The government's goal of a 10% reduction could be realized — and further government regulation avoided — if every private vehicle could use just 1 less gallon of fuel per week.

How Much Can You Save?

Tests have proven that almost anyone can make at least a 10% reduction in fuel consumption through regular maintenance and tune-ups. When a major manufacturer of spark plugs sur-

TUNE-UP

1. Check the cylinder compression to be sure the engine will really benefit from a tune-up and that it is capable of producing good fuel economy. A tune-up will be wasted on an engine in poor mechanical condition.

2. Replace spark plugs regularly. New spark plugs alone can increase fuel economy 3%.

3. Be sure the spark plugs are the correct type (heat range) for your vehicle. See the Tune-Up Specifications.

Heat range refers to the spark plug's ability to conduct heat away from the firing end. It must conduct the heat away in an even pattern to avoid becoming a source of pre-ignition, yet it must also operate hot enough to burn off conductive deposits that could cause misfiring.

The heat range is usually indicated by a number on the spark plug, part of the manufacturer's designation for each individual spark plug. The numbers in bold-face indicate the heat range in each manufacturer's identification system.

Manufacturer	Typical Designation
AC	R **45** TS
Bosch (old)	WA **145** T30
Bosch (new)	HR **8** Y
Champion	RBL **15** Y
Fram/Autolite	4**15**
Mopar	P-**62** PR
Motorcraft	BRF-**42**
NGK	BP **5** ES-15
Nippondenso	W **16** EP
Prestolite	14GR **5** 2A

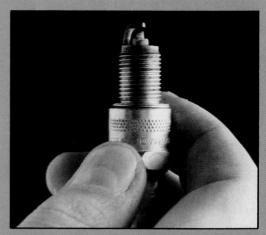

Periodically, check the spark plugs to be sure they are firing efficiently. They are excellent indicators of the internal condition of your engine.

On AC, Bosch (new), Champion, Fram/Autolite, Mopar, Motorcraft and Prestolite, a higher number indicates a hotter plug. On Bosch (old), NGK and Nippondenso, a higher number indicates a colder plug.

4. Make sure the spark plugs are properly gapped. See the Tune-Up Specifications in this book.

5. Be sure the spark plugs are firing efficiently. The illustrations on the next 2 pages show you how to "read" the firing end of the spark plug.

6. Check the ignition timing and set it to specifications. Tests show that almost all cars have incorrect ignition timing by more than 2°.

veyed over 6,000 cars nationwide, they found that a tune-up, on cars that needed one, increased fuel economy over 11%. Replacing worn plugs alone, accounted for a 3% increase. The same test also revealed that 8 out of every 10 vehicles will have some maintenance deficiency that will directly affect fuel economy, emissions or performance. Most of this mileage-robbing neglect could be prevented with regular maintenance.

Modern engines require that all of the functioning systems operate properly for maximum efficiency. A malfunction anywhere wastes fuel. You can keep your vehicle running as efficiently and economically as possible, by being aware of your vehicle's operating and performance characteristics. If your vehicle suddenly develops performance or fuel economy problems it could be due to one or more of the following:

PROBLEM	POSSIBLE CAUSE
Engine Idles Rough	Ignition timing, idle mixture, vacuum leak or something amiss in the emission control system.
Hesitates on Acceleration	Dirty carburetor or fuel filter, improper accelerator pump setting, ignition timing or fouled spark plugs.
Starts Hard or Fails to Start	Worn spark plugs, improperly set automatic choke, ice (or water) in fuel system.
Stalls Frequently	Automatic choke improperly adjusted and possible dirty air filter or fuel filter.
Performs Sluggishly	Worn spark plugs, dirty fuel or air filter, ignition timing or automatic choke out of adjustment.

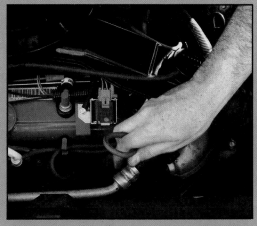

Check spark plug wires on conventional point type ignition for cracks by bending them in a loop around your finger.

Be sure that spark plug wires leading to adjacent cylinders do not run too close together. (Photo courtesy Champion Spark Plug Co.)

7. If your vehicle does not have electronic ignition, check the points, rotor and cap as specified.

8. Check the spark plug wires (used with conventional point-type ignitions) for cracks and burned or broken insulation by bending them in a loop around your finger. Cracked wires decrease fuel efficiency by failing to deliver full voltage to the spark plugs. One misfiring spark plug can cost you as much as 2 mpg.

9. Check the routing of the plug wires. Misfiring can be the result of spark plug leads to adjacent cylinders running parallel to each other and too close together. One wire tends to pick up voltage from the other causing it to fire "out of time".

10. Check all electrical and ignition circuits for voltage drop and resistance.

11. Check the distributor mechanical and/or vacuum advance mechanisms for proper functioning. The vacuum advance can be checked by twisting the distributor plate in the opposite direction of rotation. It should spring back when released.

12. Check and adjust the valve clearance on engines with mechanical lifters. The clearance should be slightly loose rather than too tight.

SPARK PLUG DIAGNOSIS

Normal

APPEARANCE: This plug is typical of one operating normally. The insulator nose varies from a light tan to grayish color with slight electrode wear. The presence of slight deposits is normal on used plugs and will have no adverse effect on engine performance. The spark plug heat range is correct for the engine and the engine is running normally.

CAUSE: Properly running engine.

RECOMMENDATION: Before reinstalling this plug, the electrodes should be cleaned and filed square. Set the gap to specifications. If the plug has been in service for more than 10-12,000 miles, the entire set should probably be replaced with a fresh set of the same heat range.

Oil Deposits

APPEARANCE: The firing end of the plug is covered with a wet, oily coating.

CAUSE: The problem is poor oil control. On high mileage engines, oil is leaking past the rings or valve guides into the combustion chamber. A common cause is also a plugged PCV valve, and a ruptured fuel pump diaphragm can also cause this condition. Oil fouled plugs such as these are often found in new or recently overhauled engines, before normal oil control is achieved, and can be cleaned and reinstalled.

RECOMMENDATION: A hotter spark plug may temporarily relieve the problem, but the engine is probably in need of work.

Incorrect Heat Range

APPEARANCE: The effects of high temperature on a spark plug are indicated by clean white, often blistered insulator. This can also be accompanied by excessive wear of the electrode, and the absence of deposits.

CAUSE: Check for the correct spark plug heat range. A plug which is too hot for the engine can result in overheating. A car operated mostly at high speeds can require a colder plug. Also check ignition timing, cooling system level, fuel mixture and leaking intake manifold.

RECOMMENDATION: If all ignition and engine adjustments are known to be correct, and no other malfunction exists, install spark plugs one heat range colder.

Carbon Deposits

APPEARANCE: Carbon fouling is easily identified by the presence of dry, soft, black, sooty deposits.

CAUSE: Changing the heat range can often lead to carbon fouling, as can prolonged slow, stop-and-start driving. If the heat range is correct, carbon fouling can be attributed to a rich fuel mixture, sticking choke, clogged air cleaner, worn breaker points, retarded timing or low compression. If only one or two plugs are carbon fouled, check for corroded or cracked wires on the affected plugs. Also look for cracks in the distributor cap between the towers of affected cylinders.

RECOMMENDATION: After the problem is corrected, these plugs can be cleaned and reinstalled if not worn severely.

MMT Fouled

APPEARANCE: Spark plugs fouled by MMT (Methycyclopentadienyl Maganese Tricarbonyl) have reddish, rusty appearance on the insulator and side electrode.

CAUSE: MMT is an anti-knock additive in gasoline used to replace lead. During the combustion process, the MMT leaves a reddish deposit on the insulator and side electrode.

RECOMMENDATION: No engine malfunction is indicated and the deposits will not affect plug performance any more than lead deposits (see Ash Deposits). MMT fouled plugs can be cleaned, regapped and reinstalled.

High Speed Glazing

APPEARANCE: Glazing appears as shiny coating on the plug, either yellow or tan in color.

CAUSE: During hard, fast acceleration, plug temperatures rise suddenly. Deposits from normal combustion have no chance to fluff-off; instead, they melt on the insulator forming an electrically conductive coating which causes misfiring.

RECOMMENDATION: Glazed plugs are not easily cleaned. They should be replaced with a fresh set of plugs of the correct heat range. If the condition recurs, using plugs with a heat range one step colder may cure the problem.

Ash (Lead) Deposits

APPEARANCE: Ash deposits are characterized by light brown or white colored deposits crusted on the side or center electrodes. In some cases it may give the plug a rusty appearance.

CAUSE: Ash deposits are normally derived from oil or fuel additives burned during normal combustion. Normally they are harmless, though excessive amounts can cause misfiring. If deposits are excessive in short mileage, the valve guides may be worn.

RECOMMENDATION: Ash-fouled plugs can be cleaned, gapped and reinstalled.

Detonation

APPEARANCE: Detonation is usually characterized by a broken plug insulator.

CAUSE: A portion of the fuel charge will begin to burn spontaneously, from the increased heat following ignition. The explosion that results applies extreme pressure to engine components, frequently damaging spark plugs and pistons.

Detonation can result by over-advanced ignition timing, inferior gasoline (low octane) lean air/fuel mixture, poor carburetion, engine lugging or an increase in compression ratio due to combustion chamber deposits or engine modification.

RECOMMENDATION: Replace the plugs after correcting the problem.

Photos Courtesy Champion Spark Plug Co.

EMISSION CONTROLS

13. Be aware of the general condition of the emission control system. It contributes to reduced pollution and should be serviced regularly to maintain efficient engine operation.

14. Check all vacuum lines for dried, cracked or brittle conditions. Something as simple as a leaking vacuum hose can cause poor performance and loss of economy.

15. Avoid tampering with the emission control system. Attempting to improve fuel econ-

FUEL SYSTEM

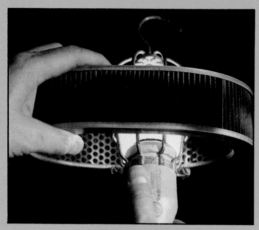

Check the air filter with a light behind it. If you can see light through the filter it can be reused.

Extremely clogged filters should be discarded and replaced with a new one.

18. Replace the air filter regularly. A dirty air filter richens the air/fuel mixture and can increase fuel consumption as much as 10%. Tests show that 1/3 of all vehicles have air filters in need of replacement.

19. Replace the fuel filter at least as often as recommended.

20. Set the idle speed and carburetor mixture to specifications.

21. Check the automatic choke. A sticking or malfunctioning choke wastes gas.

22. During the summer months, adjust the automatic choke for a leaner mixture which will produce faster engine warm-ups.

COOLING SYSTEM

29. Be sure all accessory drive belts are in good condition. Check for cracks or wear.

30. Adjust all accessory drive belts to proper tension.

31. Check all hoses for swollen areas, worn spots, or loose clamps.

32. Check coolant level in the radiator or ex-pansion tank.

33. Be sure the thermostat is operating properly. A stuck thermostat delays engine warm-up and a cold engine uses nearly twice as much fuel as a warm engine.

34. Drain and replace the engine coolant at least as often as recommended. Rust and scale

TIRES & WHEELS

38. Check the tire pressure often with a pencil type gauge. Tests by a major tire manufacturer show that 90% of all vehicles have at least 1 tire improperly inflated. Better mileage can be achieved by over-inflating tires, but never exceed the maximum inflation pressure on the side of the tire.

39. If possible, install radial tires. Radial tires deliver as much as 1/2 mpg more than bias belted tires.

40. Avoid installing super-wide tires. They only create extra rolling resistance and decrease fuel mileage. Stick to the manufacturer's recommendations.

41. Have the wheels properly balanced.

omy by tampering with emission controls is more likely to worsen fuel economy than improve it. Emission control changes on modern engines are not readily reversible.

16. Clean (or replace) the EGR valve and lines as recommended.

17. Be sure that all vacuum lines and hoses are reconnected properly after working under the hood. An unconnected or misrouted vacuum line can wreak havoc with engine performance.

23. Check for fuel leaks at the carburetor, fuel pump, fuel lines and fuel tank. Be sure all lines and connections are tight.

24. Periodically check the tightness of the carburetor and intake manifold attaching nuts and bolts. These are a common place for vacuum leaks to occur.

25. Clean the carburetor periodically and lubricate the linkage.

26. The condition of the tailpipe can be an excellent indicator of proper engine combustion. After a long drive at highway speeds, the inside of the tailpipe should be a light grey in color. Black or soot on the insides indicates an overly rich mixture.

27. Check the fuel pump pressure. The fuel pump may be supplying more fuel than the engine needs.

28. Use the proper grade of gasoline for your engine. Don't try to compensate for knocking or "pinging" by advancing the ignition timing. This practice will only increase plug temperature and the chances of detonation or pre-ignition with relatively little performance gain.

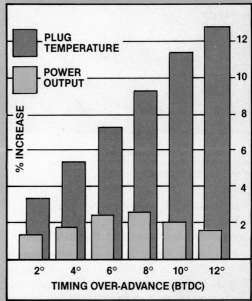

Increasing ignition timing past the specified setting results in a drastic increase in spark plug temperature with increased chance of detonation or preignition. Performance increase is considerably less. (Photo courtesy Champion Spark Plug Co.)

that form in the engine should be flushed out to allow the engine to operate at peak efficiency.

35. Clean the radiator of debris that can decrease cooling efficiency.

36. Install a flex-type or electric cooling fan, if you don't have a clutch type fan. Flex fans use curved plastic blades to push more air at low speeds when more cooling is needed; at high speeds the blades flatten out for less resistance. Electric fans only run when the engine temperature reaches a predetermined level.

37. Check the radiator cap for a worn or cracked gasket. If the cap does not seal properly, the cooling system will not function properly.

42. Be sure the front end is correctly aligned. A misaligned front end actually has wheels going in differed directions. The increased drag can reduce fuel economy by .3 mpg.

43. Correctly adjust the wheel bearings. Wheel bearings that are adjusted too tight increase rolling resistance.

Check tire pressures regularly with a reliable pocket type gauge. Be sure to check the pressure on a cold tire.

GENERAL MAINTENANCE

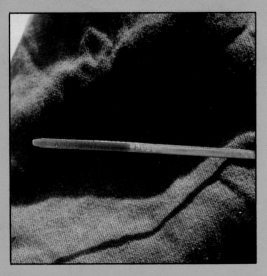

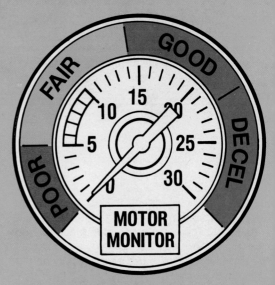

Check the fluid levels (particularly engine oil) on a regular basis. Be sure to check the oil for grit, water or other contamination.

A vacuum gauge is another excellent indicator of internal engine condition and can also be installed in the dash as a mileage indicator.

44. Periodically check the fluid levels in the engine, power steering pump, master cylinder, automatic transmission and drive axle.

45. Change the oil at the recommended interval and change the filter at every oil change. Dirty oil is thick and causes extra friction between moving parts, cutting efficiency and increasing wear. A worn engine requires more frequent tune-ups and gets progressively worse fuel economy. In general, use the lightest viscosity oil for the driving conditions you will encounter.

46. Use the recommended viscosity fluids in the transmission and axle.

47. Be sure the battery is fully charged for fast starts. A slow starting engine wastes fuel.

48. Be sure battery terminals are clean and tight.

49. Check the battery electrolyte level and add distilled water if necessary.

50. Check the exhaust system for crushed pipes, blockages and leaks.

51. Adjust the brakes. Dragging brakes or brakes that are not releasing create increased drag on the engine.

52. Install a vacuum gauge or miles-per-gallon gauge. These gauges visually indicate engine vacuum in the intake manifold. High vacuum = good mileage and low vacuum = poorer mileage. The gauge can also be an excellent indicator of internal engine conditions.

53. Be sure the clutch is properly adjusted. A slipping clutch wastes fuel.

54. Check and periodically lubricate the heat control valve in the exhaust manifold. A sticking or inoperative valve prevents engine warm-up and wastes gas.

55. Keep accurate records to check fuel economy over a period of time. A sudden drop in fuel economy may signal a need for tune-up or other maintenance.

nally, you should know how to use a digital volt-ohmmeter and be able to use it to measure resistance, voltage and current. A digital volt-ohmmeter with 10 megohms impedence is necessary to test the CCC system.

Service Precautions

CAUTION: *Whenever working on or around any computer-based microprocessor control system such as is found on most electronic fuel injection or emission control systems, always observe these general precautions to prevent the possibility of personal injury or damage to electronic components:*

• Never install or remove battery cables with the key ON or the engine running. Jumper cables should be connected with the key OFF to avoid power surges that can damage electronic control units. Engines equipped with computer controlled systems should avoid both giving and getting jump starts due to the possibility of serious damage to components from arcing in the engine compartment when connections are made with the ignition ON.

• Always remove the battery cables before charging the battery. Never use a high-output charger on an installed battery or attempt to use any type of "hot shot" (24 volt) starting aid.

• Never remove or attach wiring harness connectors with the ignition switch ON, especially to the electronic control unit. Never make or break test connections with the ignition switch ON, always turn the ignition OFF when connecting test equipment.

• Always depressurize the fuel system before attempting to disconnect any fuel lines. Fuel injected vehicles use a pressurized fuel system, and it's a good idea to exercise caution whenever disconnecting any fuel line or hose during service procedures. Take precautions to avoid a fire hazard.

• Always use clean rags and tools when working on an open fuel system and take care to prevent any dirt from entering the system. Wipe all components clean before installation and prepare a clean work area for disassembly and inspection of components. Use lint-free cloths to wipe components and avoid using any caustic cleaning solvents.

• Do not drop any components during service procedures and never apply 12 volts directly to any component (like a fuel injector) unless instructed specifically to do so. Some component electrical windings are designed to safely handle only 4 or 5 volts and can be destroyed in seconds if 12 volts are applied directly to the connector.

• Remove the electronic control unit if the vehicle is to be placed in an environment where temperatures exceed approximately 176°F (80°C), such as a paint spray booth or when arc or gas welding near the control unit location in the car.

Self-Diagnosis System

NOTE: *The following explains how to activate the Trouble Code signal light in the instrument cluster and gives an explanation of what each code means. This is not a full CCC System troubleshooting and isolation procedure.*

Before suspecting the CCC System or any of its components as faulty, check the ignition system including distributor, timing, spark plugs and wires. Check the engine compression, air cleaner, and emission control components not controlled by the ECM. Also check the intake manifold, vacuum hoses and hose connectors for leaks and the carburetor bolts for tightness. The following symptoms could indicate a possible problem with the CCC System:

1. Detonation or spark knock (ping)
2. Stalling or rough idle when cold
3. Stalling or rough idle when hot
4. Missing or erratic engine operation
5. Hesitation
6. Surges at road speeds
7. Extremely poor gasoline mileage
8. Sluggish or spongy performance
9. Hard starting when cold
10. Hard starting when hot
11. Objectionable exhaust odors (that "rotten egg" smell)

As a bulb and system check, the CHECK ENGINE or SERVICE ENGINE SOON light will come on when the ignition switch is turned to the ON position but the engine is not started. The indicator light will also produce the trouble code or codes by a series of flashes which translate as follows. When the diagnostic test terminal (ALCL) under the dash is grounded with the ignition in the ON position and the engine not running, the indicator light will flash once, pause, then flash twice is rapid succession. This is a code 12, which indicates that the diagnostic system is working. After a longer pause, the code 12 will repeat itself two or more times. The cycle will then repeat itself until the

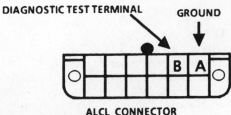

DIAGNOSTIC TEST TERMINAL   **GROUND**

ALCL CONNECTOR
To read stored trouble codes, connect terminals A and B together with a jumper wire

engine is started or the ignition is turned OFF. If the diagnostic terminal is grounded with the engine running, the system will enter the Field Service Mode. In this mode, the indicator light will show whether the system is operating in the open or closed loop mode. In the open loop mode, the indicator light will flash 2½ times per second. In closed loop, the light flashes once per second. In the Field Service Mode, the distributor will have a fixed spark advance, new trouble codes cannot be stored and the closed loop timer is bypassed.

When the engine is started, the CHECK ENGINE or SERVICE ENGINE SOON light will remain on for a few seconds, then turn off. If the light remains on, the self-diagnostic system has detected a problem. If the test terminal is then grounded as described above, the trouble code will flash three times. If more than one problem is found, each trouble code will flash three times. Trouble codes will flash in numerical order (lowest code number to highest). The trouble codes series will repeat as long as the test lead or terminal is grounded. A trouble code indicates a problem with a given circuit. For example, trouble code 14 indicates a problem in the cooling sensor circuit; this includes the coolant sensor, its electrical harness, and the Electronic Control Module (ECM). The trouble code does not, however, pinpoint exactly what is wrong with the circuit. The problem could be the result of a failed component, computer problem, or trouble in the wiring.

Since the self-diagnostic system cannot diagnose every possible fault in the system, the absence of a trouble code does not mean the system is trouble-free. To determine problems within the system which do not activate a trouble code, a system performance check must be made. This job should be left to a qualified technician.

In the case of an intermittent fault in the system, the indicator light will go out when the fault goes away, but the trouble code will remain in the memory of the ECM. Therefore, if a trouble code can be obtained even though the indicator light is not on, the trouble code must be evaluated. It must be determined if the fault is intermittent or if the engine must be at certain operating conditions (under load, etc.) before the indicator light will come on. Some trouble codes will not be recorded in the ECM until the engine has been operated at part throttle for about 5 to 18 minutes. A trouble code will be stored until terminal "R" of the ECM has been disconnected from the battery for 10 seconds. Once a problem has been repaired, the trouble memory must be cleared. An easy way to erase the computer memory

on the CCC System is to disconnect the battery terminals from the battery. If this method is used, don't forget to reset clocks and electronic preprogrammable radios. Another method is to remove the fuse marked ECM in the fuse panel. Not all models have such a fuse.

CAUTION: *To prevent ECM damage, the key must be OFF when disconnecting or reconnecting power to the ECM.*

The ECM has a "learning" ability. If the battery is disconnected to clear diagnostic codes, the learning process has to begin all over again. During this process, a change may be noted in the vehicle performance. To "teach" the ECM, make sure the engine is at normal operating temperature and drive at part throttle, with moderate acceleration and idle conditions, until normal performance returns.

WIRING HARNESS REPAIR

The ECM wiring harness electrically connects the ECM to the various sensors, switches and solenoids in the engine compartment. Most connectors in the engine compartment are protected against moisture and dirt which could create oxidation and deposits on the terminals. This protection is important because of the very low voltage and current levels found in the electronic system. The connectors have a lock which secures the male and female terminals together; a secondary lock holds the seal and terminal into the connector.

Molded-on connectors require complete replacement of the connector, requiring splicing a new connector assembly into the harness. Before making a connector repair, be certain of the type of connector. Weather-Pack and Compact Three connectors look similar but are serviced differently.

NOTE: *Use care when probing the connector or replacing terminals in them as it is possible to short between opposite terminals. If this happens to the wrong terminal pair, it is possible to damage certain components. Always use jumper wires between connectors for circuit checking. Never probe through the Weather-Pack seals.*

When diagnosing, open circuits are often difficult to locate by sight because oxidation (corrosion) or terminal misalignment are hidden by the connectors. Merely wiggling a connector on a sensor or in the wiring harness may correct the open circuit condition. This should always be considered when an open circuit or failed sensor is indicated by the trouble code in the ECM memory. Intermittent problems may also be caused by corroded or loose connections.

Weather-Pack connectors can be identified

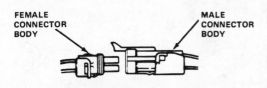

FEMALE CONNECTOR BODY

MALE CONNECTOR BODY

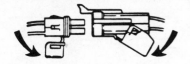

1. OPEN SECONDARY LOCK HINGE ON CONNECTOR

2. REMOVE TERMINAL USING TOOL

PUSH TO RELEASE

TERMINAL REMOVAL TOOL J-28742

3. CUT WIRE IMMEDIATELY BEHIND CABLE SEAL

WIRE
SEAL

4. REPLACE TERMINAL
   A. SLIP NEW SEAL ONTO WIRE.
   B. STRIP 5 mm (.2") OF INSULATION FROM WIRE.
   C. CRIMP TERMINAL OVER WIRE AND SEAL.

SEAL

5. PUSH TERMINAL AND CONNECTOR AND ENGAGE LOCKING TANGS.

6. CLOSE SECONDARY LOCK HINGE

Repairing Weather-Pack terminals

by the rubber seal at the rear of the connector. A special tool (J-28742) is required to remove the pin and sleeve terminals. If removal is attempted with an ordinary pick, there is a good chance that the terminal will be bent or deformed. Unlike standard blade type terminals, these cannot be straightened once they are bent. Make certain that the connectors are properly seated and that all of the sealing rings are in place when connecting leads. The hinge type flap provides a backup locking feature for the connector by retaining the terminals if the small terminal lock tangs are not positioned properly. Weather-Pack connections cannot be replaced with standard connectors.

The Compact Three connector, which looks similar to the Weather-Pack connector, is not sealed and is used where resistance to the environment is not required. The standard method of repairing a terminal may be used and a terminal tool is not required.

Wiring harnesses should be replaced with proper part number harnesses purchased from a GM dealer. When signal wires are spliced into a harness, use wire with high temperature insulation only. With the low current and voltage levels found in the system, it is important that the best possible bond at all wire splices be made by soldering the splices as illustrated. Some connectors uses on the wiring harness to connect the ECM are called Micro-Pack and terminal replacement requires a special tool.

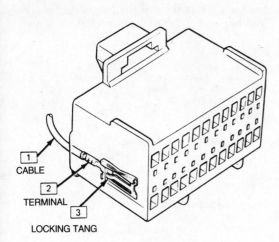

1
CABLE

2
TERMINAL

3
LOCKING TANG

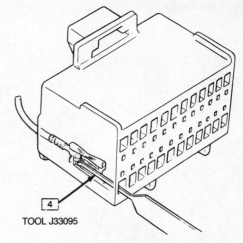

4
TOOL J33095

1. Grasp cable and push terminal to the most forward position.
2. Insert tool J33095 straight into the front of the connector cavity. Do not use conventional pick to remove terminal.

3. With tool in place, gently pull on the cable to remove terminal.
4. Visually check terminal and replace if terminal cavity or tang is damaged.
5. Install terminal into connector cavity until locking tang has snapped into position.

Repairing Micro-Pack terminals

TWISTED/SHIELDED CABLE

DRAIN WIRE
OUTER JACKET
MYLAR

1. REMOVE OUTER JACKET.
2. UNWRAP ALUMINUM/MYLAR TAPE. DO NOT REMOVE MYLAR.

TWISTED LEADS

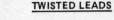

1. LOCATE DAMAGED WIRE.
2. REMOVE INSULATION AS REQUIRED.

3. UNTWIST CONDUCTORS. STRIP INSULATION AS NECESSARY.

SPLICE & SOLDER

3. SPLICE TWO WIRES TOGETHER USING SPLICE CLIPS AND ROSIN CORE SOLDER.

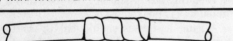

DRAIN WIRE

4. SPLICE WIRES USING SPLICE CLIPS AND ROSIN CORE SOLDER. WRAP EACH SPLICE TO INSULATE.
5. WRAP WITH MYLAR AND DRAIN (UNINSULATED) WIRE.

4. COVER SPLICE WITH TAPE TO INSULATE FROM OTHER WIRES.
5. RETWIST AS BEFORE AND TAPE WITH ELECTRICAL TAPE AND HOLD IN PLACE.

6. TAPE OVER WHOLE BUNDLE TO SECURE AS BEFORE.

Wiring harness repair

ON-CAR SERVICE

ECM Replacement

1. Make sure the ignition switch if OFF.
2. Remove the right (passenger side) kick panel to expose the ECM.
3. Disconnect the wiring harness connectors from the ECM.

4. Disconnect the ECM mounting hardware.
5. Remove the ECM from the vehicle.
6. Remove the PROM access cover from the ECM.
7. Using the rocker-type PROM removal tool, engage one end of the PROM carrier with the hook end of the tool then press on the vertical bar end of the tool and rock the engaged

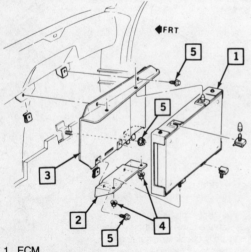

◄FRT

5 1
5
3
2 4
5

1. ECM
2. Lower ECM bracket
3. Upper ECM bracket
4. 6 N·m (37 lbs. in.)
5. Fully driven, seated and not stripped

ECM mounting behind glove box

PROM ACCESS COVER
PROM CARRIER
HARNESS CONNECTORS TO ECM
ELECTRONIC CONTROL MODULE (ECM)

Typical electronic control module (ECM)

PROM CARRIER
PROM ENGINE CALIBRATOR
CALPAC
ECM

Location of PROM and CALPAK in the ECM

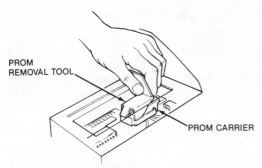

Removing the PROM using the special removal tool

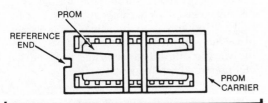

Note the position of the reference notch when installing the PROM

Note the position of the reference notch when installing the PROM

end of the PROM carrier up as far as possible. Engage the opposite end of the PROM carrier in the same manner and rock this end up as far as possible. Repeat this process until the PROM carrier and PROM are free of the PROM socket. The PROM carrier with the PROM in it should lift off the socket easily.

CAUTION: *The PROM carrier should only be removed using the appropriate tool. Other methods could cause damage to the PROM or PROM sockets.*

8. If the ECM is being replaced, transfer the PROM to the new controller body. If the PROM is being replaced, make sure the part number is correct for the vehicle being serviced. Unless specified differently, the new PROM should have the same part number as the old. Do not remove the PROM from the carrier to check the part number.

9. Install the PROM carrier into the body of the ECM. The small notch of the carrier should be aligned with the small notch in the socket. Gently press on the PROM carrier until it is seated firmly in the socket. Do not use excessive force to seat the PROM and press only on the carrier, not the PROM itself.

10. Install the access cover on the ECM then replace the ECM in the passenger compartment and reconnect the wiring harness.

11. As a functional check, turn the ignition ON and activate the trouble code readout as described earlier in this section. Trouble code 12 should flash at least four times. This indicates that the PROM is installed correctly.

12. If trouble code 51 occurs or the SER-

VICE ENGINE SOON light is on constantly with no codes, the PROM is not fully seated, installed backwards, has bent pins or is defective. If not fully seated, press firmly on the prom carrier. If the pins are bent, remove the PROM, straighten the pins and reinstall. If the pins break or crack during straightening, replace the PROM. If the PROM was installed backwards, replace it. Any time the PROM is installed backwards and the key is turned ON, the PROM is destroyed.

Oxygen Sensor Replacement

The oxygen sensor uses a permanently attached pigtail and connector. Damage or removal of the pigtail or connector could affect proper operation of the oxygen sensor. Exercise care when handling the oxygen sensor. The electrical connector and louvered end must be kept free of grease, dirt or other contaminants. Do not use cleaning solvents of any type on the oxygen sensor and do not drop it.

The oxygen sensor may be difficult to remove when engine temperature is below 120°F (48°C). When removing the sensor from the exhaust manifold, exercise caution to avoid the

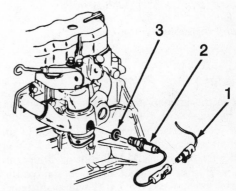

1. ECM connector
2. Oxygen sensor
3. Oxygen sensor seal

Oxygen sensor replacement on 4 cyl engine

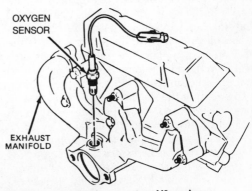

Oxygen sensor replacement on V6 engine

risk of being burned by hot metal components. Excessive force may damage threads in the exhaust manifold or exhaust pipe. Disconnect the negative battery cable and oxygen sensor pigtail, then use a suitable wrench to remove the oxygen sensor.

A special anti-seize compound is used on the oxygen sensor threads. New replacement sensors will already have the compound applied to the threads. The oxygen sensor threads must be coated with anti-seize compound before installation. If installing a used sensor, be careful not to contaminate the louvered portion of the sensor with compound when coating the threads. Tighten the oxygen sensor to 30 ft.lb. (42 Nm).

FUEL SYSTEM

NOTE: *This book contains simple testing and service procedures for for your N-Body's fuel injection system. More comprehensive testing and diagnosis procedures may be found in CHILTON'S GUIDE TO FUEL INJECTION AND FEEDBACK CARBURETORS, book part number 7488, available at most book stores and auto parts stores, or available directly from Chilton Co.*

Electric Fuel Pump

When the ignition is first turned ON without the engine running, the ECM will energize the fuel pump relay for two seconds to build up fuel pressure. If the engine is not started within two seconds, the ECM will shut off the pump and wait until the engine starts. As soon as the engine is cranked, the ECM will again energize the fuel pump relay and start the pump.

As a backup system to the fuel pump relay, the fuel pump can also be energized by the oil pressure sender. The oil pressure sender has two circuits; one operates the oil pressure indicator or gauge in the instrument cluster and the other is a normally open switch which closes when oil pressure reaches about 4 psi. If the fuel pump relay fails, the oil pressure switch will run the fuel pump. An inoperative fuel pump relay can result in long cranking times, particularly if the engine is cold. Fuel system pressure relief and testing procedures are given below. Removal procedures follow.

CAUTION: *Before servicing any part of the fuel system, it is necessary to relieve the fuel system pressure. Follow the procedure outlined below and take precautions to avoid the risk of fire.*

RELIEVING FUEL SYSTEM PRESSURE

On the four cylinder engine with throttle body (TBI) fuel injection, remove the fuse marked "Fuel Pump" from the block in the passenger compartment. Start the engine and allow it to idle until it stalls. Crank the engine an additional three seconds to make sure all fuel pressure is exhausted from the fuel lines, then turn off the key and reinstall the fuel pump fuse.

On the V6 engine with multiport (MPFI) fuel injection, connect fuel pressure gauge J-34730-1 or equivalent to the fuel pressure valve. Wrap a clean shop towel around the fitting while making connections to catch any fuel spray. Install a bleed hose onto the gauge assembly and place the end into a suitable container. Open the valve on the pressure gauge to bleed the fuel pressure from the system.

FUEL SYSTEM PRESSURE TEST

TBI System

1. Relieve fuel system pressure.
2. Remove the air cleaner and plug the THERMAC vacuum port on the throttle body.
3. Install pressure gauge J-29658 or equivalent on the throttle body side of the fuel filter at the rear of the car near the fuel tank.
4. Start the engine and read the fuel pressure on the gauge. It should be 9–13 psi.
5. Turn the ignition off, relieve the fuel system pressure and remove the fuel pressure gauge. Reconnect all fuel and vacuum lines and install the air cleaner.

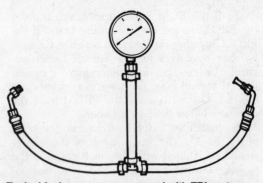

Typical fuel pressure gauge used with TBI systems

MPFI System

Depressurize the fuel system and connect pressure gauge J-34730-1 or equivalent to the fuel pressure test point (Shrader fitting) on the fuel rail. Wrap a clean shop cloth around the fitting to catch any fuel leakage when connecting the gauge. Turn the ignition ON and read the fuel pressure on the gauge. It should be 37–43 psi. Start the engine and again note the

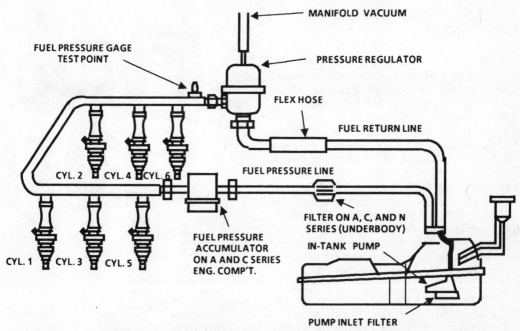

Schematic of port injection system showing fuel pressure test fitting

fuel pressure on the gauge. With the engine at idle, pressure should be 33–40 psi. This idle pressure will vary somewhat depending on barometric pressure, but in any case it should be lower. Relieve the fuel pressure and disconnect the gauge.

FUEL PUMP REPLACEMENT

1. Relieve the fuel system pressure.
2. Disconnect the negative battery cable.
3. Raise the car and support it safely.
4. Drain the fuel tank using a hand or power operated siphon. Place the drained gasoline into a suitable closed container or safety can, NOT into an open bucket or drain pan. Take precautions to avoid the risk of fire.

5. Remove the fuel tank.
6. Remove the fuel tank sending unit and pump assembly by turning the cam lock ring (located on top of the tank) counterclockwise. Lift the assembly from the fuel tank.
7. Pull the fuel pump up into the attaching hose while pulling outward from the bottom support. Exercise caution to prevent damage to the rubber insulator and strainer during removal. After the pump assembly is clear of the bottom support, pull the pump assembly out of the rubber connector for removal.
8. Installation is the reverse of removal. Inspect the fuel pump attaching hose for any signs of deterioration and replace as necessary. Check the rubber sound insulator at the bottom of the pump and replace if necessary.

Typical fuel pump assembly used with TBI system

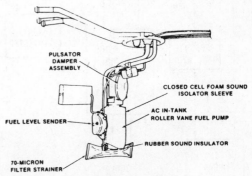

Typical fuel pump assembly used with port injection system

THROTTLE BODY INJECTION (TBI) SYSTEM

Throttle Body Fuel Injection is a completely electronic fuel delivery system which meters and injects precise amounts of fuel and air to the engine, according to the exact engine operating requirements at any given time. The TBI system is controlled by the Computer Command Control (CCC) on-board computer (ECM) which, through the monitoring of various sensors, determines the optimum air/fuel ratio and signals the TBI unit to adjust the ratio accordingly. Under normal circumstances, the system is designed to offer the owner trouble-free starting, immediate throttle response and maximum fuel efficiency regardless of weather conditions, engine rpm, temperature or load.

The main control signal for the TBI system is provided by the oxygen sensor, which is located in the exhaust manifold. The oxygen sensor tells the ECM the ratio of oxygen in the exhaust gas and the ECM changes the air/fuel ratio to the engine by controlling the fuel injector. The most efficient mixture to minimize exhaust emissions is 14.7:1, which allows the catalytic converter to operate at maximum efficiency. This constant measuring and adjust-

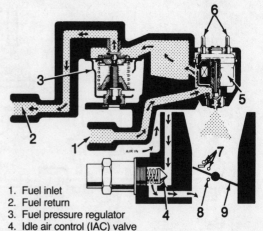

1. Fuel inlet
2. Fuel return
3. Fuel pressure regulator
4. Idle air control (IAC) valve
5. Fuel injector
6. Fuel injector connector terminals
7. Ported vacuum sources (may vary)
8. Manifold vacuum source (may vary)
9. Throttle valve

Throttle body unit operation

ing of the air/fuel ratio is referred to as "closed loop" operation.

The ECM looks at voltages from several sensors to determine how much fuel to give the engine under one of several conditions called "modes." The START MODE occurs when the ignition is first switched on. The ECM will turn on the fuel pump relay for two seconds, allowing the fuel pump to build up pressure to the TBI unit. The ECM then checks the coolant temperature sensor, throttle position sensor and crank signal from the starter to determine the proper air/fuel ratio for starting. The ECM controls the amount of fuel delivered in the START MODE by changing how long the injector is turned on and off, a process known as "pulse width." The longer the injector is on, the more fuel is delivered to the engine. If the engine floods, depressing the accelerator all the way to the floor will activate the CLEAR FLOOD MODE. The ECM pulses the injector at a 20:1 air/fuel ratio as long as the throttle stays wide open and the engine speed is below 600 rpm.

When the engine starts, the system enters the RUN MODE. This mode has two operating conditions called "open loop" and "closed loop." When the engine is first started and the engine speed is above 400 rpm, the system goes into open loop operation. In open loop, the ECM will ignore the signal from the oxygen sensor and calculate the air/fuel mixture based on inputs from the coolant and MAP sensor. The system will stay in open loop until the oxy-

FUEL CONTROL SYSTEM BLOCK DIAGRAM

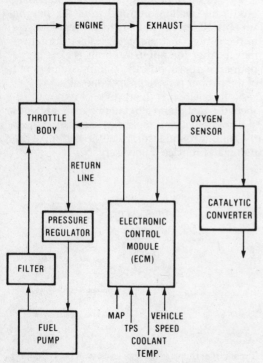

Schematic of fuel control system on GM TBI system

gen sensor heats up enough to begin operating (varying voltage output), the coolant sensor is above a specified temperature and a specific amount of time elapses after starting the engine. The specific values for these conditions vary with different engines and are stored in the PROM (computer calibrator) assembly. When the above conditions are met, the system goes into closed loop operation and the ECM will calculate the air/fuel mixture based on the signal from the oxygen sensor.

In the ACCELERATION MODE, the ECM looks at rapid changes in throttle position and manifold pressure and provides extra fuel. When deceleration occurs, the fuel remaining in the intake manifold can cause excessive emissions and backfiring. In the DECELERATION MODE, the ECM looks at changes in throttle position and manifold pressure and reduces the amount of fuel. When deceleration is very rapid, the ECM can cut off fuel completely for short periods. In the BATTERY VOLTAGE CORRECTION MODE, the ECM can compensate for weak spark due to low battery voltage by increasing the amount of fuel delivered, increasing the idle speed or increasing the ignition dwell time. Finally, in the FUEL CUT-OFF MODE, no fuel is delivered to the injectors when the engine is off. This prevents dieseling and flooding when the engine is not running.

TBI SYSTEM COMPONENTS

The basic TBI unit is made up of two major casting assemblies. The first is a throttle body with an idle air control (IAC) valve to control air flow and a throttle position sensor (TPS). The second is a fuel body with a fuel meter cover with built-in pressure regulator and a fuel injector to supply fuel to the engine. The throttle body portion of the TBI unit may contain ports located at, above or below the throttle valve which generate the vacuum signals for the EGR valve, MAP sensor and the canister purge system.

The fuel injector is a solenoid operated device controlled by the ECM. The ECM turns on the solenoid which lifts a normally closed ball valve off its seat. The fuel, which is under pressure, is injected in a conical spray pattern at the walls of the throttle body bore above the throttle valve. Fuel which is not used by the injector passes through the pressure regulator before being returned to the fuel tank. A fuel injector which does not open causes a no-start condition. An injector which is stuck partly open could cause loss of pressure after setting, so long crank times would be noticed on some engines. In addition, dieseling would occur be-

cause some fuel would be delivered to the engine after the key is turned off.

The pressure regulator is a diaphragm-operated relief valve with injector pressure on one side and air cleaner pressure on the other. The function of the regulator is to maintain a constant pressure at the injector at all times by controlling the fuel flow in the return line. The pressure regulator is serviced as part of the fuel meter cover. If the pressure regulator supplies pressure which is too low, poor performance could result. If the pressure is too high, excessive odor ("rotten egg" smell) may result.

The idle air control (IAC) valve controls engine idle speed and prevents stalling due to changes in engine load. The IAC valve is mounted in the throttle body and controls bypass air around the throttle valve. By moving a conical valve in to decrease air flow, or out to increase it, a controlled amount of air can move past the throttle valve. If the engine speed (rpm) is too low, more air is bypassed to increase rpm and vice versa. The IAC valve moves in small steps called "counts" which can be measured by some test equipment which plugs into the ALCL under the dash.

During idle, the proper position of the IAC valve is calculated by the ECM based on battery voltage, coolant temperature, engine load and engine rpm. If the rpm drops below a specified value and the throttle valve is closed, the ECM senses a near stall condition and calculates a new valve position to prevent stalling based on barometric pressure. If the IAC valve is disconnected or connected with the engine running, the IAC counts may be wrong. In this case, the IAC will reset when the vehicle speed is over 35 mph.

Fuel Injector
REMOVAL AND INSTALLATION

NOTE: *Fuel system pressure must be relieved before attempting any component removal procedures. Exercise caution when removing the fuel injector to prevent damage to the electrical connector terminals on top of the injector, injector fuel filter and the nozzle. The fuel injector is an electrical component and should not be immersed in any type of cleaner.*

1. Remove the air cleaner.

2. Disconnect the injector electrical connector by squeezing the tabs together and lifting straight up.

3. Remove the fuel meter cover as described below.

4. With the fuel meter cover gasket in place to prevent damage to the casting, use a screw-

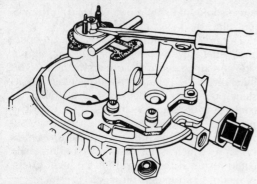

Removing TBI fuel injector

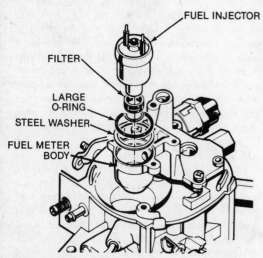

FUEL INJECTOR

FILTER

LARGE
O-RING

STEEL WASHER

FUEL METER
BODY

TBI fuel injector components

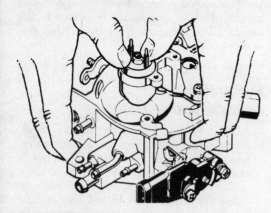

Installing TBI fuel injector

driver to lift the injector carefully until it is free of the fuel meter body.

5. Remove the small O-ring from the nozzle end of the injector, then carefully rotate the injector fuel filter back and forth to remove the filter from the base of the injector.

6. Remove and discard the fuel meter cover gasket.

7. Remove the large O-ring and steel back-up washer from the top counterbore of the fuel meter body injector cavity.

8. The fuel injector is serviced as a complete assembly only. If a problem is noted, the injector must be replaced.

9. Install the nozzle filter on the nozzle end of the injector, with the larger end of the filter facing the injector so the filter covers the raised rib at the base. Use a twisting motion to position the filter against the base of the injector.

10. Lubricate a new small O-ring with automatic transmission fluid, then push the O-ring on the nozzle end of the injector until it presses against the injector fuel filter. Install the steel back-up washer in the top counterbore of the fuel meter body injector cavity.

11. Lubricate a new large O-ring with automatic transmission fluid and install it directly over the back-up washer. Make sure the O-ring is seated properly in the cavity and is flush with the top of the fuel meter body casting surface.

NOTE: *The back-up washer and large O-ring must be installed before the injector or improper seating of the large O-ring could cause fuel to leak.*

12. Install the small O-ring on the injector, then install the injector, aligning the raised lug with the cast-in notch in the fuel meter body cavity. Push down on the injector until it is fully seated in the cavity.

13. Install the fuel meter cover, reconnect the electrical connector and install the air cleaner.

Fuel Meter Cover
REMOVAL AND INSTALLATION

CAUTION: *Do not remove the four screws securing the pressure regulator to the fuel meter cover. The pressure regulator contains a large spring under heavy compression which could cause personal injury if suddenly released. Disassembly could also cause a fuel leak between the diaphragm and the regulator container.*

1. Remove the air cleaner.

2. Disconnect the electrical connector to the fuel injector.

3. Remove the five screws and lockwashers securing the fuel meter cover to the fuel meter body. Note the location of the two short screws for reassembly.

4. Lift the fuel meter cover off of the throttle body assembly. Do not immerse the fuel meter cover in any form of cleaner or damage to the regulator diaphragms could occur.

5. Install a new dust seal into the recess on the fuel meter body.

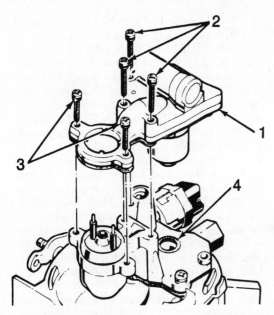

1. Fuel meter cover assembly
2. Long screws
3. Short screws
4. Dust seal

Fuel meter cover removal

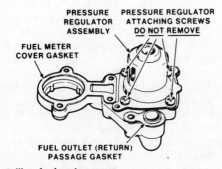

Installing fuel meter cover

6. Install new fuel outlet passage and fuel meter cover gaskets, then install the fuel meter cover, making sure the pressure regulator dust seal and cover gaskets are in place. Apply thread locking compound to the threads on the fuel meter cover attaching screws, then install the screws and torque to 28 inch lbs. (3 Nm).

7. Install the fuel injector connector and the air cleaner.

Idle Air Control Valve

REMOVAL AND INSTALLATION

1. Remove the air cleaner.
2. Remove the electrical connector from the IAC valve.
3. Remove the IAC valve using a wrench on the hex surface.

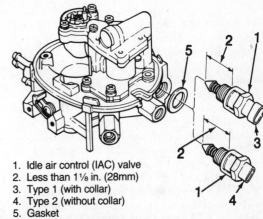

1. Idle air control (IAC) valve
2. Less than 1⅛ in. (28mm)
3. Type 1 (with collar)
4. Type 2 (without collar)
5. Gasket

Idle air control valve installation

4. Before installing the idle air control valve, measure the distance that the valve is extended from the motor housing to the end of the cone. The distance should be no greater than 1⅛ in. (28mm). If the cone is extended too far, damage may occur when the valve is installed.

5. Identify the IAC valve as having a collar at the electrical terminal end (Type 1) or without a collar (Type 2). If the extended distance is greater than 1⅛ in., reduce it as follows:

   a. Type 1: exert firm pressure on the valve to retract it. A slight side-to-side movement may help.

   b. Type 2: compress the retaining spring of the valve while turning the valve in with a clockwise motion. Return the spring to its original position with the straight portion of the spring end aligned with the flat surface of the valve.

6. Install the idle air control valve to the throttle body using a new gasket. Tighten to 13 ft.lb. (18 Nm).

7. Install the electrical connector to the idle air control valve, then install the air cleaner.

8. Start the engine and allow it to reach normal operating temperature. The ECM will reset the idle speed when the vehicle is driven above 35 mph.

Fuel Pump Relay

The fuel pump relay is mounted in the engine compartment. Other than checking for loose connections, the only service possible is replacement of the relay.

MULTIPORT FUEL INJECTION (MFI) SYSTEM

Like the TBI system, multiport fuel injection is a completely electronic fuel delivery system which meters precise amounts of fuel and air to the engine, according to the exact engine operating requirements at any given time. The major differences between the two types of fuel injection are the components used and the manner in which fuel is delivered to the combustion chambers.

The main control signal for the MFI system is provided by the oxygen sensor, which is located in the exhaust manifold. The oxygen sensor tells the ECM the ratio of oxygen in the exhaust gas and the ECM changes the air/fuel ratio to the engine by controlling the fuel injectors. The most efficient mixture to minimize exhaust emissions is 14.7:1, which allows the catalytic converter to operate at maximum efficiency. This constant measuring and adjusting of the air/fuel ratio is referred to as "closed loop" operation.

The ECM looks at voltages from several sensors to determine how much fuel to give the engine under one of several conditions called "modes." The START MODE occurs when the ignition is first switched on. The ECM will turn on the fuel pump relay for two seconds, allowing the fuel pump to build up pressure in the fuel system. The ECM then checks the coolant temperature sensor, throttle position sensor and crank signal from the starter to determine the proper air/fuel ratio for starting. The ECM controls the amount of fuel delivered in the START MODE by changing how long the injectors are turned on and off, a process known as "pulse width." The longer the injectors are on, the more fuel is delivered to the engine. If the engine floods, depressing the accelerator all the way to the floor will activate the CLEAR FLOOD MODE. The ECM pulses the injector at a 20:1 air/fuel ratio as long as the throttle stays wide open and the engine speed is below 600 rpm.

When the engine starts the system enters the RUN MODE. This mode has two operating conditions called "open loop" and "closed loop." When the engine is first started and the engine speed is above 400 rpm, the system goes into open loop operation. In open loop, the ECM will ignore the signal from the oxygen sensor and calculate the air/fuel mixture based on inputs from the coolant and MAP sensor. The system will stay in open loop until the oxygen sensor heats up enough to begin operating (varying voltage output), the coolant sensor is above a specified temperature and a specific amount of time elapses after starting the engine. The specific values for these conditions vary with different engines and are stored in the PROM (computer calibrator) assembly. When the above conditions are met, the system goes into closed loop operation and the

ECM will calculate the air/fuel mixture based on the signal from the oxygen sensor.

In the ACCELERATION MODE, the ECM looks at rapid changes in throttle position and manifold pressure and provides extra fuel. When deceleration occurs, the fuel remaining in the intake manifold can cause excessive emissions and backfiring. In the DECELERATION MODE, the ECM looks at changes in throttle position and manifold pressure and reduces the amount of fuel. When deceleration is very rapid, the ECM can cut off fuel completely for short periods. In the BATTERY VOLTAGE CORRECTION MODE, the ECM can compensate for weak spark due to low battery voltage by increasing the amount of fuel delivered, increasing the idle speed or increasing the ignition dwell time. Finally, in the FUEL CUT-OFF MODE, no fuel is delivered to the injectors when the engine is off. This prevents dieseling and flooding when the engine is not running.

MFI SYSTEM COMPONENTS

The MFI fuel control system includes the fuel injectors, throttle body, fuel rail, fuel pressure regulator, idle air control (IAC) valve, fuel pump and fuel pump relay. The throttle body has a throttle valve to control the amount of air delivered to the engine and contains vacuum ports located at, above or below the throttle valve which generate vacuum signals for various components. The throttle position switch (TPS) and idle air control (AIC) valve are mounted on the throttle body.

The fuel rail is mounted to the top of the engine and distributes fuel to the individual injectors. Fuel is pumped to the input end of the rail, flows through the rail and then through the pressure regulator. The regulator keeps the fuel pressure to the injectors constant, with remaining fuel returned to the fuel tank. Each fuel injector (there are six) is a solenoid operated device controlled by the electronic control module (ECM), which energizes the solenoid to open a valve and allow fuel delivery. The pressurized fuel is injected in a conical spray pattern at the opening of each intake valve, with unused fuel being returned to the tank through the pressure regulator.

The pressure regulator is a diaphragm operated relief valve with injector pressure on one side and manifold pressure on the other. The regulator is designed to maintain a constant pressure at the injector at all times and compensates for engine load by increasing fuel pressure when it senses low engine vacuum. The pressure regulator is mounted on the fuel rail and is serviced separately. If fuel pressure is too low, poor performance could result. If fuel pressure is too high, excessive odor ("rotten egg" smell) and a trouble code 45 may result.

The idle air control (IAC) valve controls engine idle speed and prevents stalling due to changes in engine load. The IAC valve is mounted in the throttle body and controls bypass air around the throttle valve. By moving a conical valve in to decrease air flow, or out to increase it, a controlled amount of air can move past the throttle valve. If the engine speed (rpm) is too low, more air is bypassed to increase rpm and vice versa. The IAC valve moves in small steps called "counts" which can be measured by some test equipment which plugs into the ALCL under the dash.

During idle, the proper position of the IAC valve is calculated by the ECM based on battery voltage, coolant temperature, engine load and engine rpm. If the rpm drops below a specified value and the throttle valve is closed, the ECM senses a near stall condition and calculates a new valve position to prevent stalling based on barometric pressure. If the IAC valve is disconnected or connected with the engine running, the IAC counts may be wrong. In this case, the IAC will reset when the ignition is turned ON and then OFF.

Different designs are used for the IAC valve and any replacement part should be checked before installation to make sure it is the correct type. The IAC valve affects only the idle characteristics of the vehicle. If open fully, too much air will be allowed into the manifold and idle speed will be high. If stuck closed, too little air will be allowed into the manifold and the idle speed will be low. If stuck partly open, the idle may be rough and will not respond to engine load changes.

Fuel Rail and Injectors
REMOVAL AND INSTALLATION

NOTE: *Fuel pressure must be relieved before attempting to remove any fuel system components. After servicing fuel system components, turn the key ON and allow the system to pressurize, then check for fuel leaks before starting the engine. Exercise caution when removing the injectors to prevent damage to the electrical connector pins on the injector and the nozzle. Do not immerse the injector in any kind of cleaning solvent.*

1. Depressurize the fuel system as described earlier in this chapter.
2. Make sure the ignition is OFF, then remove the injector electrical connectors. Note the connector locks which must be released.

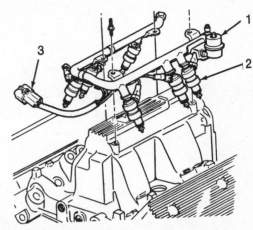

1. Pressure regulator
2. Fuel injector
3. Harness connector

Fuel rail assembly on port injection system

3. Remove the fuel rail by disconnecting the fuel feed line, then removing the four retaining bolts that fasten the fuel rail to the intake manifold.
4. Remove the injector(s) from the intake manifold by pulling upward. If the injectors were removed with the fuel rail as an assembly, remove them from the rail with a twisting motion.
5. If the original injectors are being installed, new O-rings must be used. If a new injector is being installed, O-rings are supplied with the part.
6. Install the remaining components in the reverse order of removal. Reconnect the fuel line, turn the ignition ON and check for fuel leaks before starting the engine.

Idle Air Control Valve
REMOVAL AND INSTALLATION

1. Remove the air cleaner.
2. Remove the electrical connector from the IAC valve.
3. Remove the IAC valve using a wrench on the hex surface.
4. Before installing the idle air control valve, measure the distance that the valve is extended from the motor housing to the end of the cone. The distance should be no greater than 1⅛ in. (28mm). If the cone is extended too far, damage may occur when the valve is installed.
5. Identify the IAC valve as having a collar at the electrical terminal end (Type 1) or without a collar (Type 2). If the extended distance is greater than 1⅛ in., reduce it as follows:

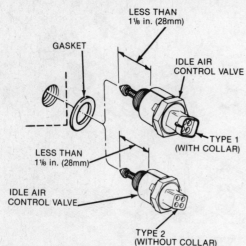

Idle air control valve installation

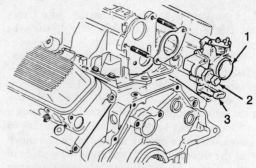

1. Throttle body assembly
2. Idle air control motor (IAC)
3. Throttle position sensor (TPS)

Throttle body removal on V6 engine

a. Type 1: exert firm pressure on the valve to retract it. A slight side-to-side movement may help.

b. Type 2: compress the retaining spring of the valve while turning the valve in with a clockwise motion. Return the spring to its original position with the straight portion of the spring end aligned with the flat surface of the valve.

6. Install the idle air control valve to the throttle body using a new gasket. Tighten to 13 ft.lb. (18 Nm).

7. Install the electrical connector to the idle air control valve, then install the air cleaner.

8. Start the engine and allow it to reach normal operating temperature. The ECM will reset the IAC valve when the ignition is switched ON and then OFF.

Chassis Electrical

5

UNDERSTANDING AND TROUBLESHOOTING ELECTRICAL SYSTEMS

For any electrical system to operate, it must make a complete circuit. This simply means that the power flow from the battery must make a complete circle. When an electrical component is operating, power flows from the battery to the component, passes through the component causing it to perform its function (lighting a light bulb), and then returns to the battery through the ground of the circuit. This ground is usually (but not always) the metal part of the car or truck on which the electrical component is mounted.

Perhaps the easiest way to visualize this is to think of connecting a light bulb with two wires attached to it to the battery. If one of the two wires attached to the light bulb were attached to the negative post of the battery and the other were attached to the positive post of the battery, you would have a complete circuit. Current from the battery would flow to the light bulb, causing it to light, and return to the negative post of the battery.

The normal automotive circuit differs from this simple example in two ways. First, instead of having a return wire from the bulb to the battery, the light bulb returns the current to the battery through the chassis of the vehicle. Since the negative battery cable is attached to the chassis and the chassis is made of electrically conductive metal, the chassis of the vehicle can serve as ground wire to complete the circuit. Secondly, most automotive circuits contain switches to turn components on and off as required.

Every complete circuit from a power source must include a component which is using the power from the power source. If you were to disconnect the light bulb from the wires and touch the two wires together (don't do this) the power supply wire to the component would be grounded before the normal ground connection for the circuit.

Because grounding a wire from a power source makes a complete circuit (less the required component to use the power) this phenomenon is called a short circuit. Common causes are: broken insulation (exposing the metal wire to a metal part of the car or truck), or a shorted switch.

Some electrical components which require a large amount of current to operate also have a relay in their circuit. Since these circuits carry a large amount of current, the thickness of the wire in the circuit (gauge size) is also greater. If this large wire were connected from the component to the control switch on the instrument panel, and then back to the component, a voltage drop would occur in the circuit. To prevent this potential drop in voltage, an electromagnetic switch (relay) is used. The large wires in the circuit are connected from the battery to one side of the relay, and from the opposite side of the relay to the component. The relay is normally open, preventing current from passing through the circuit. An additional, smaller, wire is connected from the relay to the control switch for the circuit. When the control switch is turned on, it grounds the smaller wire from the relay and completes the circuit. This closes the relay and allows current to flow from the battery to the component. The horn, headlight, and starter circuits are three which use relays.

It is possible for larger surges of current to pass through the electrical system of your car or truck. If this surge of current were to reach an electrical component, it could burn it out. To prevent this, fuses, circuit breakers or fusible links are connected into the current supply wires of most of the major electrical systems. When an electrical current of excessive power passes throughout the component's fuse, the fuse blows out and breaks the circuit, saving the component from destruction.

A circuit breaker is basically a self-repairing fuse. The circuit breaker opens the circuit the same way a fuse does. However, when either the short is removed from the circuit or the surge subsides, the circuit breaker resets itself and does not have to be replaced as a fuse does.

A fuse link is a wire that acts as a fuse. It is normally connected between the starter relay and the main wiring harness. This connection is usually under the hood. The fuse link (if installed) protects all the chassis electrical components, and is the probable cause of trouble when none of the electrical components function, unless the battery is disconnected or dead.

Electrical problems generally fall into one of three areas:

1. The component that is not functioning is not receiving current.

2. The component itself is not functioning.

3. The component is not properly grounded.

The electrical system can be checked with a test light and a jumper wire. A test light is a device that looks like a pointed screwdriver with a wire attached to it and has a light bulb in its handle. A jumper wire is a piece of insulated wire with an alligator clip attached to each end.

If a component is not working, you must follow a systematic plan to determine which of the three causes is the villain.

1. Turn on the switch that controls the inoperable component.

2. Disconnect the power supply wire from the component.

3. Attach the ground wire on the test light to a good metal ground.

4. Touch the probe end of the test light to the end of the power supply wire that was disconnected from the component. If the component is receiving current, the test light will go on.

NOTE: *Some components work only when the ignition switch is turned on.*

5. If the test light does not go on, then the problem is in the circuit between the battery and the component. This includes all the switches, fuses and relays in the system. Follow the wire that runs back to the battery. The problem is an open circuit between the battery and the component. If the fuse is blown and, when replaced, immediately blows again, there is a short circuit in the system which must be located and repaired. If there is a switch in the system, bypass it with a jumper wire. This is done by connecting one end of the jumper wire to the power supply wire into the switch and the other end of the jumper wire to the wire coming out of the switch. If the test light lights with the jumper wire installed, the switch or whatever was bypassed is defective.

NOTE: *Never substitute the jumper wire for the component, since it is required to use the power from the power source.*

6. If the bulb in the test light goes on, then the current is getting to the component that is not working. This eliminates the first of the three possible causes. Connect the power supply wire and connect a jumper wire from the component to a good metal ground. Do this with the switch which controls the component turned on, and also the ignition switch turned on if it is required for the component to work. If the component works with the jumper wire installed, then it has a bad ground. This is usually caused by the metal area on which the component mounts to the chassis being coated with some type of foreign matter (corrosion, grease, etc.).

7. If neither test located the source of the trouble, then the component itself is defective. Remember that for any electrical system to work, all connections must be clean and tight.

NOTE: *Some electrical components (like ignition modules) require the use of a heat-dissipating silicone compound in order to function properly. This silicone compound must not be removed and should not be confused with the foreign matter mentioned above.*

WIRING DIAGRAMS

Wiring diagrams have been left out of this book. As cars have become more complex and available with longer and longer option lists, wiring diagrams have grown in size and complexity also. It has become virtually impossible to provide a readable reproduction in a reasonable number of pages.

HEATER

Blower Motor
REMOVAL AND INSTALLATION

1. Disconnect the negative battery cable.

2. Disconnect the blower motor electrical connector.

3. Disconnect the relay bracket.

4. Raise the vehicle and support it safely.

5. Remove the blower motor retaining screws and nuts, then remove the blower motor from the firewall.

6. Installation is the reverse of removal.

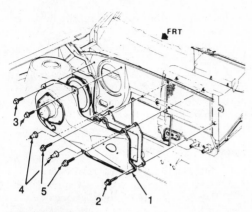

1. Blower assembly
2. Install first
3. Install second
4. 23 inch lbs.
5. 30 inch lbs.

Removing blower motor assembly

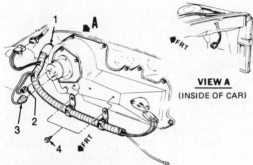

VIEW A
(INSIDE OF CAR)

1. Heater module wiring harness
2. Blower motor ground
3. Blower motor feed
4. 12 inch lbs.

Blower motor wiring connections

Heater Core

REMOVAL AND INSTALLATION

1. Disconnect the negative battery cable.
2. Drain the cooling system.

CAUTION: *When draining the coolant, keep in mind that cats and dogs are attracted by the ethelyne glycol antifreeze, and are quite likely to drink any that is left in an uncovered container or in puddles on the ground. This will prove fatal in sufficient quantity. Always drain the coolant into a sealable container. Coolant should be reused unless it is contaminated or several years old.*

3. Remove the console extensions.
4. Remove the console air ducts.
5. Remove the hush panel.
6. Remove the hot air plenum.
7. Remove the heater core housing.
8. Raise the vehicle and support it safely.
9. Remove the heater core hoses.

10. Lower the vehicle, then remove the heater core. The core may contain some coolant, so take precautions to avoid damage to the carpet or upholstery in the passenger compartment when removing the core.

11. Installation is the reverse of removal. Refill the cooling system.

Radio

REMOVAL AND INSTALLATION

NOTE: *Do not operate the radio with the speaker leads disconnected. Operating the radio without an electrical load will damage the output transistors.*

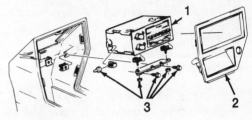

1. Radio
2. Radio trim plate
3. Fully driven, seated and not stripped

Typical console radio installation

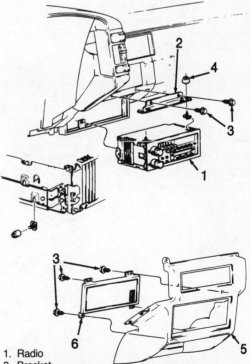

1. Radio
2. Bracket
3. Fully driven, seated and not stripped
4. Tighten to 23 inch lbs.
5. Lower center trim cover
6. Cover used without radio

Typical in-dash radio mounting

Grand Am

1. Disconnect the battery.
2. Remove the right console extension.
3. Remove the rear main plate.
4. Remove the radio screws and connectors and remove the radio.
5. Installation is the reverse of removal.

Calais

WITH AUTO-CALCULATOR

1. Remove the radio trim plate by pulling it rearward.
2. Remove the screws from the radio mounting bracket.
3. Pull the radio rearward and disconnect the wiring.
4. Remove the radio.
5. Installation is the reverse of removal. Make sure all connections are tight.

WITHOUT AUTO-CALCULATOR

1. Open the ashtray and remove the insert.
2. Locate the locking tangs on each side of the ashtray. Each tang has a tab on the right side.
3. Using a small screwdriver, depress the tab on the right side of the locking tang.
4. Pull the lower ashtray assembly out to the second stop and depress the tangs again.
5. Lower the ashtray assembly.

6. Remove the screws from the upper ashtray assembly.
7. Remove the trim plate with the upper ashtray assembly.
8. Remove the mounting screws from the radio.
9. Slide the radio rearward and disconnect the wiring. Remove the radio.
10. Installation is the reverse of removal.

Somerset and Skylark

1. Remove the left hand trim cover.
2. Remove the right side switch trim plate.
3. Remove the mounting screws.
4. Pull the radio out enough to disconnect the electrical connectors and antenna. Disconnect the clock connector, if equipped.
5. Remove the radio.
6. Installation is the reverse of removal. Make sure all connections are tight.

WINDSHIELD WIPERS

Wiper Arm

REMOVAL AND INSTALLATION

1. Using tool J-8966 or equivalent, insert a pop rivet completely through the hole located next to the pivot on the arm and lift the arm off the transmission shaft.
2. Installation is the reverse of removal. If adjustment is required, proceed as follows.

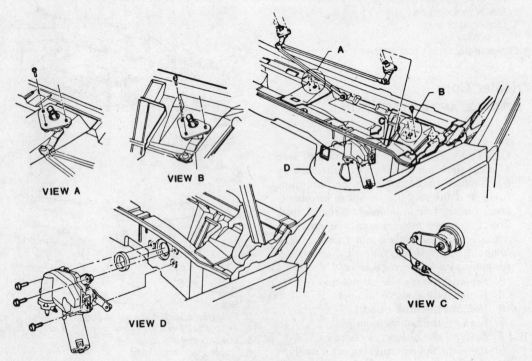

VIEW A

VIEW B

VIEW C

VIEW D

Wiper motor and transmission

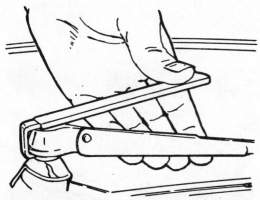

The wiper arms can be removed with the aid of this special tool

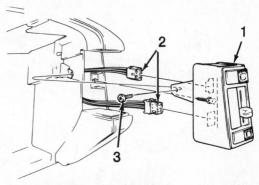

1. Windshield wiper and rear window defogger switch
2. Wiper and rear window defogger switch connector
3. Fully driven, seated and not stripped

Wiper and rear defogger switch-Calais shown

3. Remove the right arm and blade assembly.

4. Loosen, but do not remove, the wiper transmission drive link-to-motor crank arm attaching nuts.

5. Rotate the left arm assembly to a position slightly below the blade stops.

6. Tighten the attaching nuts on the transmission drive link(s) to motor crank arm to 8–11 ft.lb. (6–8 Nm).

7. Position the right arm and blade assembly slightly below the blade stop and install the arm assembly to the transmission shaft.

8. Lift the right and left arm and blade assemblies over the stops.

9. Check the wipe pattern and park position. The correct park position and outwipe dimensions are determined with the wipers operating at low speed on a wet windshield.

Wiper Blade

REMOVAL AND INSTALLATION

The wiper blade is retained to the wiper arm pin by spring tension. To remove the blade assembly, insert a screwdriver between the wiper arm and wiper blade assembly. Twist the screwdriver gently until the blade assembly is released from the wiper arm pin.

Wiper Blade Element

REMOVAL AND INSTALLATION

The N-series wiper blade element uses a spring-type clip on the end of the element. To remove the element, squeeze the clip, then pull down and out. Slide the element out of the housing retaining tabs. To install, slide the element into the housing retaining tabs and snap the clip into place.

INSTRUMENT CLUSTER AND GAUGES

Instrument Panel

REMOVAL AND INSTALLATION

The N-Body instrument cluster has been designed to allow removal of all control switches, instruments and gauges from the driver's side of the instrument panel. Trim covers are held in place by screws or clips. Electrical connectors for the headlight switch, cluster connectors, windshield wiper and rear defogger switch are locked to the cluster carrier and remain in place when the cluster or switches are removed. The cluster housing contains the speedometer, gauges, telltales and instrument panel bulbs. When removing or installing any electrical components, disconnect the negative battery cable to prevent possible short circuits which could lead to personal injury or damage to electronic components.

NOTE: *When replacing a speedometer or odometer assembly, Federal Law requires the odometer reading of the replacement unit to be set to register the same mileage as the prior odometer. If the same mileage cannot be set, the law requires that the replacement odometer be set to zero and a label be installed on the driver's door frame to show previous odometer reading and the date of replacement.*

LIGHTING

Headlamps

REMOVAL AND INSTALLATION

1. Remove the grille panel headlight bezel.
2. Remove the sealed beam retainer screws. Do not touch the aiming screws.

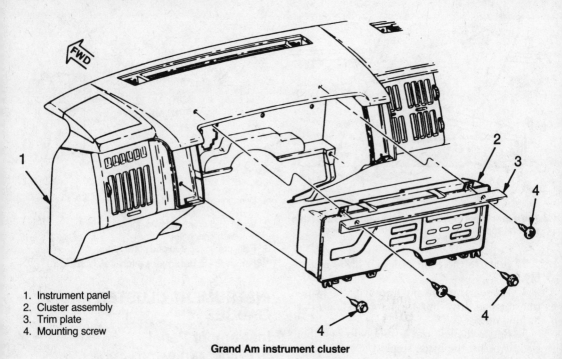

1. Instrument panel
2. Cluster assembly
3. Trim plate
4. Mounting screw

Grand Am instrument cluster

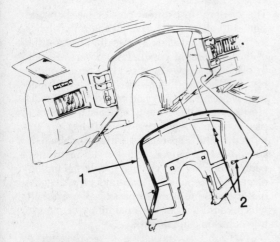

1. Cluster trim plate
2. Fully driven, seated and not stripped

Instrument cluster trim plate-Calais shown

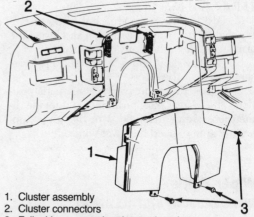

1. Cluster assembly
2. Cluster connectors
3. Fully driven, seated and not stripped

Calais instrument cluster

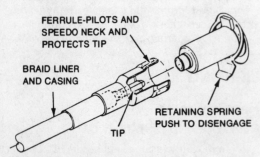

FERRULE-PILOTS AND
SPEEDO NECK AND
PROTECTS TIP

BRAID LINER
AND CASING

RETAINING SPRING
PUSH TO DISENGAGE

TIP

Speedometer cable disengagement at the speedometer

3. Pull the headlamp forward and disconnect the wiring harness connector.

4. Reverse the procedure to install the new headlamp. Aim the headlight if necessary.

HEADLIGHT AIMING

The headlights must be aimed properly to get the right amount of light on the road. With halogen sealed beam units, proper aiming is even more important as the increased range and power of these lights cam make even slight variations from the recommended aiming hazardous to approaching traffic. The headlamps are aimed by turning the vertical or horizontal aim screws. The vehicle should be at its normal

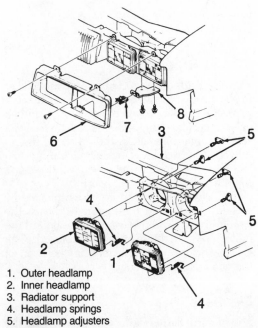

1. Outer headlamp
2. Inner headlamp
3. Radiator support
4. Headlamp springs
5. Headlamp adjusters
6. Bezel
7. Retainer
8. Bracket

Typical headlamp and bezel mounting

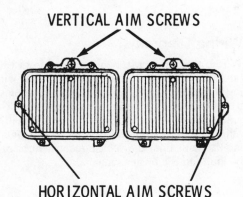

VERTICAL AIM SCREWS

HORIZONTAL AIM SCREWS
Location of headlamp aiming screws

weight with the spare tire, normal fluid levels and the fuel tank at least half full. Tires should be uniformly inflated to the proper pressure. If the car normally carries an unusual load in the rear or tows a trailer, these loads should be on the car when the headlamps are aimed.

Headlight Switch
REMOVAL AND INSTALLATION

1. Remove the steering column collar.
2. Remove the screws from the steering column opening filler.
3. Remove the cluster trim plate.

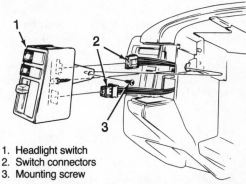

1. Headlight switch
2. Switch connectors
3. Mounting screw

Typical headlamp switch installation

4. Remove the screw mounting the headlight switch to the instrument panel pad.
5. Pull the headlight switch rearward and unplug both connectors, then remove the switch.
6. Installation is the reverse of removal.

CIRCUIT PROTECTION

Fusible Links

A fusible link is a protective device used in an electrical circuit. When the current increases beyond a certain amperage, the fusible metal of the wire link melts, thus breaking the electrical circuit and preventing further damage to other components and wiring. Whenever a fusible link is melted because of a short circuit, correct the cause before installing a new link.

The N-Body cars have five fusible links. Four are at the starter and one is located behind the battery. They protect the starting and charging circuits, lighting, cooling fan and electronic control module (ECM).

To replace a fusible link, cut off the burned link beyond the original splice. Replace the link with a new one of the same rating. If the splice has two wires, two repair links are required,

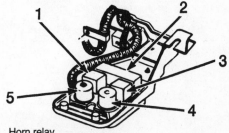

1. Horn relay
2. Seat belt, key and headlight buzzer
3. Vacant with fuel injection
4. Hazard flasher
5. Turn signal flasher

Typical convenience center. Not used on all models

one for each wire. Connect the new fusible link to the wire, then crimp or solder securely.

CAUTION: *Use only replacements of the same electrical capacity as the original link, available from a dealer or parts jobber. Replacements of a different electrical value will not provide adequate system protection and could lead to ECM damage.*

Fuses

Fuses protect all the major electrical systems in the car. In case of an electrical overload, the fuse melts, breaking the circuit and stopping the flow of electricity.

If a fuse blows, the cause should be investigated and corrected before installing a new fuse, a task usually easier suggested than accomplished. Because each fuse protects a limited number of components, the job is narrowed down somewhat, but finding the source of an electrical problem can be both tedious and time consuming. Begin the investigation by looking for obvious fraying, loose connections, breaks in insulation, etc., using the techniques outlined at the beginning of this chapter. If you are patient and persistent and approach the problem logically (that is, don't start replacing electrical components randomly), you will eventually find the solution.

The amperage of each fuse and the circuit it protects are marked on the fusebox or the fusebox cover. In addition, the amperage of the fuse is marked on the plastic fuse body so that it faces out when installed. Replacing a fuse with one of a higher amperage rating is not recommended and could cause electrical damage. A suspected blown fuse can easily be pulled out and inspected; the clear plastic body gives full view of the element to blade construction for visual inspection.

Circuit Breakers

The headlights are protected by a circuit breaker in the headlamp switch. If the circuit breaker trips, the headlights will either flash on and off or stay off altogether. The circuit breaker resets automatically after the overload is removed. There are also two circuit breakers in the fuse box, one for the power windows and the other for all power accessories.

The windshield wipers are also protected by a circuit breaker. If the motor overheats, the circuit breaker will trip, remaining off until the motor cools or the overload is removed. One common cause of overheating is operation of the wipers in heavy snow.

Flashers

The hazard flasher is located forward of the console in all N-Body models. The turn signal flasher is located behind the instrument panel, on the left hand side of the steering column. In both cases, replacement is accomplished by unplugging the old flasher and plugging in a new one.

Wiring Diagrams

Wiring diagrams have been omitted from this book. As cars have become more complex, wiring diagrams have grown in size and complexity as well. It has become impossible to provide a readable reproduction in a reasonable number of pages. Information on ordering wiring diagrams from the vehicle manufacturer can be found in the owner's manual.

6

MANUAL TRANSAXLE

Because of the complexity of the transaxle, no overhaul procedures are given in this book. However, removal and installation, adjustment and halfshaft removal, installation and overhaul are covered.

REMOVAL AND INSTALLATION

1. Disconnect the negative battery cable.

2. Install an engine support fixture such as J-28467 or equivalent, then raise the engine enough to take pressure off the motor mounts. Attach the hook to the engine lift ring, if equipped.

3. Remove the left sound insulator, if equipped with hydraulic clutch.

4. Disconnect the clutch master cylinder pushrod from the clutch pedal, if equipped with hydraulic clutch.

5. Disconnect the clutch slave cylinder from the transaxle support bracket and lay it aside.

6. Remove the transaxle mount attaching bolts.

7. Remove the transaxle mount bracket attaching bolts and nuts.

8. Disconnect the shift cables and retaining clamp at the transaxle.

9. Disconnect the ground cables at the transaxle mounting stud.

10. Raise the car and support it safely. Drain the transaxle.

11. Remove the left front tire and wheel assembly.

12. Remove the left front inner splash shield.

13. Disconnect the transaxle front strut.

14. Disconnect the transaxle front strut bracket.

15. Remove the clutch housing cover bolts.
CAUTION: *The clutch driven disc contains asbestos, which has been determined to be a cancer causing agent. Never clean clutch*

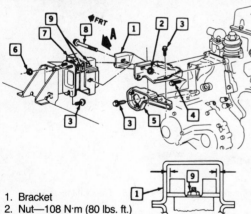

1. Bracket
2. Nut—108 N·m (80 lbs. ft.)
3. Bolt—54 N·m (40 lbs. ft.)
4. Bolt—75 N·m (56 lbs. ft.)
5. Support—only with hydraulic clutch
6. Nut—30 N·m (23 lbs. ft.)
7. Rear mount
8. Bolt
9. Nut—25 N·m (18 lbs. ft.)
   These nuts must be tightened last and should be tightened to provide equal gaps

Typical rear transaxle mount

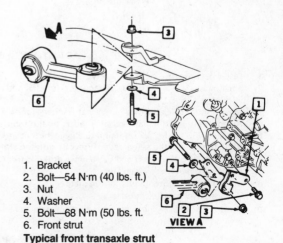

1. Bracket
2. Bolt—54 N·m (40 lbs. ft.)
3. Nut
4. Washer
5. Bolt—68 N·m (50 lbs. ft.
6. Front strut

Typical front transaxle strut

surfaces with compressed air! Avoid inhaling any dust from any clutch surface! When cleaning clutch surfaces, use a commercially available brake cleaning fluid.

16. Disconnect the speedometer cable or sensor at the transaxle.

17. Disconnect the stabilizer bar at the left suspension support and control arm.

18. Disconnect the ball joint from the steering knuckle.

19. Disconnect the left suspension support attaching bolts and remove the support and control arm as an assembly.

20. Disconnect the drive axles at the transaxle and remove the left shaft from the trans-

axle. See Drive Axle Removal for procedures.

21. Attach the transaxle case to a suitable jack. Make sure the transaxle will not slip off the jack during removal.

22. Remove the transaxle to engine mounting bolts.

23. Remove the transaxle by sliding it towards the driver side, away from the engine. Carefully lower the jack, guiding the right drive axle out of the transaxle and move the transaxle from under the car.

24. Installation is the reverse of removal. When installing the transaxle, guide the right drive axle into its bore as the transaxle is being raised. The right hand drive axle cannot be

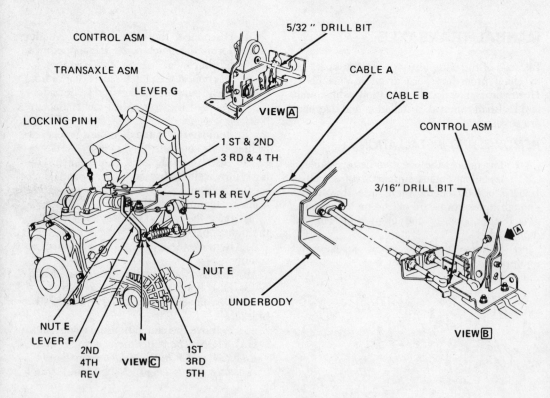

ADJUSTMENT PROCEDURE

1. Disconnect negative cable at battery.
2. Shift transaxle into third gear. Remove lock pin (H) and reinstall with tapered end down. This will lock transaxle in third gear.
3. Loosen shift cable attaching nuts (E) at transaxle levers (G) and (F).
4. Remove console trim plate and slide shifter boot up shifter handle. Remove console.
5. Install a 5/32" or No. 22 drill bit into alignment hole at side of shifter assembly, as shown in View A.
6. Align the hole in the select lever (View B) with the slot in the shifter plate and install a 3/16" drill bit.
7. Tighten nuts E at levers G and F. Remove drill bits from alignments holes at the shifter. Remove lockpin (H) and reinstall with tapered end up.
8. Install console, shifter boot and trim plate.
9. Connect negative cable at battery.
10. Road test vehicle to check for a good neutral gate feel during shifting. It may be necessary to fine tune the adjustment after road testing.

Manual shift linkage adjustment

readily installed after the transaxle is attached to the engine.

DRIVE AXLE

REMOVAL AND INSTALLATION

NOTE: *Some vehicles use a silicone (gray) boot on the right hand inboard joint. Use boot protector J-33162 or equivalent on these boots during removal. All other boots are made of thermoplastic material (black) and do not require the use of a boot protector.*

1. Raise the vehicle and install jackstands under the engine cradle.

2. Lower the vehicle slightly so that the weight rests on the cradle and not on the lower control arms.

3. Remove the tires and wheels.

4. Install a drift punch through the brake rotor cooling holes to lock the rotor in place.

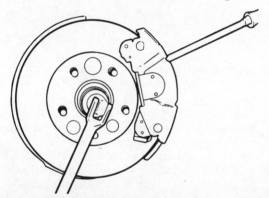

Removing and installing hub nut

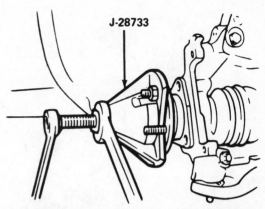

Loosening splines between hub and drive axle

Clean the drive axle threads of dirt, then lubricate and remove the hub nut and washer using a suitable socket and breaker bar.

5. Remove the caliper mounting bolts and support the caliper with wire or string. Do not let the caliper hang by the brake hose.

6. Remove the brake rotor.

7. Remove the lower ball joint nut.

8. Remove the stabilizer bolt from the lower control arm.

9. Install tool J-28733, or equivalent, and press the drive axle in and away from the hub. The drive axle should only be pressed in until the press fit between the drive axle and hub is loose.

CAUTION: *Be careful not to press the drive axle in too far as damage to the joint may occur.*

10. Separate and remove the lower ball joint from the steering knuckle.

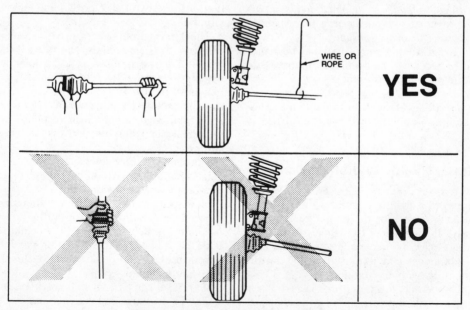

Precautions for handling the Tri-pot joints

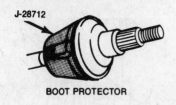

BOOT PROTECTOR

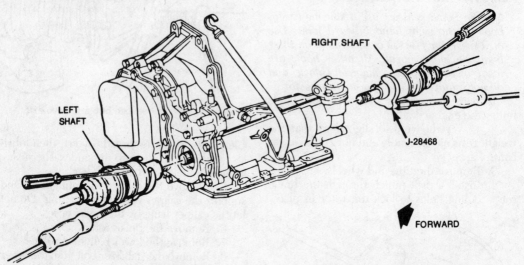

Halfshaft removal; the special tools are attached to slide hammers in this diagram

11. Separate the drive axle from the hub by pulling the hub assembly out away from the drive axle.

NOTE: *On vehicles equipped with Tri-Pot joints, care must be taken not to allow the joints to become overextended. When either end or both ends of the shaft are disconnected, overextending the joint could result in separation of internal components. This could cause failure of the joint, so it's important to handle the drive axle in a manner that prevents overextension.*

12. Install slide hammer tool and boot protector, if necessary, and remove the drive axle from the differential assembly.

13. Installation is the reverse of removal. Start the splines of the drive axle into the transaxle and push until the axle snaps into place.

Constant Velocity Joints

Front wheel drive vehicles present several unique problems to engineers because the driveshaft must do three things, simultaneously. It must allow the wheels to turn for steering, telescope to compensate for road surface vibrations, and it must transmit torque continuously without vibration.

To compensate for these three factors a two-joint driveshaft allows the front wheels to perform these functions. This driveshaft mates disc type straight groove ball joint design with the bell type Rzeppa CV universal joint. The Rzeppa joint on the outboard end of each driveshaft provides steering ability by allowing drive wheels to steer up to 43° while transmitting all available torque to the wheels. The inboard joint allows telescoping (up to 1 ½ in.) through the rolling actions of balls in straight grooves and operates at angles up to 20°. The combined action of these two ball type U-joints eliminates vibration.

The typical front wheel drive vehicle uses two driveshaft assemblies, one to each driving wheel. Each assembly has a CV-joint at the wheel end is called the inboard joint. This joint may be either the ball or Tri-Pot type. It allows the slip motion required when the driveshaft must shorten or lengthen in response to suspension action when traveling over an irregular surface.

Constant velocity joints are precision machined parts that have difficult jobs to perform in a hostile environment. They are exposed to heat, shock, torque, and many thousands of miles of service. For this reason, the lubricants used are specially formulated to be compatible with the rubber boot and give proper lubrication. Most CV-joint repair kits have this special lubricant included.

NOTE: *Wear pattern in a used ball or Tri-Pot CV-joint are impossible to match during reassembly. If there are any signs of wear,*

1. Race, C.V. joint outer
2. Cage, C.V. joint
3. Race, C.V. joint inner
4. Ring, shaft retaining
5. Ball (6)
6. Clamp, seal retaining
7. Seal, C.V. joint
8. Clamp, seal retaining
9. Shaft, axle (L.H.)
10. Seal, tri-pot joint
11. Spider, tri-pot joint
12. Roller, needle
13. Ball, tri-pot joint (3)
14. This no. not used
15. Housing assy., tri-pot (L.H.)
16. Housing assy., tri-pot (R.H.)
17. Shaft, damper & axle (R.H.)
18. Ring, spacer
19. Ring, race retaining
20. Clamp, seal retaining
21. Retainer, needle
22. Ring, needle retainer
23. Ring, joint retaining
24. Ring, deflector

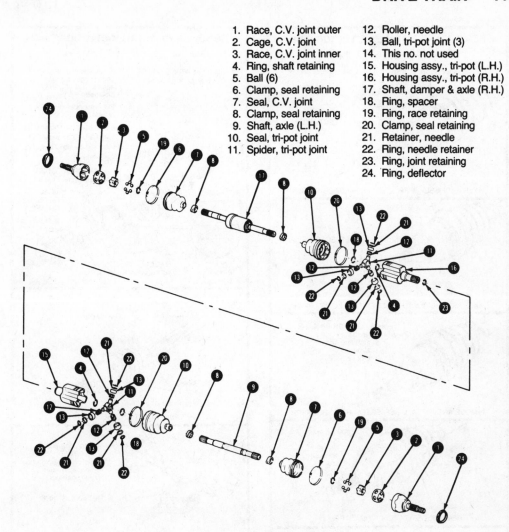

Tri-pot joint exploded view

abnormal operating noise, corrosion, or heat discoloration, the joint must be replaced.

TROUBLESHOOTING

Noises from the engine, drive axles, suspension and steering in the front drive cars can be misleading to the untrained ear. Ideally a smooth road serves best for detecting operating condition(s) that cause noise.

• A humming noise could indicate that early stage of insufficient or incorrect lubricant.

• Worn driveshaft joints will cause a continuous knock at low speeds.

• A popping or clicking sound on sharp turns indicates trouble in the outer or wheel end joint.

• The click noise at acceleration from coasting or deceleration from a load pull indicated two possibilities: damaged inner or transaxle joint or differential problem(s).

• An inner joint will create a vibration during acceleration due to plunging action hanging up and releasing repeatedly. Probable cause would be foreign particles or lack of lubrication, or improper assembly.

• Remember that tires, suspension, engine, and exhaust system are all up front to add their noises.

• Make a check with front wheels elevated off ground. Spin the wheels by hand to determine if wheel bearing could be noisy or if out of round tires are causing vibration. Many wheel bearings are prelubed and sealed at the factory.

CAUTION: Personal injury can occur from spinning wheels by engine power. Spinning a wheel at excess speed may cause damage to CV-joints that could be operating at angles too steep when wheels are allowed to hang. Over speeding might also cause damage to tires and the differential.

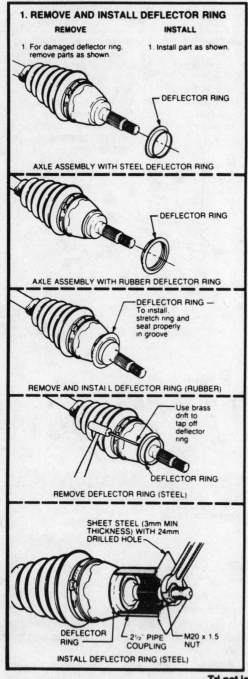

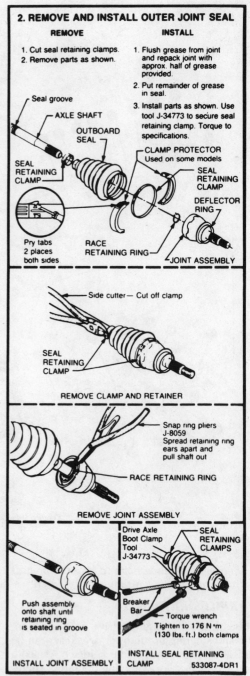

Tri-pot joint overhaul

TRI-POT JOINT OVERHAUL

For overhaul of these joints, follow the picture sequence:

Hub and Bearing
REMOVAL AND INSTALLATION

NOTE: *Several special tools are required for this procedure.*

1. Raise and support the front end on jackstands, allowing the wheels to hang.
2. Remove the front wheels.
3. Install drive axle boot seal protector tool J-28712 on the outer CV joints and J-34754 on the inner Tri-Pot joints.
4. Insert a long punch through the caliper and into the rotor to keep it from turning.
5. Clean the axle threads and lubricate them with a thread lubricant.

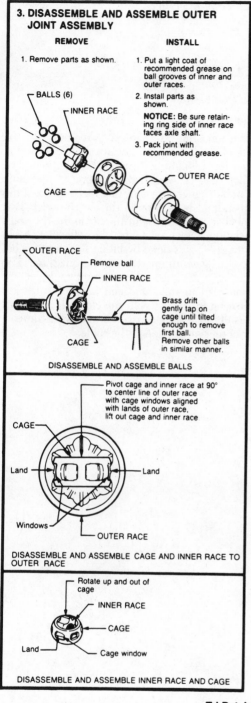

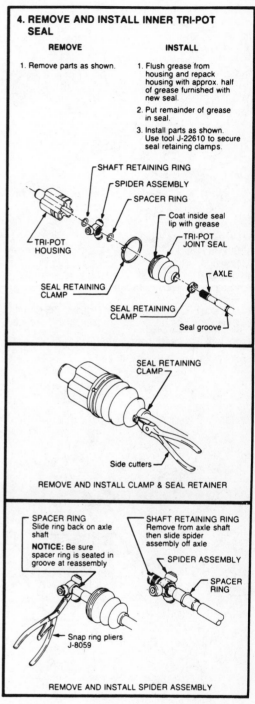

Tri-Pot Joint Overhaul

6. Remove the hub nut and washer.

7. Remove and support the caliper out of the way.

8. Remove the rotor.

9. Using puller J-28733, loosen the splined fit between the hub and shaft.

10. Remove the three hub attaching bolts, shield, hub and bearing assembly, and O-ring.

NOTE: *The hub and bearing are serviced as an assembly only.*

11. Remove the bearing seal from the knuckle.

12. Installation is the reverse of removal. Use a new O-ring and bearing seal. Lubricate the new bearing seal and the bearing with wheel bearing grease. Tighten the hub bolts to 40 ft.lb.

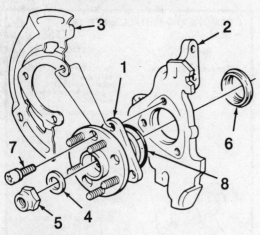

1. Hub and bearing assembly
2. Steering knuckle
3. Shield
4. Washer
5. Hub nut-180 ft. lbs. (245 Nm)
6. Seal
7. Hub and bearing retaining bolt-70 ft. lbs. (95 Nm)
8. O-ring

Front hub and bearing assembly

(55 Nm); the caliper bolts to 28 ft.lb. (38 Nm); the hub nut to 185 ft.lb. (260 Nm).

CLUTCH

ADJUSTMENT

Cable Clutch

The adjusting mechanism is mounted to the clutch pedal and bracket assembly. The cable is a fixed length and cannot be lengthened or shortened; however, the position of the cable can be changed by adjusting the position of the quandrant in relation to the clutch pedal. This mechanism makes adjustments in the quadrant position which changes the effective cable length. This is done by lifting the clutch pedal to disengage the pawl from the quadrant. The spring in the hub of the quadrant applies a tension load to the cable and keeps the release bearing in contact with the clutch levers. This results in a balanced condition, with the correct tension applied to the cable.

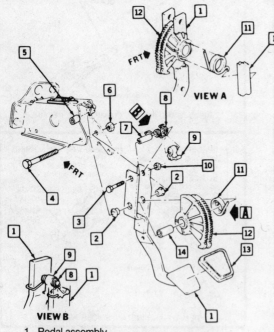

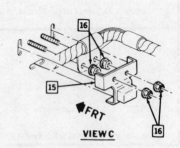

1. Pedal assembly
   Pedal must swing freely after assembling. Pedal must have a minimum travel of 46° without contacting carpet or sound barrier.
2. Bushing
3. Bolt/screw
4. Bolt/screw
5. Bumper
   Assemble bumper past both tangs on clutch pedal bracket assembly
6. 35 N·m (26 lbs. ft.)
7. Spacer
8. Spring
9. Pawl
   With pedal against bumper, pawl teeth must clear O.D. of detent teeth and snap into engagement when pedal is moved.
10. 5 N·m (44 lbs. in.)
11. Spring
12. Detent
13. Cover
14. Spacer
15. Bracket
16. Nut

Exploded view of clutch pedal assembly

Clutch Diagnosis

Condition	Probable Cause	Correction
Fails to Release (Pedal pressed to floor-shift lever does not move freely in and out of reverse gear without gear clash	Improper pedal travel. Faulty driven disc. Fork and bearing not assembled properly. Clutch disc hub binding on input shaft splines. Clutch disc warped or bent. Clutch-to-flywheel bolts loose.	Check for floor mat under pedal or misassembled bump stop. Replace disc. Install properly and* lubricate fingers at release bearing with wheel bearing grease. Repair or replace. Replace disc. Torque bolts to spec. Bleed air from system. *Very lightly lubricate fingers.
Slipping	Improper operation. Oil soaked driven disc. Worn facing or facing torn from disc. Warped pressure plate or flywheel. Weak diaphragm spring. Driven plate not seated in. Driven plate overheated.	Correct as required. Install new disc and correct leak at its source. Replace disc. Replace pressure plate or flywheel. Replace pressure plate. Make 30 to 40 normal starts. CAUTION: Do Not Overheat Allow to cool.
Grabbing (Chattering)	Oil on facing. Burned or glazed facings. Worn splines on input shaft. Warped pressure plate or flywheel. Burned or smeared resin on flywheel or pressure plate.	Install new disc and correct leak to engine or transaxle. Replace input shaft. Replace pressure plate or flywheel. Sand off if superficial, replace burned or heat checked parts.
Rattling-Transmission Click	Release fork loose. Oil in driven plate damper. Driven plate damper spring failure. Low engine idle speed. Broken return spring in slave cylinder.	Install properly. Replace driven disc. Replace driven disc. Adjust idle speed. Replace spring.
Release Bearing Noise with Clutch Fully Engaged	Improper operation. Release bearing binding. Fork shaft improperly installed. Faulty bearing.	Correct as required. Clean, relubricate, check for burrs, nicks, etc. Install properly. Replace bearing.
Noisy	Worn release bearing. Fork shaft improperly installed.	Replace bearing. Install properly and lubricate fork fingers at bearing.
Pedal Stays on Floor	Bind in linkage or release bearing. Fork shaft binds in housing.	Lubricate and free up linkage and release bearing. Free up shaft and lubricate.
Hard Pedal Effort	Driven plate, worn. Fork shaft binds in housing.	Replace driven plate. Free up shaft and lubricate.

As the clutch friction material wears, the cable must be lengthened. This is accomplished by simply pulling the clutch pedal up to its rubber bumper. This action forces the pawl against its stop and rotates it out of mesh with the quadrant teeth, allowing the cable to play out until the quadrant spring load is balanced against the load applied by the release bearing. This adjustment procedure is required every 5000 miles or so.

Hydraulic Clutch

This clutch release system consists of a clutch master cylinder with an integral or remote reservoir and a slave cylinder connected to the master cylinder by a hydraulic line, much like the brake system. The clutch master cylinder is mounted to the front of the dash and the slave cylinder is mounted to the transaxle support bracket. The clutch master cylinder is operated directly off the clutch pedal by a pushrod.

When the clutch pedal is depressed, hydraulic fluid under pressure from the master cylinder flows into the slave cylinder. As the hydraulic force reaches the slave cylinder, the push rod movement rotates the clutch fork which forces the release bearing into the clutch diaphragm and disengages the clutch. The hydraulic clutch system provides automatic clutch adjustment, so no adjustment of the clutch linkage or pedal position is required.

NOTE: *When adding fluid to the clutch master cylinder, use Delco Supreme No. 11 brake fluid or an equivalent that meets DOT 3 specifications. Do not use mineral or parafin base oil in the clutch hydraulic system as these fluids will damage the rubber parts in the cylinders.*

Clutch Cable

REMOVAL AND INSTALLATION

1. Support the clutch pedal upward against the bumper stop to release the pawl from the quadrant.

2. Disconnect the end of the cable from the clutch release lever at the transaxle. Be careful and prevent the cable from snapping toward the rear of the car. The quadrant in the adjusting mechanism can be damaged by allowing the cable to snap back.

3. Disconnect the clutch cable from the quadrant. Lift the locking pawl away from the quadrant, then slide the cable out on the right side of the quadrant.

4. From the engine side of the cowl, disconnect the two upper nuts holding the cable retainer to the upper studs. Disconnect the cable from the bracket mounted to the transaxle and remove the cable.

5. Inspect the clutch cable for signs of fraying, kinks, worn ends or excessive cable friction. Replace the cable if any of these problems are noted.

6. To install the cable, place the gasket in position on the two upper studs, then position the cable with the retaining flange against the bracket.

7. Attach the end of the cable to the quadrant, being sure to route the cable underneath the pawl. Attach the two upper nuts to the retainer mounting studs and tighten.

8. Attach the cable to the bracket mounted to the transaxle.

9. Support the clutch pedal upward against the bumper to release the pawl from the quadrant. Attach the outer end of the cable to the clutch release lever.

NOTE: *Be sure not to yank on the cable, since overloading the cable could damage the quadrant.*

10. Check clutch operation and adjust by lifting the clutch pedal up to allow the mechanism to adjust the cable length. Depress the pedal slowly several times to set the pawl into mesh with the quadrant teeth.

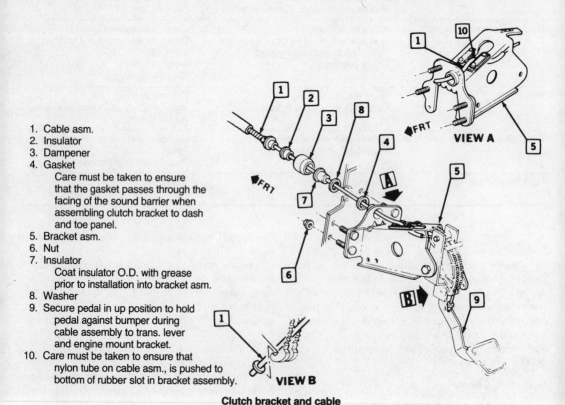

1. Cable asm.
2. Insulator
3. Dampener
4. Gasket
   Care must be taken to ensure that the gasket passes through the facing of the sound barrier when assembling clutch bracket to dash and toe panel.
5. Bracket asm.
6. Nut
7. Insulator
   Coat insulator O.D. with grease prior to installation into bracket asm.
8. Washer
9. Secure pedal in up position to hold pedal against bumper during cable assembly to trans. lever and engine mount bracket.
10. Care must be taken to ensure that nylon tube on cable asm., is pushed to bottom of rubber slot in bracket assembly.

Clutch bracket and cable

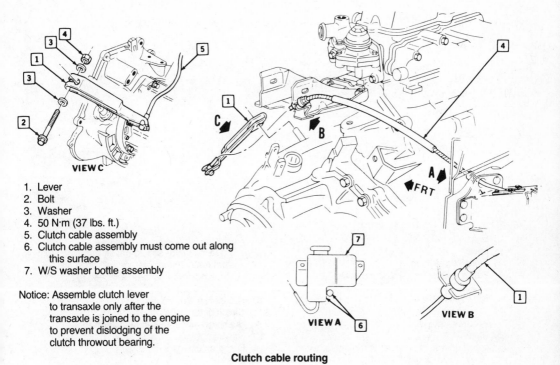

1. Lever
2. Bolt
3. Washer
4. 50 N·m (37 lbs. ft.)
5. Clutch cable assembly
6. Clutch cable assembly must come out along this surface
7. W/S washer bottle assembly

Notice: Assemble clutch lever to transaxle only after the transaxle is joined to the engine to prevent dislodging of the clutch throwout bearing.

Clutch cable routing

Hydraulic Clutch System

The hydraulic clutch system is serviced as a complete unit and has been bled of air and filled with fluid at the factory. Individual components of the system are not available separately.

BLEEDING

Bleeding is necessary whenever any part of the system has been disconnected or the level of fluid in the reservoir has been allowed to fall so low that air has been drawn into the master cylinder. Never use fluid which has been bled from a system to fill the reservoir as it may be aerated, have too much moisture content or be contaminated.

1. Clean dirt and grease from the cap to ensure no foreign substances enter the system.
2. Remove the cap and diaphragm and fill the reservoir to the top with approved DOT 3 brake fluid only.
3. Loosen the bleed screw, located in the slave cylinder body next to the inlet connection.
4. Fluid will begin to move from the master cylinder down the line to the slave cylinder. It is important that the reservoir be kept full for efficient gravity fill. It is not necessary to pump the clutch pedal.
5. Bubbles may appear at the bleeder screw as air is expelled from the system. When the slave cylinder is full, a steady stream of fluid will come from the outlet. At this point, tighten the bleeder screw. Be careful not to over-tighten the screw.
6. Assemble the diaphragm and cap to the reservoir after making sure the fluid level is full. If engagement problems are still noted, repeat the bleeding procedure.

Clutch Master and Slave Cylinders

REMOVAL AND INSTALLATION

4 Cylinder Engine

1. Disconnect the negative battery cable.
2. Remove the sound insulator from inside the car.
3. Disconnect the clutch master cylinder push rod from the clutch pedal.
4. Remove the clutch master cylinder retaining nuts at the front of the dash and disconnect the remote reservoir, if equipped.
5. Remove the slave cylinder retaining nuts at the transaxle.
6. Remove the hydraulic system as a unit from the vehicle. Note that the hydraulic system is replaced as a unit. Individual components are not available.
7. Install the slave cylinder to transaxle support bracket aligning the push rod into the pocket on the lever. Tighten the retaining nuts evenly to prevent damage to the slave cylinder.

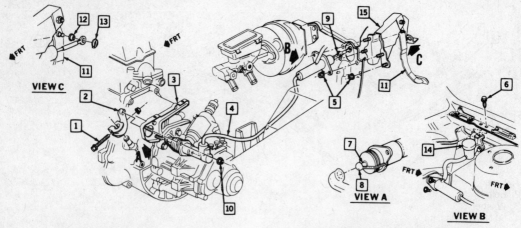

1. Bolt 50 N·m (36 lbs. ft.)
2. Lever
3. Transaxle support
4. Clutch master and actuator cylinder
   assembly
5. Nut 27 N·m (20 lbs. ft.)
6. Bolt 9 N·m (80 lbs. in.)
7. Actuator rod
8. Button
   Button end of strap must remain between
   lever and actuator rod after assembly.
   The straps will break on first clutch
   pedal application.

9. Restrictor
   Pedal restrictor should not be removed
   from replacement system until after
   slave cylinder has been attached to
   transaxle support.
10. Nut 22 N·m (16 lbs. ft.)
11. Clutch pedal
12. Bushing—lubricate before installing
13. Retainer
14. Remote fluid reservoir
15. Bracket

Hydraulic clutch system

NOTE: *Do not remove the plastic push rod retainer from the slave cylinder. The straps will break on the first clutch pedal application.*

8. Position the clutch master cylinder to the front of the dash. Install the retaining nuts and tighten evenly to prevent damage to the master cylinder. Install the remote reservoir, if equipped.

9. Remove the pedal restrictor from the push rod. Lube the push rod bushing on the clutch pedal. Connect the push rod to the clutch pedal and install the retaining clip.

10. If equipped with cruise control, check the switch adjustment at the clutch pedal bracket. When adjusting cruise control switch, do not exert more than a 20 lb. upward force on the clutch pedal or damage to the master cylinder push rod retaining ring can result.

11. Install the hush panel and depress the clutch pedal several times to break the retaining straps on the slave cylinder push rod. Do not remove the plastic button on the end of the push rod.

12. If a new hydraulic system was installed, bleeding should not be necessary. If the old system was reinstalled, or if any lines were opened, bleed the system as described above. Reconnect the negative battery cable.

V6 Engine

1. Remove the air intake duct from the air cleaner.

2. Disconnect the negative battery cable, then disconnect the positive cable.

3. Remove the left fender brace.

4. Loosen the battery hold down clamp bolt and remove the battery.

5. Disconnect the manifold air temperature sensor lead at the air cleaner.

6. Disconnect the mass air flow sensor lead.

7. Remove the PCV hose retaining clamp from the air intake duct.

8. Remove the clamp retaining the air intake duct to the throttle body.

9. Remove the mass air flow sensor mounting bolt.

10. Remove the air cleaner bracket mounting bolts at the battery tray.

11. Remove the air cleaner, mass air flow sensor and air intake duct as an assembly.

12. Disconnect the electrical lead at the washer bottle, then remove the attaching bolts and washer bottle from the car.

13. If equipped with cruise control, remove the mounting bracket retaining nuts from the strut tower.

14. Remove the sound insulator from inside the car.

15. Disconnect the clutch master cylinder push rod from the clutch pedal.

16. Remove the clutch master cylinder retaining nuts at the front of the dash and remote reservoir, if equipped.

17. Remove the slave cylinder retaining nuts at the transaxle.

18. Remove the hydraulic system as a unit from the vehicle.

19. To install, follow Steps 7–12 of the 4 cyl procedure, above.

Pressure Plate and Clutch Disc
REMOVAL AND INSTALLATION

NOTE: *Prior to any service that requires the removal of the slave cylinder on cars equipped with a hydraulic clutch, the master cylinder pushrod must be disconnected from the clutch pedal. Permanent damage to the slave cylinder will occur if the clutch pedal is depressed while the slave cylinder is disconnected.*

1. Disconnect the negative battery cable.

2. Remove the sound insulator from inside the car.

3. Disconnect the clutch master cylinder push rod from the clutch pedal, if equipped.

4. Remove the transaxle assembly as outlined under "Manual Transaxle Removal," above.

5. Mark the relationship of the pressure plate assembly to the flywheel for reassembly in the same position for proper balance.

6. Loosen the attaching bolts one turn at a time, until spring pressure is relieved. Loosen the bolts in sequence, moving from one side to the other with every turn so as not to distort the pressure plate.

7. Support the pressure plate, then remove the bolts. Remove the pressure plate and driven disc, noting the flywheel side of the disc if it is to be reinstalled. Do not attempt further disassembly of the pressure plate.

CAUTION: *The clutch driven disc contains asbestos, which has been determined to be a cancer causing agent. Never clean clutch surfaces with compressed air and avoid inhaling any dust from the clutch surface. When cleaning clutch surfaces, use a commercially available brake cleaning fluid.*

8. Inspect the clutch disc, pressure plate, flywheel, clutch fork and pivot shaft assembly and release bearing. Replace parts as required. Inspect the bearing retainer outer surface of the transaxle.

9. Clean the pressure plate and flywheel mating surface and the bearing retainer outer surface of all oil, grease, metal deposits, etc.

10. Position the clutch disc and pressure plate in relative installed position and support with a clutch centering tool J-29074, or equivalent. The driven disc is installed with the damper springs offset toward the transaxle. Stamped letters on the driven disc identify the flywheel side.

11. Install the pressure plate assembly-to-flywheel bolts evenly and gradually, in sequence, with the pressure plate mated to the alignment marks made earlier. Remove the alignment tool and torque the pressure plate mounting bolts to 15 ft.lb. (20 Nm).

12. Lightly lubricate the clutch fork ends which contact the bearing and pack the inside

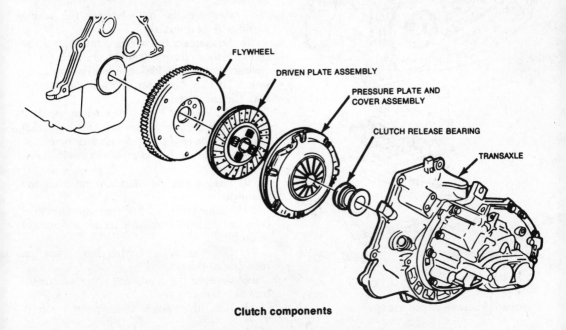

FLYWHEEL

DRIVEN PLATE ASSEMBLY

PRESSURE PLATE AND COVER ASSEMBLY

CLUTCH RELEASE BEARING

TRANSAXLE

Clutch components

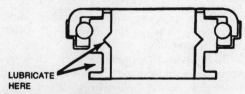

LUBRICATE HERE

Release bearing lubrication

diameter recess of the release bearing with grease No. 1051344 or equivalent. On five speed transaxles, make sure bearing pads are located on the fork ends (pads must be indexed) and both spring ends are in fork holes with the spring completely seated in the bearing groove.

13. Install the transaxle and remaining components in the reverse order of removal.

NOTE: *The clutch lever must not be moved toward the flywheel until the transaxle is bolted to the engine or damage to the transaxle could occur.*

AUTOMATIC TRANSAXLE

CHANGING FLUID AND FILTER

1. Raise the vehicle and support it safely.
2. Place a drain pan under the transaxle oil pan.
3. Remove the oil pan bolts from the front and sides.
4. Loosen rear pan bolts about four turns each.
5. Carefully pry the oil pan loose and allow the fluid to drain.

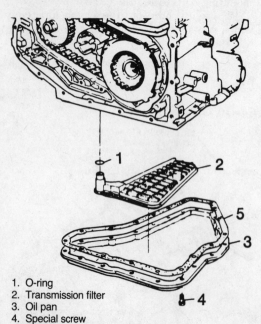

1. O-ring
2. Transmission filter
3. Oil pan
4. Special screw
5. Gasket

Automatic transaxle oil pan and filter

6. Remove the remaining oil pan bolts, pan and gasket.
7. Remove the transmission filter/screen and seal.
8. Check the oil pan and screen for metal particles, clutch facing material, rubber particles and engine coolant. If contamination is found, find the cause and correct it.
9. Clean all gasket mating surfaces on the oil pan and transaxle case. Remove all traces of the old gasket. Wash the oil pan in solvent and blow dry.
10. Install the screen, using a new filter and seal. Coat the seal with petroleum jelly.
11. Install the pan, using a new gasket, then lower the car and refill the transaxle with the proper quantity of Dexron®II or equivalent. Start the engine and run at slow idle (do not race the engine) with the gear selector in Park, then recheck the fluid level.

REMOVAL AND INSTALLATION

NOTE: *This procedure requires the use of special tools to support the engine and remove the axle shafts during service.*

1. Disconnect the negative battery cable.
2. Remove the air cleaner assembly. On V6 engines, remove the mass air flow sensor and air intake duct.
3. Disconnect the throttle valve (TV) cable at the throttle lever and transaxle.
4. Remove the transaxle dipstick and dipstick tube.
5. Install engine support J-28467 or equivalent.
6. Insert a ¼ x 2 in. bolt in the hole at the front right motor mount to maintain driveline alignment.
7. Remove the nut securing the wiring harness to the transaxle.
8. Disconnect the wiring connectors at the speed sensor, torque converter clutch (TCC) connector and the Park/Neutral/Backup lamp switch. It may be easier to reach the last one with the car raised.

NOTE: *When a T-latch type wiring connector is disconnected, care must be taken that it is reconnected properly. An improper connection will result in intermittent loss of switch function.*

9. Disconnect the shift linkage from the transaxle.
10. Remove the top two transaxle-to-engine bolts and left upper transaxle mount and bracket assembly.
11. Disconnect the rubber hose from the transaxle to the vent pipe.
12. Remove the remaining upper engine-to-transaxle bolts.
13. Raise the vehicle and support it safely.

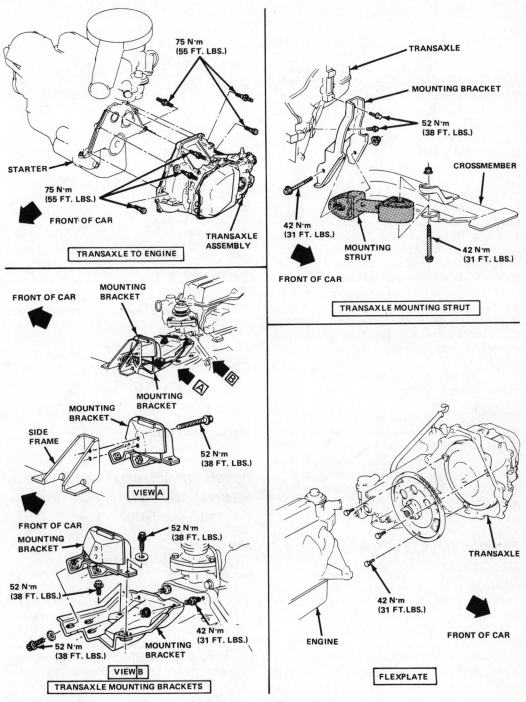

Typical transaxle mounts

If a chain hoist was used to support the engine, make sure tension is maintained while the car is being raised. Raise the vehicle high enough to permit the transaxle to be removed from underneath.

14. Remove both front tires.

15. Drain the transmission fluid.

16. Disconnect the shift linkage and bracket from the transaxle.

17. Some vehicles may use a silicone (gray) boot on the inboard axle joint. Use boot seal protector J-33162 or equivalent on these boots. All other drive axle boots are made from a thermo-plastic material (black) and do not re-

quire the use of a boot seal protector before continuing.

18. Disconnect both ball joints from their control arms.

19. Remove both drive axles and support as described under "Drive Axle Removal."

20. Disconnect the transaxle mounting strut.

21. Remove the left stabilizer bar link pin bolt.

22. Remove the left stabilizer bar frame bushing clamp nuts.

23. Disconnect the left frame support assembly.

24. Remove the transaxle converter cover.

25. Using a scribe, mark the relationship of the flex plate to the torque converter for reassembly in the same position. Remove the torque converter-to-flexplate bolts.

26. Disconnect the transaxle cooler lines and plug them to prevent fluid leakage.

27. Disconnect the transaxle to engine support bracket.

28. Position a suitable jack under the transaxle. The jack should be placed so the transaxle is held securely and won't slip off during removal.

29. Remove the remaining transaxle-to-engine mounting bolts and remove the transaxle from beneath the car.

30. Installation is the reverse of removal. Place a small amount of light grease on the torque converter pilot hub and make sure the torque converter is properly seated in the oil pump. Torque the torque converter-to-flexplate bolts to 46 ft.lb. (62 Nm). Check the TV cable adjustment.

Throttle Valve (TV) Cable
ADJUSTMENT

Adjustment of the throttle valve cable must be made by rotating the throttle lever at the throttle body. Do not use the accelerator pedal to rotate the throttle lever. The engine should be off for this procedure.

1. Depress and hold down the metal readjust tab at the engine end of the TV cable.

2. Move the slider until it stops against the fitting.

3. Release the readjustment tab.

4. Rotate the throttle lever to its full travel position. The slider must move (ratchet) toward the lever when the lever is rotated to its full travel position.

5. Check that the cable moves freely. The cable may appear to function properly with the engine stopped and cold. Recheck after the engine is warm.

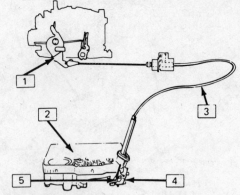

1. Throttle lever
2. Control valve asm.
3. T.V. cable
4. T.V. lever and bracket asm.
5. T.V. link

Throttle valve cable

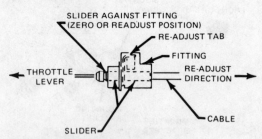

Throttle valve cable adjuster

Park/Neutral/Backup Lamp Switch
REMOVAL AND INSTALLATION

1. Disconnect the shift linkage.

2. Disconnect the electrical connector at the transaxle switch.

3. Remove the mounting bolts, then remove the switch.

4. If installing the old switch, place the shift shaft in Neutral. Align the flats of the shift shaft with the switch, then loosely install the mounting bolts. Insert a gauge pin in the service adjustment hole and rotate the switch until the pin drops in to a depth of $\frac{9}{64}$ in. (9mm), then tighten the mounting bolts and remove the gauge pin.

5. If installing a new switch, place the shift shaft in Neutral and align the flats of the shift shaft to the flats in the switch. Install the mounting bolts and tighten. If the bolt holes do not align with the mounting boss on the transaxle, check that the shift shaft is in Neutral. Do not rotate the switch, as it is pinned in the Neutral position. If the switch has been rotated and the pin broken, use the procedure in Step 4.

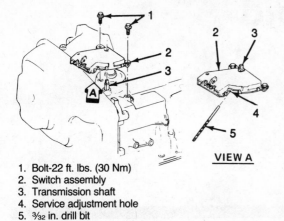

1. Bolt-22 ft. lbs. (30 Nm)
2. Switch assembly
3. Transmission shaft
4. Service adjustment hole
5. ³⁄₃₂ in. drill bit

Park/Neutral/Backup lamp switch

VIEW A

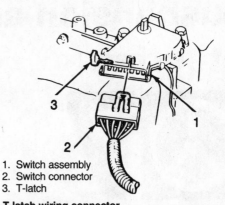

1. Switch assembly
2. Switch connector
3. T-latch

T-latch wiring connector

6. Check that the engine will only start in Park and Neutral. If not, perform the switch adjustment procedure.

ADJUSTMENT

1. Place the shift lever in Neutral.
2. Loosen the switch mounting bolts.
3. Rotate the switch on the shaft assembly to align the service adjustment hole with the carrier tang hole.
4. Insert a ³⁄₃₂ in. (2.34mm) diameter gauge pin (or drill bit) to a depth of ⅝ in. (15mm).
5. Tighten the mounting bolts and remove the gauge pin.
6. Check that the engine will only start in Park and Neutral. If not, repeat the adjustment procedure.

Suspension and Steering

7

FRONT SUSPENSION

The front suspension on all N-Body models is a MacPherson strut design. This combination strut and shock absorber adapts to front wheel drive. The lower control arm pivots from the engine cradle, which has isolation mounts to the body and conventional rubber bushings for the lower control arm pivots. The upper end of the strut is isolated by a rubber mount which contains a nonservicable bearing for wheel turning.

The lower end of the wheel steering knuckle pivots on a ball stud for wheel turning. The ball stud is retained in the lower control arm and the steering knuckle clamps to the stud portion.

All front suspension fasteners are an important attaching part in that it could affect the performance of vital parts and systems and/or could result in major repair expense. They must be replaced with one of the same part number or with an equivalent part if replacement becomes necessary. Do not use a replacement part of lesser quality or substitute design. Never attempt to heat, quench or straighten any front suspension part. If bent or damaged, the part should be replaced.

MacPherson Strut

REMOVAL AND INSTALLATION

NOTE: *Before removing front suspension components, their positions should be marked so they may assembled correctly. Scribe the knuckle along the lower outboard strut radius (A), the strut flange on the inboard side along the curve of the knuckle (B) and make a chisel mark across the strut/knuckle interface (C). When reassembling, carefully match the marks to the components.*

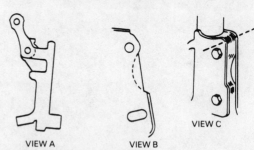

VIEW A   VIEW B   VIEW C

Scribing the strut and knuckle

1. Remove the three nuts attaching the top of the strut assembly to the body.
2. Raise the car and support it safely.
3. Place jackstands under the frame.
4. Lower the car slightly so that the weight rests on the jackstands and not on the control arms.
5. Remove the front tire.

CAUTION: *Whenever working near the drive axles, take care to prevent the inner Tri-Pot joints from being overextended. Overextension of the joint could result in separation of internal components which could go undetected and result in failure of the joint.*

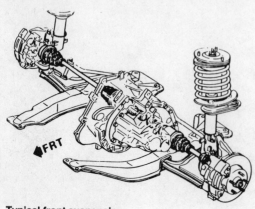

Typical front suspension

6. Some vehicles may use a silicone (gray) boot on the inboard axle joint. Use boot protector J-33162 or equivalent on these boots. All other boots are made from a thermoplastic material (black) and do not require the use of a boot seal protector.

7. Disconnect the brake line bracket from the strut assembly.

8. Remove the strut to steering knuckle bolts.

9. Remove the strut assembly from the vehicle. Care should be taken to avoid chipping or cracking the spring coating when handling the front suspension coil spring assembly.

10. Installation is the reverse of removal.

DISASSEMBLY

NOTICE: Care should be taken to avoid chipping or cracking the spring coating when handling the front suspension coil spring.

1. Mount Strut Compressor J-34013 in Holding Fixture J-3289-20.

2. Mount strut into Strut Compressor. Notice that Strut Compressor has strut mounting holes drilled for specific car lines.

3. Compress strut approx. ½ its height after initial contact with top cap. NEVER BOTTOM SPRING OR DAMPENER ROD.

4. Remove the nut from the strut dampener shaft and place the J-34013-27 Guiding Rod on top of the dampener shaft. Use this rod to guide the dampener shaft straight down through the bearing cap while decompressing the spring. Remove components.

5. Perform services as required.

ASSEMBLY

1. Install bearing cap into Strut Compressor if previously removed.

2. Mount strut into Strut Compressor using bottom locking pin only. Extend dampener shaft and install clamp J-34013-20 on dampener shaft.

3. Install spring over dampener and swing assembly up so upper locking pin can be installed. Install upper insulator, shield, bumper, and upper spring seat. Be sure flat on upper spring seat is facing in proper direction. The spring seat flat should be facing the same direction as the centerline of strut assembly spindle.

4. Install Guiding Rod and turn forcing screw while Guiding Rod centers the assembly. When threads on dampener shaft are visable, remove Guiding Rod and install nut.

5. Tighten nut to a torque of 85 N·m (65 lbs. ft.). Use a crowsfoot line wrench while holding dampener shaft with socket.

6. Remove clamp.

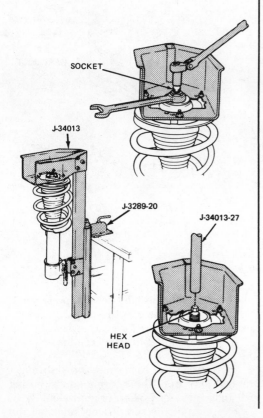

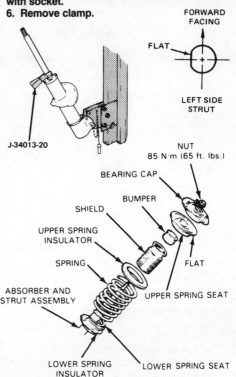

MacPherson strut disassembly procedures

The internal piston rod, cylinder assembly, & fluid can be replaced utilizing a service cartridge and nut. Internal threads are located immediately below a cut line groove.

1. Clamp strut in vise. Do not overclamp! Excessive clamping may damage tube and/or bracket.

2. Locate cut line groove as shown. It is important to locate groove as accurately as possible because mislocation will result in thread damage.

   Cut around groove with a pipe cutter until reservoir tube is completely cut through.

3. Remove and discard end cap, cylinder, and piston-rod assembly.

   Remove strut from vise and discard fluid.

4. Reclamp strut in vise.

   Tool J-25589 can be used to flare and deburr cut edge of reservoir tube to accept service nut. Place tool on open end of reservoir tube.

   Strike tool with a mallet or hammer.

until tool's flat outer surface rests on reservoir tube.

Remove the tool and discard.

At this time, try nut to assure positive start and smooth threading into reservoir tube threads. Remove nut after this check.

Flaring cup must be placed in contact with tube so there is no gap between cup and tube when struck.

5. Place strut cartridge in reservoir tube.

   Turn cartridge until it settles into indentations at base of tube so cartridge cannot be easily turned.

   Place nut over cartridge.

6. Using tool (J 29778) for 53mm hex nut and a torque wrench, tighten to 190-230 N·m (140-170 ft. lbs.) in upright mounting position. Stroke the piston rod once or twice to check for proper operation.

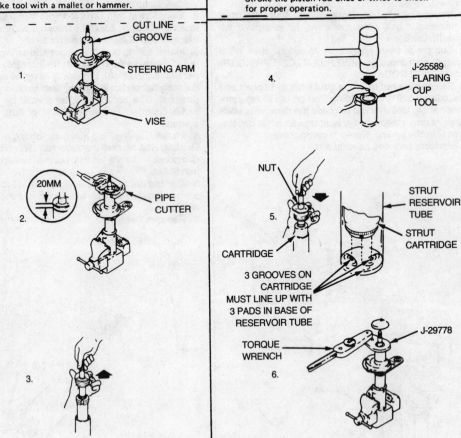

Replacing strut cartridge

Ball Joint

REMOVAL AND INSTALLATION

1. Raise the car and support it safely.
2. Place jackstands under the frame.
3. Lower the car slightly so the weight rests on the jackstands and not the control arm.
4. Remove the front tire.
5. If a silicone (gray) boot is used on the inboard axle joint, install boot seal protector J-33162 or equivalent. If a thermoplastic (black) boot is used, no protector is necessary.

6. Remove the cotter pin from the ball joint castle nut.

7. Remove the castle nut and disconnect the ball joint from the steering knuckle using ball joint separator J-34505 or equivalent.

8. Drill out the three rivets retaining the ball joint.

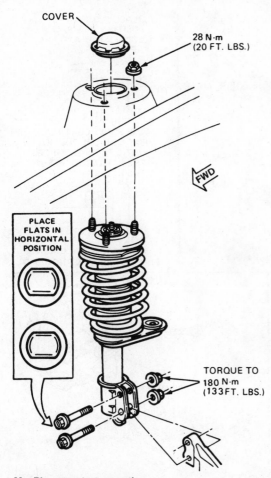

MacPherson strut mounting

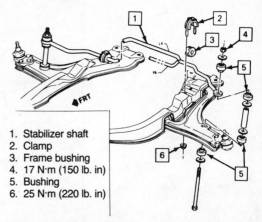

1. Stabilizer shaft
2. Clamp
3. Frame bushing
4. 17 N·m (150 lb. in)
5. Bushing
6. 25 N·m (220 lb. in)

Stabilizer shaft mounting

3. Disconnect the stabilizer shaft from the control arms.

4. Disconnect the stabilizer shaft from the support assemblies.

5. Loosen the front bolts and remove the rear and center bolts from the support assemblies to lower them enough to remove the stabilizer shaft.

6. Remove the stabilizer shaft and bushings.

7. Installation is the reverse of removal. Torque the support assembly bolts to 65 ft.lb. (90 Nm); the stabilizer shaft to support assembly nuts to 18 ft.lb. (25 Nm); and the stabilizer shaft to control arm nuts to 15 ft.lb. (20 Nm).

Lower Control Arm
REMOVAL AND INSTALLATION

1. Raise the car and support it safely on jackstands. Place the jackstands under the frame so that the suspension hangs freely.

2. Remove the tire.

3. Disconnect the stabilizer shaft from the control arm and/or support assembly.

4. Disconnect the ball joint from the steering knuckle using separator tool J-29330 or equivalent. See "Ball Joint Removal."

5. To remove the support assembly with the control arm attached, remove the bolts mounting the support assembly to the car. To remove the control arm only, remove the control arm to support assembly bolts.

6. Installation is the reverse of removal. Torque the ball joint castle nut to 45 ft.lb. (60 Nm). If the support assembly was removed, tighten the rear bolts first to 65 ft.lb. (88 Nm); the center bolts second to 66 ft.lb. (90 Nm); and the front bolts last to 65 ft.lb. (88 Nm). Tighten the control arm pivot bolts to 60 ft.lb. (85 Nm) with the weight of the car on the control arm.

CAUTION: *Be careful not to damage the drive axle boot when drilling out the ball joint rivets.*

9. Loosen the stabilizer shaft bushing assembly nut.

10. Remove the ball joint from the control arm.

11. Installation is the reverse of removal. Tighten the ball joint retaining nuts to 50 ft.lb. (68 Nm); the stabilizer bushing clamp bolts to 15 ft.lb. (20 Nm); and the ball joint castle nut to 45 ft.lb. (60 Nm). Install a new cotter pin.

NOTE: *The front end alignment should be checked and adjusted whenever the strut assemblies are removed.*

Stabilizer Shaft and Bushings
REMOVAL AND INSTALLATION

1. Raise the car and support it safely with jackstands, allowing the front suspension to hang freely.

2. Remove the front tire.

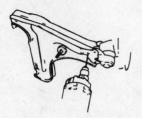

USING 1/8" DRILL, DRILL A PILOT HOLE COMPLETELY THROUGH THE RIVET.

DRILL PILOT HOLE

USING A 1/2" OR 13mm DRILL, DRILL COMPLETELY THROUGH THE RIVET. REMOVE BALL JOINT. DO NOT USE EXCESSIVE FORCE TO REMOVE BALL JOINT.

DRILL FINAL HOLE

PLACE J 29330 INTO POSITION AS SHOWN. LOOSEN NUT AND BACK OFF UNTIL . . .

J29330

KNUCKLE

. . . THE NUT CONTACTS THE TOOL. CONTINUE BACKING OFF THE NUT UNTIL THE NUT FORCES THE BALL STUD OUT OF THE KNUCKLE.

SEPARATING BALL JOINT FROM KNUCKLE USING J29330

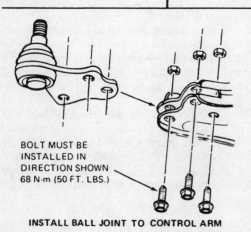

BOLT MUST BE INSTALLED IN DIRECTION SHOWN 68 N·m (50 FT. LBS.)

INSTALL BALL JOINT TO CONTROL ARM

60 N·m (44 FT. LBS.)

FWD

Removing ball joint assembly

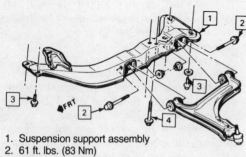

1. Suspension support assembly
2. 61 ft. lbs. (83 Nm)
3. 65 ft. lbs. (88 Nm)
4. 66 ft. lbs. (90 Nm)

Control arm and lower support assembly

Front Hub, Bearing and Seal
REMOVAL AND INSTALLATION

NOTE: *This procedure requires the use of a number of special tools.*

1. Raise the car and support it safely with jackstands. Place the jackstands under the frame so that the front suspension hangs freely.

2. Remove the front tire.

3. If a silicone (gray) boot is used on the

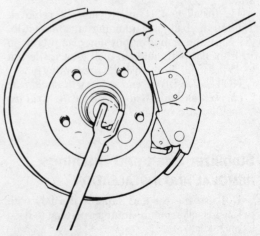

Removing hub nut

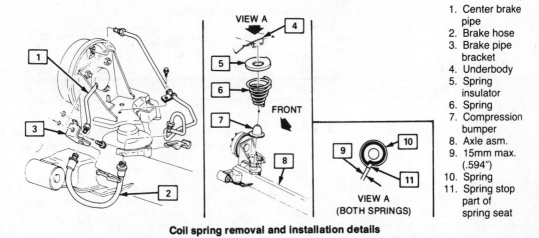

1. Center brake pipe
2. Brake hose
3. Brake pipe bracket
4. Underbody
5. Spring insulator
6. Spring
7. Compression bumper
8. Axle asm.
9. 15mm max. (.594")
10. Spring
11. Spring stop part of spring seat

VIEW A
FRONT
VIEW A
(BOTH SPRINGS)

Coil spring removal and installation details

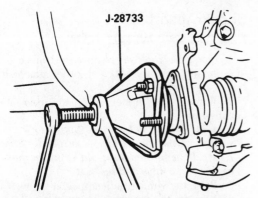

J-28733

Loosening the splines between the drive axle and hub

inboard axle joint, place boot seal protector J-33162 or equivalent. If a thermoplastic (black) boot is used, no seal protector is necessary.

4. Insert a drift punch through the rotor cooling vanes to lock the rotor in place and remove the hub nut. Clean the drive axle threads of all dirt and grease.

5. Remove the brake caliper mounting bolts and remove the caliper from the spindle assembly. Support the caliper with string or wire. Do not allow it to hang by the brake hose.

6. Remove the brake rotor.

7. Attach tool J-28733 or equivalent and separate the hub and drive axle.

8. Remove the three hub and bearing retaining bolts, shield, hub and bearing assembly and O-ring.

NOTE: *The hub and bearing are replaced as an assembly.*

9. Using a punch, tap the seal toward the engine. When the seal is removed from the steering knuckle, cut it off the drive axle using wire cutters. The factory seal is installed from the engine side of the steering knuckle, but the service replacement is installed from the wheel side of the steering knuckle.

10. Install the new hub and bearing seal in the steering knuckle using a suitable hub seal installer tool.

11. The remainder of the installation is in reverse order of removal. Lubricate the hub and bearing seal with grease and install a new O-ring around the hub and bearing assembly. Tighten the hub and bearing bolts to 40 ft.lb. (55 Nm). Tighten the hub nut to 185 ft.lb. (260 Nm).

Front End Alignment

Front alignment refers to the angular relationship between the front wheels, the front suspension attaching parts and the ground. Camber is the tilting of the front wheels from the vertical when viewed from the front of the car. When the wheels tilt outward at the top, the camber is said to be positive (+); when the wheels tilt inward at the top, the camber is said to be negative (−). The amount of tilt is measured in degrees from the vertical and this measurement is called camber angle.

Toe-in is the turning in of the front wheels.

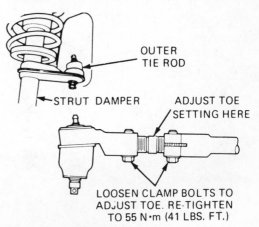

OUTER TIE ROD

STRUT DAMPER   ADJUST TOE SETTING HERE

LOOSEN CLAMP BOLTS TO ADJUST TOE. RE-TIGHTEN TO 55 N·m (41 LBS. FT.)

Toe setting adjustment

Wheel Alignment Specifications

Year	Model	Caster		Camber		Toe-In (in.)	Steering Axis (deg) Inclination
		Range (deg)	Pref. Setting (deg)	Range (deg)	Pref. Setting (deg)		
'85–'86	All	⅔P to 2⅔P	1⅔P	⅕P to 1½P	⅚P	⅛ OUT	—

The actual amount of toe-in is normally only a fraction of one degree. The purpose of the toe-in specification is to insure parallel rolling of the front wheels. Excessive toe-in or toe-out may increase tire wear. Toe-in also serves to offset the small deflections of the wheel support system which occur when the car is rolling forward. In other words, even when the wheels are set to toe-in slightly when the car is standing still, they tend to roll parallel on the road when the car is moving.

Toe setting is the only adjustment normally required. However, in special circumstances such as damage due to road hazard, collision, etc., camber adjustment may be required. To perform a camber adjustment, the bottom hole in the strut mounting must be slotted. Caster is not adjustable.

REAR SUSPENSION

All N-Body vehicles use a semi-independent rear suspension system which consists of an axle with trailing arms and twisting cross beam, two coil springs, two shock absorbers, two upper spring insulators and two spring compression bumpers. The axle assembly attaches to the underbody through a rubber bushing located at the front of each control arm; the brackets are integral with the underbody side rails. A ser-

viceable stabilizer bar is available as an option and is attached to the inside of the axle beam and to the lower surface of the control arms as a subassembly of the axle.

A single unit hub and bearing assembly is bolted to both ends of the rear axle assembly. This hub and bearing assembly is a sealed unit and the bearing is not replaceable separately.

Shock Absorber

REMOVAL AND INSTALLATION

1. Open the trunk and remove the trim cover (if equipped) over the shock absorber attaching bolts.
2. Remove the upper shock absorber attaching nut.
CAUTION: *Do not remove both shock absorbers at the same time, as suspending the rear axle at full length could result in damage to brake lines and hoses.*
3. Raise the vehicle and support it safely.
4. Remove the lower attaching bolt and remove the shock absorber.
5. Installation is the reverse of removal.

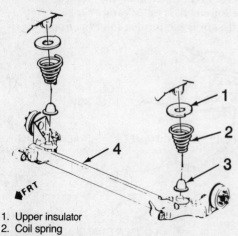

1. Upper insulator
2. Coil spring
3. Lower insulator
4. Axle assembly

Typical rear suspension

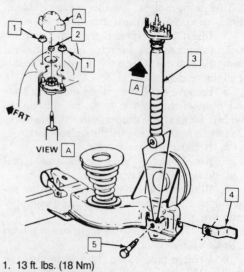

1. 13 ft. lbs. (18 Nm)
2. 28 ft. lbs. (38 Nm)
3. Shock absorber
4. 35 ft. lbs. (48 Nm)
5. Tab nut
A. Arrow should point to left side

Rear shock absorber mounting

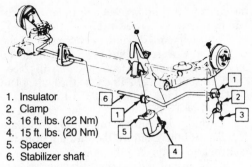

1. Insulator
2. Clamp
3. 16 ft. lbs. (22 Nm)
4. 15 ft. lbs. (20 Nm)
5. Spacer
6. Stabilizer shaft

Stabilizer shaft mounting

Stabilizer Bar
REMOVAL AND INSTALLATION

1. Raise the vehicle and support it safely with jackstands.

2. Remove the nuts and bolts at both the axle and control arm attachments and remove the bracket, insulator and stabilizer bar.

3. Install the U-bolts, upper clamp, spacer and insulator in the trailing axle. Position the stabilizer bar in the insulators and loosely install the lower clamp and nuts.

4. Attach the end of the stabilizer bar to the control arms and torque all nuts to 15 ft.lb. (20 Nm).

5. Tighten the axle attaching nut, then lower the vehicle.

Springs and Insulators
REMOVAL AND INSTALLATION

1. Raise the vehicle and support the rear axle with a hydraulic jack.

2. Install jackstands under the frame.

3. Remove the rear tires.

4. Remove the right and left brake line bracket attaching screws from the body and allow the brake line to hang free.

5. Remove both shock absorber lower mounting bolts with the rear axle supported by the hydraulic jack.

6. Carefully lower the rear axle and remove the springs and/or insulators.

CAUTION: *Do not suspend the rear axle by the brake hoses or damage to the hoses could result. Lower the axle just enough to remove the springs and support it during all service procedures.*

7. Installation is the reverse of removal. Position the springs and insulators in their seats and raise the axle. The ends of the upper coil on the spring must be positioned in the seat of the body and within the limits. Prior to installing the spring it will be necessary to install the upper insulators to the body with adhesive to keep it in position while raising the axle assembly and springs.

Rear Hub and Bearing Assembly
REMOVAL AND INSTALLATION

1. Raise the vehicle and support it safely.

2. Remove the tire.

3. Remove the brake drum. Do not hammer on the brake drum during removal or damage to the assembly could result.

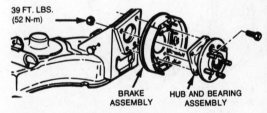

39 FT. LBS.
(52 N-m)

BRAKE
ASSEMBLY

HUB AND BEARING
ASSEMBLY

Rear hub and bearing assembly

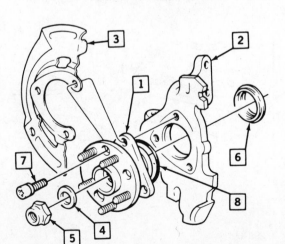

1. Hub and bearing assembly
2. Steering knuckle
3. Shield
4. Washer
5. Hub nut 245 N·m (180 ft. lbs.)
6. Seal
7. Hub and bearing retaining bolt (55 torx) 95 N·m (70 ft. lbs.)
8. "O" ring

Front wheel bearing

4. Remove the four hub and bearing assembly to rear axle attaching bolts, then remove the hub and bearing assembly from the axle. The top rear attaching bolt will not clear the brake shoe when removing the hub and bearing assembly. Partially remove the hub prior to removing this bolt.

5. Installation is the reverse of removal.

Control Arm Bushings

REMOVAL AND INSTALLATION

NOTE: *This procedure requires the use of a number of special tools.*

1. Raise the vehicle and support it safely.

2. Remove the tire and support the body with jackstands.

3. If replacing the right bushing, disconnect the brake line from the body. If the left bushing is being replaced, disconnect the brake line bracket from the body and the parking brake cable from its hook guide on the body.

NOTE: *Replace the bushings one at a time.*

4. Remove the nut, bolt and washer from the control arm and bracket attachment and rotate the control arm downward.

5. Install tool J-29376-1 or equivalent on the control arm over the bushing and tighten the attaching nuts until the tool is securely in place.

6. Install J-21474-19 bolt through plate J-29376-7 and install into J-29376-1 receiver.

7. Place J-29376-6 remover into position on the bushing and install nut J-21474-18 onto J-21474-19 bolt. Remove the bushing from the control arm by turning the bolt.

8. To install the bushing, first install tool J-29376-1 on the control arm.

9. Install J-21474-19 bolt through plate J-29376-7 and install into J-29376-1 receiver.

10. Install the bushing on the bolt and position it into the housing. Align bushing installation arrow with the arrow on the receiver for proper indexing of the bushing.

11. Install nut J-21474-18 onto bolt J-21474-19, then press the bushing into the control arm by turning the bolt. When the bushing is in its proper position, the end flange will be flush against the face of the control arm.

12. Use a screw-type jackstand to position the control arm into the bracket and install the bolt and nut. Do not torque the bolt at this time. It is necessary to torque the bolt with the vehicle at standing height.

13. The remainder of the installation is in the reverse order of removal.

STEERING

Steering Wheel

REMOVAL AND INSTALLATION

CAUTION: *Disconnect the negative battery cable before removing the steering wheel. When installing a steering wheel, make sure the turn signal lever is in the neutral position.*

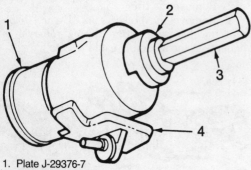

1. Plate J-29376-7
2. Remove J-29376-6
3. Nut J-21474-18
4. Receiver J-29376-1

Control arm bushing removal tools

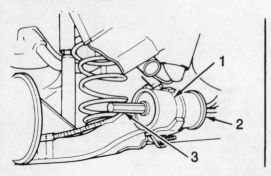

1. Receiver J-29376-1
2. Plate J-29376-7
3. Nut J-21474-18
4. Installer J-29376-4
5. Index marks

Installing control arm bushings

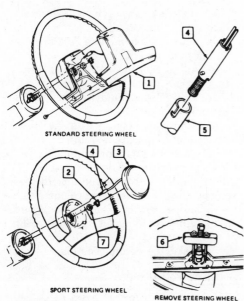

STANDARD STEERING WHEEL

SPORT STEERING WHEEL

REMOVE STEERING WHEEL

1. Pad
2. Retainer
3. Cap
4. Horn lead
5. Cam tower
6. J-1859-03 or BT-61-9
7. Nut—41 N·m (30 ft. lbs.)

Steering wheel mounting

1. Remove the trim retaining screws from behind the wheel. On wheel with a center cap, pull off the cap.

2. Lift off the trim and pull the horn wires from the turn signal cancelling cam.

3. Remove the retainer and the steering wheel nut.

4. Mark the wheel-to-shaft relationship and then remove the steering wheel using a suitable puller.

5. To install, place the wheel on the shaft and align the previously make marks. Tighten the mounting nut.

6. Insert the horn wires into the cancelling cam, then install the center trim and reconnect the battery cable.

Turn Signal Switch
REMOVAL AND INSTALLATION

1. Remove the steering wheel as described above.

2. Loosen the cover screws, pry the cover off with a screwdriver, then lift the cover off the shaft.

3. Position the U-shaped lockplate compressor on the end of the steering shaft and compress the lock plate by turning the shaft nut clockwise. Pry the wire snapring out of the shaft groove.

4. Remove the tool and lift the lockplate off the shaft.

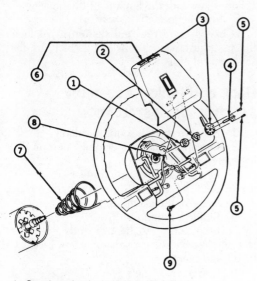

1. Steering wheel nut 41 N·m (30 ft. lbs.)
2. Steering wheel nut retainer
3. Telescoping adjuster lever
4. Steering shaft lock knob bolt
5. Steering shaft lock knob bolt positioning screw (2)
6. Steering wheel pad
7. Horn contact spring
8. Horn lead
9. Fully driven, seated and not stripped

Tilt wheel mounting

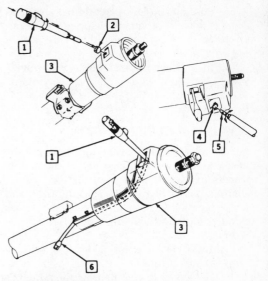

1. Turn signal lever
2. Insulator
3. Housing
4. Switch notch
5. Tang
6. Cruise control wiring

Multi-function switch removal

5. Slip the cancelling cam, upper bearing preload spring and thrust washer off the shaft.

6. Remove the turn signal lever. Push the flasher knob in and unscrew it. Remove the button retaining screw and remove the button, spring and knob.

7. Pull the switch connector out the mast jacket and tape the upper part to help switch removal. Attach a long piece of wire to the turn signal switch connector. When installing the turn signal switch, feed this wire through the column first, then use the wire to pull the switch connector into position. On tilt wheels, place the turn signal and shifter housing in low position and remove the harness cover.

8. Remove the three switch mounting screws and remove the switch by pulling it straight up while guiding the wiring harness cover through the column.

9. Install the replacement switch by working the connector and cover down through the housing and under the bracket. On tilt models, the connector is worked down through the housing, under the bracket, and then the cover is installed on the harness.

10. Install the switch mounting screws and the connector on the mast jacket bracket. Install the column-to-dash trim plate.

11. Install the flasher knob and the turn signal lever.

12. With the turn signal lever in neutral and the flasher knob out, slide the thrust washer, upper bearing preload spring and cancelling cam on the shaft.

13. Position the lock plate on the shaft and press it down until a new snapring can be inserted in the shaft groove. Always use a new snapring when assembling.

14. Install the cover and the steering wheel.

Ignition Switch
REMOVAL AND INSTALLATION

The switch is located on the upper side of the lower steering column area and is completely inaccessible without first lowering the steering column. The switch is actuated by a rod and rack assembly. A gear on the end of the lock cylinder engages the toothed upper end of the rod.

1. Lower the steering column; be sure to properly support it.

2. Disconnect the wiring from the switch.

3. Remove the two switch screws and remove the switch assembly.

4. Before installing, place the slider on the new switch in one of the following positions, depending on the steering column and accessories:

   a. Standard column with key release—extreme left detent

   b. Standard column with Park Lock—one detent from extreme left

   c. All other standard columns—two detents from extreme left

   d. Adjustable column with key release—extreme right detent

   e. Adjustable column with Park Lock—one detent from extreme right

   f. All other adjustable columns—two detents from extreme right

5. Install the activating rod into the switch and assembly the switch to the column. Tighten the mounting screws. Do not use oversize screws as they could impair the collapsibility of the column.

6. Reinstall the steering column.

Ignition Lock Cylinder
REMOVAL AND INSTALLATION

1. Place the lock in the RUN position.

2. Remove the lock plate, turn signal switch and buzzer switch.

3. Remove the screw and lock cylinder. CAUTION: *If the screw is dropped on removal, it could fall into the column, requiring complete disassembly to retrieve the screw.*

4. Rotate the cylinder clockwise to align the cylinder key with the keyway in the housing.

5. Push the lock all the way in.

6. Install the screw and tighten to 14 inch lbs. for adjustable columns and 25 inch lbs. for standard columns.

Rack and Pinion Assembly
REMOVAL AND INSTALLATION

1. Remove the left sound insulator.

2. Disconnect the upper pinch bolt on the coupling assembly.

3. Disconnect the clamp nuts.

4. Raise the car and support it safely.

5. Remove the clamp nut.

6. Remove both front tires.

7. Disconnect the tie rod ends from the steering knuckles using separator tool J-24319-01 or equivalent.

8. Lower the vehicle.

9. Disconnect the fluid line retainer.

10. Disconnect the fluid lines at the steering gear from the pump.

11. Move the steering gear forward and remove the lower pinch bolt on the coupling assembly.

12. Disconnect the coupling from the steering gear.

13. Remove the rack and pinion assembly

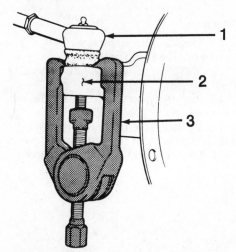

1. Tie rod end
2. Steering knuckle
3. Tie rod end puller J-24319-01

Separating tie rod end from the knuckle

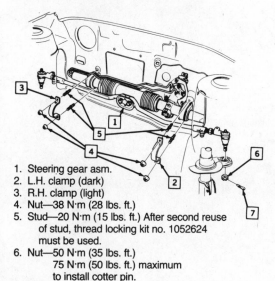

1. Steering gear asm.
2. L.H. clamp (dark)
3. R.H. clamp (light)
4. Nut—38 N·m (28 lbs. ft.)
5. Stud—20 N·m (15 lbs. ft.) After second reuse
   of stud, thread locking kit no. 1052624
   must be used.
6. Nut—50 N·m (35 lbs. ft.)
       75 N·m (50 lbs. ft.) maximum
       to install cotter pin.
7. Cotter pin

Rack and pinion mounting

with the dash seal through the left wheel opening.

14. Installation is the reverse of removal. Refill the power steering pump and bleed the system.

BLEEDING THE POWER STEERING SYSTEM

If the power steering hydraulic system has been serviced, an accurate fluid level reading cannot be obtained unless air is bled from the system.

1. With the wheels turned all the way to the left, add power steering fluid to the COLD mark on the fluid level indicator.

2. Start the engine and check the fluid level at fast idle. Add fluid, if necessary to bring the level up to the COLD mark.

3. Bleed air from the system by turning the wheels from side to side without hitting the stops. Keep the fluid level just above the internal pump casting or at the COLD mark. Fluid with air in it has a light tan or red appearance.

4. Return the wheels to the center position and continue running the engine for two or three minutes.

5. Road test the vehicle to check steering function and recheck the fluid level with the system at its normal operating temperature. Fluid should be at the HOT mark.

Power Steering Pump
REMOVAL AND INSTALLATION
4 Cylinder Engine

1. Remove the drive belt.
2. Disconnect the fluid lines from the pump.

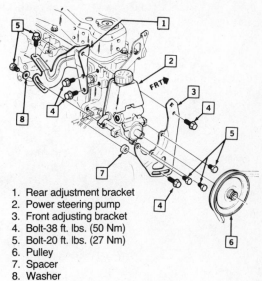

1. Rear adjustment bracket
2. Power steering pump
3. Front adjusting bracket
4. Bolt-38 ft. lbs. (50 Nm)
5. Bolt-20 ft. lbs. (27 Nm)
6. Pulley
7. Spacer
8. Washer

4 cyl power steering pump mounting

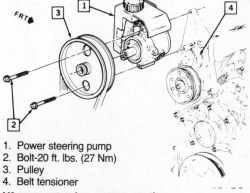

1. Power steering pump
2. Bolt-20 ft. lbs. (27 Nm)
3. Pulley
4. Belt tensioner

V6 power steering pump mounting

3. Remove the front adjustment bracket-to-rear adjustment bracket bolt.

4. Remove the front adjustment bracket-to-engine bolt and spacer.

5. Remove the pump with the front adjustment bracket attached.

6. Transfer the pulley and front adjustment bracket to the new pump, if necessary.

7. Installation is the reverse of removal. Adjust the belt tension and fill the system with power steering fluid. Bleed the system of air as described above.

V6 Engine

1. Remove the serpentine drive belt.

2. Remove the pump mounting bolts.

3. Pull the pump forward and disconnect the fluid lines.

4. Remove the pump and transfer the pulley as necessary.

5. Installation is the reverse of removal. Install the drive belt, fill the system with power steering fluid and bleed as described above.

UNDERSTANDING THE BRAKE SYSTEM

Hydraulic System

A hydraulic system is used to actuate the brakes. The system transports the power required to force the frictional surfaces of the braking system together from the pedal to the individual braking units at each wheel. A hydraulic system is used for three reasons. First, fluid under pressure can be carried to all parts of the automobile by small hoses (some of which are flexible) without taking up a significant amount of room or posing routing problems. Second, liquid is noncompressible; a hydraulic system can transport force without modifying or reducing that force. Third, a great mechanical advantage can be given to the brake pedal end of the system and the foot pressure required to actuate the brakes can be reduced by making the surface area of the master cylinder pistons smaller than that of any of the pistons in the wheel cylinders or calipers.

The master cylinder consists of a fluid reservoir and a double cylinder and piston assembly. Double type (or dual) master cylinders are designed to separate the front and rear braking systems hydraulically in case of a leak. Steel lines carry the brake fluid to a point on the vehicle's frame near each of the vehicle's wheels. The fluid is then carried to the slave cylinders by flexible tubes in order to allow for suspension and steering movements.

In drum brake systems, the slave cylinders are called wheel cylinders. Each wheel cylinder contains two pistons, one at either end, which push outward in opposite directions. In disc brake systems, the slave cylinders are part of the calipers. Anywhere from one to four cylinders are used to force the brake pads against the disc, but all cylinders contain one piston only. All slave cylinder pistons employ some type of seal (usually made of rubber) to minimize the leakage of fluid around the piston. A rubber dust boot seals the outer end of the cylinder against dust and dirt. The boot fits around the outer end of the piston on disc brake calipers and around the brake actuating rods on wheel cylinders.

When at rest the entire system, from the pistons in the master cylinder to those in the wheel cylinders or calipers, is full of brake fluid. Upon application of the brake pedal, fluid trapped in front of the master cylinder pistons is forced through the lines to the slave cylinders where it forces the pistons outward and applies the brakes. The motion of the pistons is opposed by return springs mounted outside the cylinder in drum brakes and by internal springs or spring seals in disc brakes.

Upon releasing the brake pedal, a spring located inside the master cylinder immediately returns the master cylinder pistons to the normal position. The pistons contain check valves and the master cylinder has compensating ports drilled in it. These are uncovered as the pistons reach their normal position. The piston check valves allow fluid to flow toward the wheel cylinders or calipers as the pistons withdraw. Then, as the return springs force the brake pads or shoes into the released position, the excess fluid returns to the master cylinder fluid reservoir through the compensating ports. It is during the time the pedal is in the released position that any fluid that has leaked out of the system will be replaced through the compensating ports.

Dual circuit master cylinders employ two pistons, located one behind the other, in the same cylinder. The primary piston is actuated directly by the mechanical linkage from the brake pedal. The secondary piston is actuated by fluid trapped between the two pistons. If a leak develops in front of the secondary piston, it moves forward until it bottoms against the front of the master cylinder and the fluid trapped between the pistons will operate the rear brakes. If the rear brakes develop a leak, the primary piston will move forward until direct contact with the secondary piston takes place and it will force the secondary piston to actuate the front brakes. In either case, the brake pedal moves farther when the brakes are applied and less braking power is available.

All dual-circuit systems use a distributor switch to warn the driver when only half of the brake system is operational. This switch is located in a valve body which is mounted on the master cylinder. A hydraulic piston receives pressure from both circuits, each circuit's pressure being applied to one end of the piston. When the pressures are in balance, the piston remains stationary. When one circuit has a leak, the greater pressure in that circuit during application of the brakes will push the piston to one side, closing the distributor switch and activating the brake warning light.

In disc brake systems, this valve body also contains a metering valve and, in some cases, a proportioning valve. The metering valve keeps pressure from traveling to the disc brakes on the front wheels until the brake shoes on the rear wheels have contacted the drums, ensuring that the front brakes will never be used alone. The proportioning valve throttles the pressure to the rear brakes so as to avoid rear wheel lockup during very hard braking.

These valves may be tested by removing the lines to the front and rear brake systems and installing special brake pressure testing gauges. Front and rear system pressures are then compared as the pedal is gradually depressed. Specifications vary with the manufacturer and design of the brake system. Brake system warning lights may be tested by depressing the brake pedal and holding it while opening one of the wheel cylinder bleeding screws. If this does not cause the light to go on, substitute a new lamp, make continuity checks or replace the switch, as necessary.

The hydraulic system may be checked for leaks by applying pressure to the pedal gradually and steadily. If the pedal sinks very slowly to the floor, the system has a leak. This is not to be confused with the springy or spongy feel due to the compression of air within the lines. If the system leaks, there will be a gradual change in the position of the pedal with a constant pressure. Check for leaks along all lines and at wheel cylinders. If no external leaks are apparent, the problem is inside the master cylinder.

Disc Brakes

Instead of the traditional expanding brakes that press outward against a circular drum, disc brake systems utilize a cast iron disc with brake pads positioned on either side of it. Braking effect is achieved in a manner similar to the way you would squeeze a spinning phonograph record between your fingers. The disc (rotor) is a one-piece casting with cooling fins between the two braking surfaces. This enables air to circulate between the braking surfaces, making them less sensitive to heat buildup and more resistant to fade. Dirt and water do not affect braking action since contaminants are thrown off by the centrifugal action of the rotor or scraped off by the pads. In addition, the equal clamping action of the two brake pads tends to ensure uniform, straightline stops. All disc brakes are inherently self-adjusting.

Drum Brakes

Drum brakes employ two brake shoes mounted on a stationary backing plate. These shoes are positioned inside a circular cast iron drum which rotates with the wheel assembly. The shoes are held in place by springs; this allows them to slide toward the drums when the brakes are applied, while keeping the linings and drums in alignment. The shoes are actuated by a wheel cylinder which is mounted at the top of the backing plate. When the brakes are applied, hydraulic pressure forces the wheel cylinders two actuating links outward. Since these links bear directly against the top of the brake shoes, the tops of the shoes are then forced outward against the inner side of the drum. This action forces the bottoms of the two shoes to contact the brake drum by rotating the entire assembly slightly (known as servo action). When pressure within the wheel cylinder is relaxed, return springs pull the shoes back away from the drum.

The drum brakes are designed to be self-adjusting during application with the vehicle moving in reverse. This motion causes both shoes to rotate very slightly with the drum, rocking an adjusting lever and thereby causing rotation of the adjusting screw by means of an actuating lever.

Power Brake Booster

Power brakes operate just as standard brake systems except in the actuation of the master cylinder pistons. A vacuum diaphragm is located on the front of the master cylinder and assists the driver in applying the brakes, reducing both the effort and travel that must be put into moving the brake pedal.

The vacuum diaphragm housing is connected to the intake manifold by a vacuum hose. A check valve is placed at the point where the hose enters the diaphragm housing, so that during periods of low manifold vacuum brake assist vacuum will not be lost.

Depressing the brake pedal closes off the vacuum source and allows atmospheric pressure to enter one side of the diaphragm. This causes the master cylinder pistons to move and apply the brakes. When the brake pedal is released, vacuum is applied to both sides of the diaphragm and return springs return the diaphragm and master cylinder pistons to the released position. If the vacuum fails, the brake pedal rod will butt against the end of the master cylinder actuating rod and direct mechanical application will occur as the pedal is depressed.

The hydraulic and mechanical problems that apply to conventional brake systems also apply to power brakes and should be checked for if the following tests do not reveal the problem. Test for a vacuum leak in the following manner:

1. Operate the engine at idle with the transaxle in Neutral without touching the brake pedal for one minute.

2. Turn off the engine and wait one minute.

3. Test for the presence of assist vacuum by depressing the brake pedal and releasing it several times. Light application will produce less and less pedal travel, if vacuum is present. If there is no vacuum, air is leaking into the system somewhere.

Test for system operation as follows:

1. Pump the brake pedal (with the engine off) until the supply vacuum is entirely gone.

2. Put a light, steady pressure on the pedal.

3. Start the engine and operate it at idle with the transaxle in Neutral. If the system is operating, the brake pedal should fall toward the floor if constant pressure is maintained on the pedal.

Power brake systems may be tested for hydraulic leaks just as ordinary systems are tested, except that the engine should be idling with the transaxle in Neutral throughout the test.

BRAKE SYSTEM

All models have a diagonally-split hydraulic system. This differs from conventional practice in that the left front and right rear brakes are on one hydraulic circuit and the right front and left rear are on the other.

A diagonally-split system necessitates the use of a special master cylinder design. The N-Body master cylinder incorporates the functions of a standard tandem master cylinder, plus a warning light switch and proportioning valves. Additionally, the master cylinder is designed with a quick take-up feature which provides a large volume of fluid to the brakes at low pressure when the brakes are initially applied. The low pressure fluid acts to quickly fill the large displacement requirements of the system.

The front disc brakes are single piston sliding caliper units. Fluid pressure acts equally against the piston and the bottom of the piston bore in the caliper. This forces the piston outward until the pad contacts the rotor. The force on the caliper bore forces the caliper to slide over, carrying the other pad into contact with the other side of the rotor. The disc brakes are self-adjusting.

Rear drum brakes are conventional duo-servo units. A dual piston wheel cylinder, mounted to the top of the backing plate, actuates both brake shoes. Wheel cylinder force to the shoes is supplemented by the tendency of the shoes to wrap into the drum (servo action). An actuating link, pivot and lever serve to automatically engage the adjuster as the brakes are applied when the car is moving in reverse. Provisions for manual adjustment are also provided. The rear brakes also serve as the parking brakes; linkage is mechanical. Vacuum boost is standard, and the booster is a conventional tandem vacuum unit.

BRAKE ADJUSTMENT

Disc Brakes

The front disc brakes are inherently self-adjusting. No adjustments ar necessary or possible.

Drum Brakes

The drum brakes are designed to self-adjust when applied with the car moving in reverse. However, they can also be adjusted manually. This manual adjustment should also be performed whenever the linings are replaced.

1. Use a punch to knock out the stamped area on the brake backing plate. If this is done with the drum installed on the car, the drum must be removed and all metal cleaned out of the brake compartment. After adjustments are complete, a hole cover (part no. 4874119 or equivalent) must be inserted to prevent the entry of dirt and water into the brakes.

2. Use an awl, screwdriver, or adjusting tool made for this purpose to turn the brake adjusting screw star wheel. Expand the shoes until the drum can just barely be turned by hand. The drag should be equal for both wheels.

3. Back off the adjusting screw at each wheel 12 notches. If the shoes still drag lightly on the drum, back the adjusting screw off an additional one or two notches. The brakes should be free of drag when the screw has been backed off approximately 12 notches. Heavy drag at this point indicates tight parking brake cables.

4. Once all adjustments are complete, install the hole cover in the backing plate and check the parking brake adjustment.

Master Cylinder

REMOVAL AND INSTALLATION

1. Disconnect the electrical connector at the warning switch.

2. Disconnect and plug the hydraulic lines to prevent the entry of dirt into the system.

3. Drain the brake fluid from the master cylinder and discard. Exercise caution when handling the brake fluid as it will damage painted surfaces.

4. Remove the attaching nuts, then lift the master cylinder clear of the brake power booster unit.

5. Installation is the reverse of removal. Bleed the brake system.

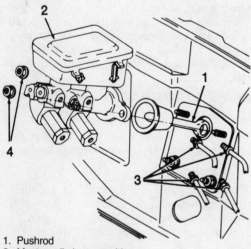

1. Pushrod
2. Master cylinder assembly
3. Tube nut
4. Nut

Master cylinder mounting

OVERHAUL

1. Remove the master cylinder from the car.

2. Empty any remaining brake fluid from the reservoir.

3. Secure the master cylinder in a soft-jawed vise by clamping it on the mounting flange.

4. Using a small prybar, carefully lever the reservoir from the master cylinder body.

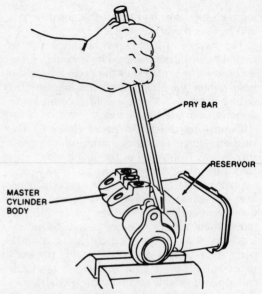

Removing the master cylinder reservoir

5. Remove the lockring while depressing the primary piston with a suitable blunt drift.

6. Use compressed air applied at the rear outlet to force out the pistons, retainer and spring.

7. Wash all parts in denatured alcohol and inspect for wear, scoring or other defects. Replace any parts found to be suspect. If any defect is found in the master cylinder bore, the entire cylinder must be replaced.

NOTE: *The master cylinder cannot be honed and no abrasives are to be used in the bore.*

8. Assemble the master cylinder components in reverse order of disassembly. Lubricate all parts and seals with clean brake fluid. Install the reservoir by pushing in with a rocking motion.

9. Bench bleeding the master cylinder reduces the possibility of getting air into the lines when the unit is installed. Connect two short pieces of brake line to the outlet fittings, then bend them until the free end is below the fluid level in the master cylinder reservoirs.

10. Fill the reservoirs with fresh brake fluid, then slowly pump the piston with a suitable blunt drift until no more air bubbles appear in the reservoirs.

11. Disconnect the two short lines, top up the brake fluid level and install the reservoir cap.

12. Install the master cylinder on the car. Attach the lines, but do not tighten them. Force out any air that might have been trapped at the connection by slowly depressing the brake pedal, then tighten the lines before releasing the pedal. Bleed the brake system as described below.

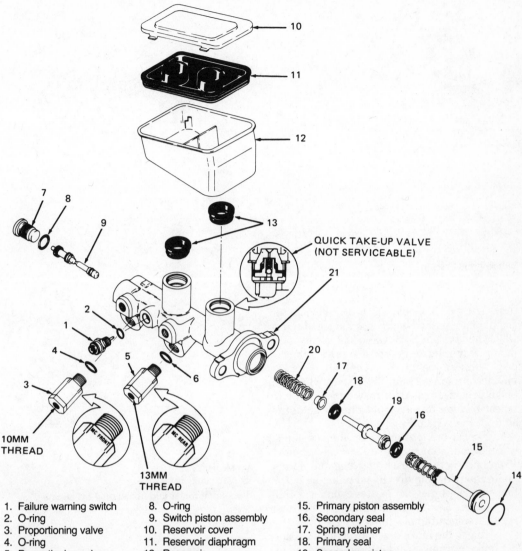

1. Failure warning switch
2. O-ring
3. Proportioning valve
4. O-ring
5. Proportioning valve
6. O-ring
7. Plug
8. O-ring
9. Switch piston assembly
10. Reservoir cover
11. Reservoir diaphragm
12. Reservoir
13. Reservoir grommet
14. Lock ring
15. Primary piston assembly
16. Secondary seal
17. Spring retainer
18. Primary seal
19. Secondary piston
20. Spring
21. Cylinder body

Exploded view of the master cylinder

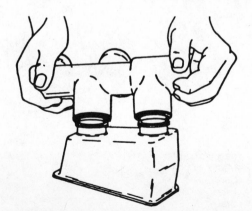

Install the master cylinder body to the reservoir with a rocking motion

BLEEDING THE BRAKE SYSTEM

On diagonally split brake systems, start the manual bleeding procedure with the right rear, then the left front; right rear, then right front.

1. Clean the bleeder screw at each wheel.

2. Attach a small rubber hose to the bleed screw and place the end in a clear container of fresh brake fluid.

3. Fill the master cylinder with fresh brake fluid. The master cylinder reservoir should be checked and topped up often during the bleeding procedure.

4. Have an assistant slowly pump up the brake pedal and hold pressure.

5. Open the bleeder screw about one-quarter

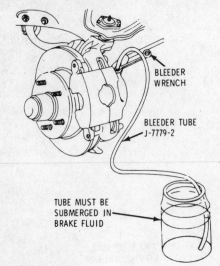

Bleeding the brakes

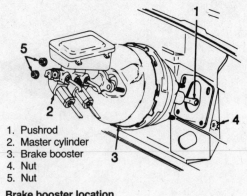

1. Pushrod
2. Master cylinder
3. Brake booster
4. Nut
5. Nut

Brake booster location

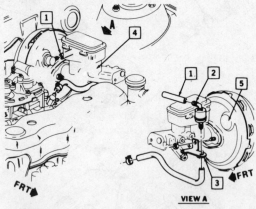

1. Hose
2. Filter
3. Support
4. Master cylinder
5. Vacuum booster

Vacuum booster and hoses on 4 cyl engine

turn. The pedal should fall to the floor as air and fluid are pushed out. Close the bleed screw while the assistant holds the pedal to the floor, then slowly release the pedal and wait 15 seconds. Repeat the process until no more air bubbles are forced from the system when the brake pedal is applied. It may be necessary to repeat this ten or more times to get all of the air from the system.

6. Repeat this procedure on the remaining wheel cylinders and calipers. Remember to wait 15 seconds between each bleeding and do not pump the pedal rapidly. Rapid pumping of the brake pedal pushes the master cylinder secondary piston down the bore in a manner that makes it difficult to bleed the system.

7. Check the brake pedal for sponginess and the brake warning light for indication of unbalanced pressure. Repeat the entire bleeding procedure to correct either of these two conditions.

Brake Booster

REMOVAL AND INSTALLATION

1. Working inside the car, detach the brake pushrod from the brake pedal.

2. Disconnect the hydraulic lines from the front of the master cylinder and the vacuum line from the engine.

3. Remove the nuts from the mounting studs which hold the unit to the dash panel and remove the booster and master cylinder as an assembly. Continue disassembly to separate the booster and master cylinder on the bench.

4. Installation is the reverse of removal. Clean the mounting surfaces before installing the booster and bleed the brake system.

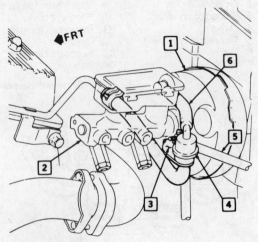

1. Vacuum booster
2. Master cylinder
3. Support
4. Filter
5. Brace
6. Hose

Vacuum booster and hoses on V6 engine

TROUBLESHOOTING

The following items are in addition to those listed in Chapter 10 "Troubleshooting." Check those items first.

Hard Pedal

1. Faulty vacuum check valve.
2. Vacuum hose kinked, collapsed, plugged, leaking or improperly connected.
3. Internal leak in unit.
4. Damaged vacuum cylinder.
5. Damaged valve plunger.
6. Broken or faulty springs.
7. Broken plunger stem.

Grabbing Brakes

1. Damaged vacuum cylinder.
2. Faulty vacuum check valve.
3. Vacuum hose leaking or improperly connected.
4. Broken plunger stem.

Pedal Goes To Floor

Generally, when this problem occurs it is not caused by the power brake booster. In rare cases, a broken plunger stem may be at fault.

OVERHAUL

Most power brake boosters are serviced by replacement only. In many cases, repair parts are simply not available. In addition, a good many special tools are required for rebuilding these units and for these reasons it is most practical to replace a failed booster with a new or remanufactured unit.

FRONT DISC BRAKES

Brake Pads

REMOVAL AND INSTALLATION

CAUTION: *Brake pads contain asbestos, which has been determined to be a carcinogenic (cancer-causing) material. Never clean the brake surfaces with compressed air and avoid inhaling any dust from any brake surface. When cleaning brake surfaces, use a commercially available brake cleaning fluid and wear a particle mask during service procedures.*

1. Remove half of the brake fluid from the master cylinder using a siphon bulb. Be careful not to spill any brake fluid on painted surfaces as it will damage the paint. If brake fluid is accidentally spilled, flush the area with water immediately.

2. Position a large C-clamp or pliers over the caliper with the screw end against the outboard brake pad. Tighten the clamp or pliers

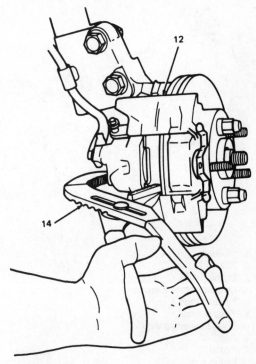

12. Caliper
14. Pliers

Compressing the piston

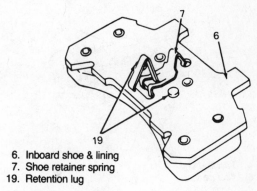

6. Inboard shoe & lining
7. Shoe retainer spring
19. Retention lug

Inboard pad and retainer

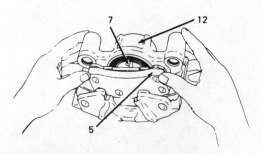

5. Inboard shoe & lining
7. Shoe retainer spring
12. Caliper housing

Installing the inboard pad

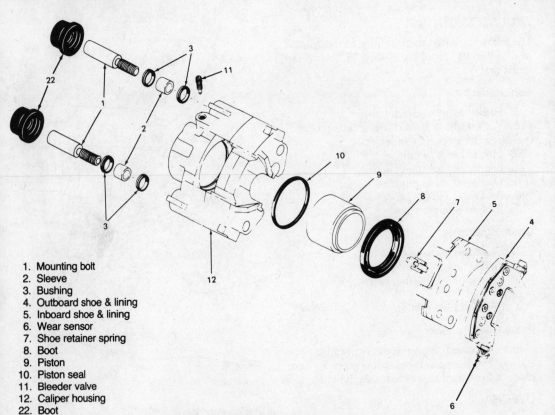

1. Mounting bolt
2. Sleeve
3. Bushing
4. Outboard shoe & lining
5. Inboard shoe & lining
6. Wear sensor
7. Shoe retainer spring
8. Boot
9. Piston
10. Piston seal
11. Bleeder valve
12. Caliper housing
22. Boot

Caliper exploded view

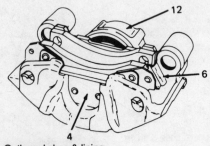

4. Outboard shoe & lining
6. Wear sensor
12. Caliper housing

Installing the outboard pad

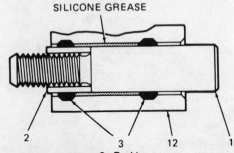

SILICONE GREASE

1. Mounting bolt   3. Bushing
2. Sleeve   12. Caliper housing

Lubrication points

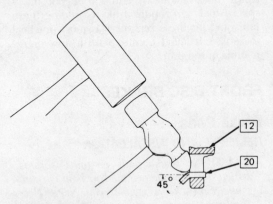

12. Caliper body
20. Outboard shoe tab

Bending the outboard pad tabs

until the caliper is pushed out enough to bottom the piston.

3. Remove the C-clamp.

4. Remove the mounting pins and lift off the caliper. Do not let the caliper hang by the brake hose at any time during service. Use a piece of wire or string to support the caliper assembly if necessary.

5. Unbend the outboard pad retaining tabs and lift out the pad.

6. Lift out the inboard pad.

7. Remove and discard the sleeves and bushings.

8. Lightly lubricate the new sleeves and bushings with silicone lubricant.

9. Installation is the reverse of removal. Make sure the outboard pads are installed with the wear sensor at the leading edge of the pad. Bend the outboard pad tabs to retain the pad, using the method shown in the accompanying illustration. Torque the caliper mounting pins to 30–35 ft.lb.

Brake Caliper
REMOVAL AND INSTALLATION

1. Raise the vehicle and support it safely on jackstands.

2. Remove the front tire.

3. Working on one side at a time, disconnect the hydraulic line from the caliper and plug the end to prevent the entry of dirt and loss of brake fluid.

4. Remove the caliper mounting pins and slide the caliper off the disc.

5. Remove the disc pads from the caliper or mounting adapter. If the old pads are to be reused, mark them so they may be installed in their original positions.

6. Remove the caliper bleed screw and drain the fluid. Clean the outside of the caliper and mount it securely in a soft-jawed vise. Be careful when securing the caliper; it could be damaged by the vise.

7. Place some shop rags or a thin piece of wood in the caliper right in front of the piston. Wear safety goggles and apply a small amount of compressed air to the caliper hydraulic line inlet and force the piston from its bore.

CAUTION: *Do not attempt to catch the piston with your fingers or personal injury could result. Apply short, light bursts of air pressure to free the piston.*

8. Use a non-metallic tool to pry the seal from the piston. Discard the seal and dust boot.

9. Clean all parts in denatured alcohol.

10. Inspect the piston and bore for any wear or damage. Light scratches or scoring may be removed from the piston or bore with crocus cloth. Don't use anything more abrasive than crocus cloth. Heavy scoring, pitting and rust cannot be removed and parts with these conditions must be replaced. When in doubt, replace the part.

11. Assembly is the reverse of disassembly. Make sure that no lint is present on the parts. Lubricate the bore, piston and seal with clean brake fluid. Bleed the brake system after the caliper is installed.

Disc Brake Rotor
RUNOUT

Manufacturers differ widely on permissible runout, but too much can sometimes be felt as a pulsation at the brake pedal. A wobble pump effect is created when a rotor is not perfectly smooth and the pad hits the high spots, forcing fluid back into the master cylinder. This alternating pressure causes a pulsating feeling which can be felt at the pedal when the brakes are applied. This excessive runout also causes the brakes to be out of adjustment because disc brakes are self-adjusting; they are designed so that the pads drag on the rotor at all times and therefore compensate for wear.

To check the actual runout of the rotor, first tighten the wheel spindle nut to a snug bearing adjustment, end play removed. Fasten a dial indicator on the suspension at a convenient location so that the indicator stylus contacts the rotor face approximately one inch from its outer edge. Set the dial indicator to zero, then check the total indicator reading while turning the rotor one full revolution. If the rotor is warped beyond the runout specification, it can sometimes be successfully machined.

REMOVAL AND INSTALLATION

For rotor removal and installation, see Hub and Bearing Removal and Installation in Chapter 6.

REAR DRUM BRAKES

Brake Drum and Shoes
REMOVAL AND INSTALLATION

CAUTION: *Brake shoes contain asbestos, which has been determined to be a carcinogenic (cancer-causing) material. Never clean the brake surfaces with compressed air and avoid inhaling any dust from any brake surface. When cleaning brake surfaces, use a commercially available brake cleaning fluid and wear a particle mask during service procedures.*

1. Raise the vehicle and support it safely on jackstands.

2. Remove the rear tire.

3. Matchmark the position of the brake drum and axle, then pull the drum off the axle. If replacing the rear shoes, it's a good idea to leave one side assembled to use as a model when installing the brake springs on the opposite side.

4. Using suitable brake spring pliers, remove the brake return springs after noting their position for reassembly.

5. Using pliers or a suitable brake tool, remove the holddown springs and lever pivot, then remove the holddown pins.

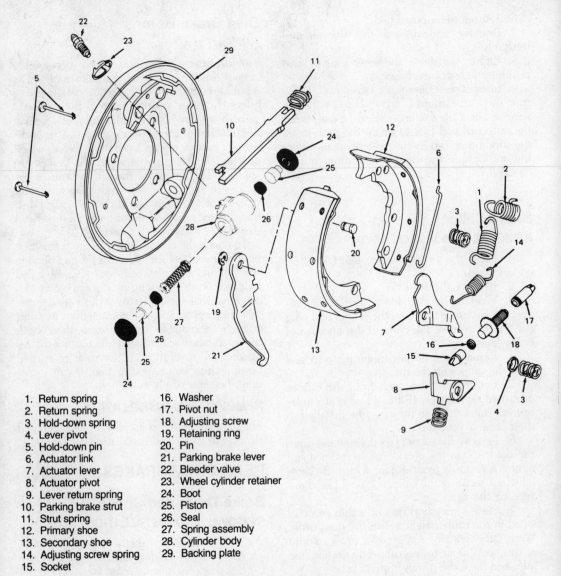

1. Return spring
2. Return spring
3. Hold-down spring
4. Lever pivot
5. Hold-down pin
6. Actuator link
7. Actuator lever
8. Actuator pivot
9. Lever return spring
10. Parking brake strut
11. Strut spring
12. Primary shoe
13. Secondary shoe
14. Adjusting screw spring
15. Socket
16. Washer
17. Pivot nut
18. Adjusting screw
19. Retaining ring
20. Pin
21. Parking brake lever
22. Bleeder valve
23. Wheel cylinder retainer
24. Boot
25. Piston
26. Seal
27. Spring assembly
28. Cylinder body
29. Backing plate

Drum brake components

6. Lift up on the actuating lever and remove the link.

7. Remove the actuator lever, pivot and return spring.

8. Remove the parking brake strut and spring.

9. Note the position of the adjusting spring, disconnect the parking brake cable and remove the brake shoes.

10. Inspect all brake parts and replace any that are questionable.

11. Assemble the brake shoes in reverse order of disassembly. Install the shoes so that the shoe with the shorter amount of brake material (primary) is facing the front of the car. The threads on the adjusters should be cleaned and lubricated with silicone grease. When install-

ing, the coil spring should not be over the adjuster.

Wheel Cylinders
REMOVAL AND INSTALLATION

1. Raise the vehicle and support it safely on jackstands.

2. Remove the tire. Mark and remove the brake drum as described above.

3. Remove the brake shoes and springs.

4. Clean the area around the brake line, disconnect and cap the brake line at the wheel cylinder.

5. Insert two awls, 1/8 in. diameter, into the access slots between the wheel cylinder pilot

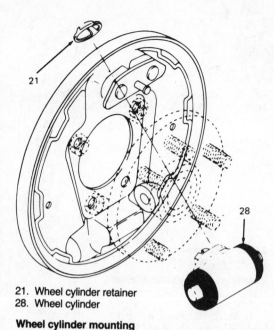

21. Wheel cylinder retainer
28. Wheel cylinder

Wheel cylinder mounting

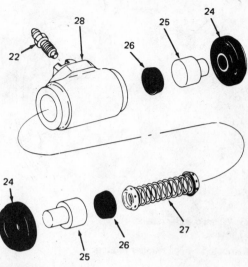

22. Bleeder valve
24. Boot
25. Piston
26. Seal
27. Spring assembly
28. Wheel cylinder body

Exploded view of a wheel cylinder

and the retainer locking tabs. Bend both tabs away simultaneously.

6. Remove the wheel cylinder.

7. To install, position the wheel cylinder in place and hold it there with a wood block between the cylinder and the flange.

8. Install a new retainer on the cylinder using a 1⅛ in. 12 point socket and extension.

9. Install the brake shoes, springs and drum and bleed the brakes as described previously.

Parking Brake
ADJUSTMENT

1. Depress the parking brake pedal exactly three ratchet clicks.

2. Raise the vehicle and support it safely with jackstands.

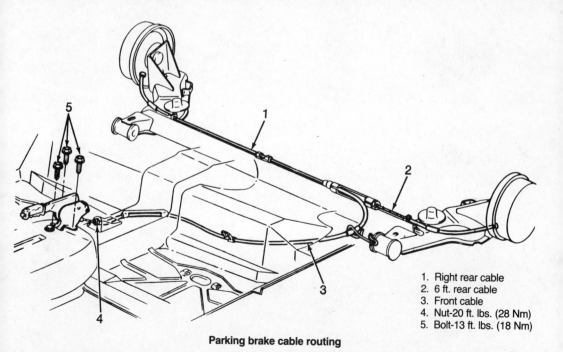

1. Right rear cable
2. 6 ft. rear cable
3. Front cable
4. Nut-20 ft. lbs. (28 Nm)
5. Bolt-13 ft. lbs. (18 Nm)

Parking brake cable routing

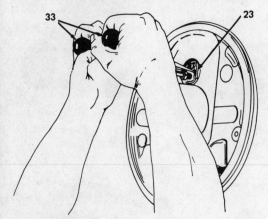

23. Wheel cylinder retainer
33. Awls

Removing wheel cylinder retainer

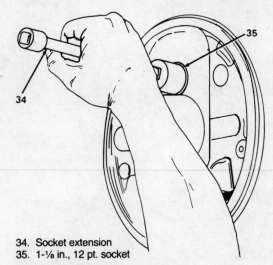

34. Socket extension
35. 1-⅛ in., 12 pt. socket

Installing wheel cylinder retainer

3. Check that the equalizer nut groove is liberally lubricated with chassis lube. Tighten the adjusting nut until the right rear wheel can just be turned to the rear with both hands, but is locked when forward rotation is attempted.

4. With the mechanism totally disengaged, both rear wheels should turn freely in either direction with no brake drag. Do not adjust the parking brake so tightly as to cause brake drag.

EXTERIOR

Doors

REMOVAL AND INSTALLATION

1. Mark the locations of the door hinge strap (upper and lower) on the door.
2. Remove the inner belt sealing strip.
3. Remove the door trim panel.

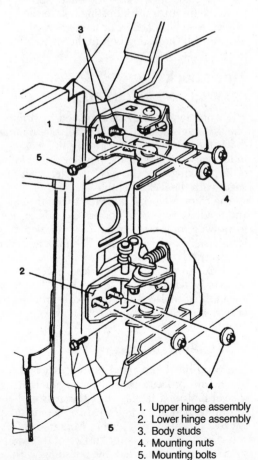

1. Upper hinge assembly
2. Lower hinge assembly
3. Body studs
4. Mounting nuts
5. Mounting bolts

Door hinge assembly

4. Remove the armrest support brackets.
5. Remove the water deflector.
6. Disconnect all wiring harness connectors to door electrical components.
7. Remove the rubber conduit from the door.
8. Remove the wiring harness from the door.
9. Support the door and remove the hinge-to-door attaching bolts using a suitable flexible head ratchet and 13mm socket.
10. Remove the door with the aid of an assistant.
11. Installation is the reverse of removal. Check the alignment of the door to the body and lock to striker engagement. Adjust the door if necessary as described below.

DOOR ADJUSTMENT

The hinges are bolted to the door and body. Elongated holes in the hinge straps allow for minimal door adjustment. The factory installed hinges have a small screw installed in the upper front corner which is a locating hole and not required for service hinges. If the door is adjusted rearward, determine if the door jamb switch must be replaced.

Adjust the door up or down by loosening the hinge-to-door mounting bolts and repositioning the door as necessary. Adjust the door fore and aft by loosening the hinge-to-body nuts and repositioning the door as necessary. Once all adjustments are complete, tighten the mounting bolts and check door operation.

Door Locks

REMOVAL AND INSTALLATION

1. Make sure the door glass is in the full up position.
2. Remove the door trim panel.
3. Remove the water deflector.
4. Disconnect the lock cylinder-to-lock rod.

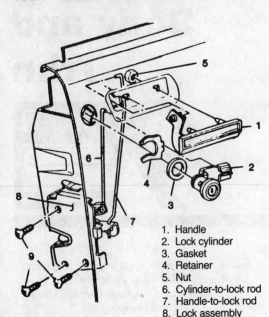

1. Handle
2. Lock cylinder
3. Gasket
4. Retainer
5. Nut
6. Cylinder-to-lock rod
7. Handle-to-lock rod
8. Lock assembly
9. Screws

Exploded view of the outside handle and lock assembly

5. Remove the lock retainer.
6. Remove the lock cylinder and gasket.
7. Installation is the reverse of removal.

Hood

REMOVAL AND INSTALLATION

1. Open the hood and scribe alignment marks along the hinges.
2. Have an assistant support the hood.
3. Remove the strut mounting screws at the hood and swing them down out of the way. Disconnect the hood light connector, if equipped.
4. Remove the hood hinge mounting bolts and lift off the hood.
5. Installation is the reverse of removal. Align the scribe marks when installing the hood hinge bolts.

Hood Release Cable

REMOVAL AND INSTALLATION

The one-piece hood latch release cable includes the pull handle, control cable and housing. The control cable is installed on the left shroud side panel. A sealing grommet attached to the dash panel completes the assembly.

1. Disconnect the cable from the latch assembly. Block the latch to prevent the hood from locking until the cable has been replaced.
2. Remove the pull handle mounting screws and move the handle and bezel away from the kick panel.

3. Remove the grommet from the dash panel by turning it to the left and pulling the cable through the hole in the dash. Remove the cable from the passenger compartment side of the firewall.
4. Installation is the reverse of removal. Apply a soapy solution to the grommet to ease installation into the firewall. Use strip caulk sealer on grommet-to-dash and cable-to-grommet area for waterproofing.

Trunk Lid

REMOVAL, INSTALLATION AND ADJUSTMENT

Open the trunk lid and scribe alignment marks along the hinges. Have an assistant support the trunk lid and remove the mounting bolts. Lift the lid clear of the body. Install in reverse order. If alignment is necessary, loosen the mounting bolts for front-to-rear or side-to-side adjustments. To raise or lower the trunk lid height, raise or lower the rubber bumpers. The rear compartment lid extension springs are adjustable to increase or decrease lifting effort. To increase the amount of effort needed to raise the trunk lid, or decrease the effort needed to close the lid, turn the adjusting bolt to the left. To decrease lifting effort or increase closing effort, turn the adjusting bolt to the right.

Trunk Lock

REMOVAL AND INSTALLATION

The trunk lock cylinder is removed by drilling out the rivets with a 5/32 in. drill bit, pulling down the retainer and removing the lock cylinder rearward. Install the new lock in reverse order, making sure the lock cylinder shaft engages with the lock assembly.

The trunk lid lock is attached to the trunk lid and is adjustable up and down and side to side to provide for proper trunk lid operation and lock-to-striker engagement. If equipped with an electric lid release, a solenoid is bolted to the lock. Some models may also have a deck lid ajar switch mounted to the lock. The lock assembly is replaced or adjusted by removing or loosening the mounting bolts.

Windshield

The windshield is bonded to the body and replacement procedures require a number of special tools and talents. For this reason, it is recommended that windshield replacement be left to a qualified repair shop. Minor scratches and abrasions on the outer surface of the windshield may be removed by polishing with a special repair kit, available from the dealer or aftermarket sources. Follow the directions included in the polishing kit.

INTERIOR

Door Panels

REMOVAL AND INSTALLATION

NOTE: *When removing a door trim panel that has a power window switch attached, the ignition switch must be in the off position. This will eliminate the possibility of shorting out the switch when removing the switch from the harness.*

1. Remove the door armrest/pull handle by removing the mounting screws. Some armrests may have covers over the mounting screws that must be carefully pried off to gain access.

2. Remove the plug covering the inside handle cover plate retaining screw and remove the screw.

3. Remove the lock knob and the screw behind the lock knob.

4. Remove the inside handle escutcheon by sliding the cover plate forward until the retainers on the escutcheon disengage from the holes in the trim panel.

5. Remove the window regulator handle us-

ing tool J-9886 or equivalent to disengage the handle lock clip.

6. Remove the inner belt sealing strip by using a small, flat-bladed tool at the top rear of the door panel and lifting up on the sealing strip.

7. Remove the trim panel by grasping the panel at the lower outboard edges and pulling inboard on the panel until the lower fasteners are disengaged, then grasping the top outboard edges of the panel and lifting up and outboard to disengage the retainers from the door panel.

8. Disconnect all electrical connectors and remove the door panel.

9. Installation is the reverse of removal. Connect all electrical connectors before mounting the door panel to the door assembly.

Window Regulator

REMOVAL AND INSTALLATION

The doors incorporate a lightweight tape drive regulator design. The tape length used on the manual regulator is $46\frac{9}{16}$ in. (1183mm); electric regulator tape length is $40\frac{13}{16}$ in. (1037mm). The service tape is $54\frac{1}{6}$ in. (1385mm) and must be cut to the specified length when replacing the tape.

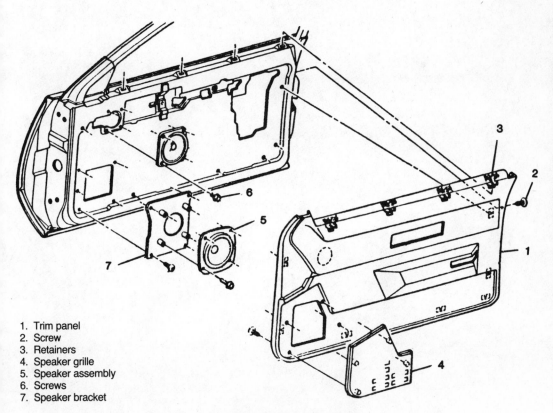

1. Trim panel
2. Screw
3. Retainers
4. Speaker grille
5. Speaker assembly
6. Screws
7. Speaker bracket

Typical door trim panel mounting

1. Remove the inner belt sealing strip.
2. Remove the door panel.
3. Remove the armrest support brackets.
4. Remove the water deflector.
5. Block the window glass in the full up position.
6. Remove the rivets using a ¼ in. drill bit.
7. Disconnect the electrical connector if equipped with power windows.

8. Remove the regulator by moving it until the guide is disengaged from the sash channel on the glass, then lifting the regulator out through the access hole in the door inner panel.
9. If the electric window motor is being replaced, remove it from the regulator on the bench by drilling out the rivets.
10. Installation is the reverse of removal.

Troubleshooting

10

This section is designed to aid in the quick, accurate diagnosis of automotive problems. While automotive repairs can be made by many people, accurate troubleshooting is a rare skill for the amateur and professional alike.

In its simplest state, troubleshooting is an exercise in logic. It is essential to realize that an automobile is really composed of a series of systems. Some of these systems are interrelated; others are not. Automobiles operate within a framework of logical rules and physical laws, and the key to troubleshooting is a good understanding of all the automotive systems.

This section breaks the car or truck down into its component systems, allowing the problem to be isolated. The charts and diagnostic road maps list the most common problems and the most probable causes of trouble. Obviously it would be impossible to list every possible problem that could happen along with every possible cause, but it will locate MOST problems and eliminate a lot of unnecessary guesswork. The systematic format will locate problems within a given system, but, because many automotive systems are interrelated, the solution to your particular problem may be found in a number of systems on the car or truck.

USING THE TROUBLESHOOTING CHARTS

This book contains all of the specific information that the average do-it-yourself mechanic needs to repair and maintain his or her car or truck. The troubleshooting charts are designed to be used in conjunction with the specific procedures and information in the text. For instance, troubleshooting a point-type ignition system is fairly standard for all models, but you may be directed to the text to find procedures for troubleshooting an individual type of electronic ignition. You will also have to refer to the specification charts throughout the book for specifications applicable to your car or truck.

TOOLS AND EQUIPMENT

The tools illustrated in Chapter 1 (plus two more diagnostic pieces) will be adequate to troubleshoot most problems. The two other tools needed are a voltmeter and an ohmmeter. These can be purchased separately or in combination, known as a VOM meter.

In the event that other tools are required, they will be noted in the procedures.

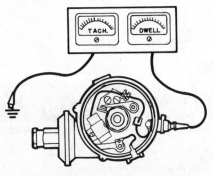

Tach-dwell hooked-up to distributor

Troubleshooting Engine Problems

See Chapters 2, 3, 4 for more information and service procedures.

Index to Systems

System	To Test	Group
Battery	Engine need not be running	1
Starting system	Engine need not be running	2
Primary electrical system	Engine need not be running	3
Secondary electrical system	Engine need not be running	4
Fuel system	Engine need not be running	5
Engine compression	Engine need not be running	6
Engine vacuum	Engine must be running	7
Secondary electrical system	Engine must be running	8
Valve train	Engine must be running	9
Exhaust system	Engine must be running	10
Cooling system	Engine must be running	11
Engine lubrication	Engine must be running	12

Index to Problems

Problem: Symptom	Begin at Specific Diagnosis, Number ____
Engine Won't Start:	
Starter doesn't turn	1.1, 2.1
Starter turns, engine doesn't	2.1
Starter turns engine very slowly	1.1, 2.4
Starter turns engine normally	3.1, 4.1
Starter turns engine very quickly	6.1
Engine fires intermittently	4.1
Engine fires consistently	5.1, 6.1
Engine Runs Poorly:	
Hard starting	3.1, 4.1, 5.1, 8.1
Rough idle	4.1, 5.1, 8.1
Stalling	3.1, 4.1, 5.1, 8.1
Engine dies at high speeds	4.1, 5.1
Hesitation (on acceleration from standing stop)	5.1, 8.1
Poor pickup	4.1, 5.1, 8.1
Lack of power	3.1, 4.1, 5.1, 8.1
Backfire through the carburetor	4.1, 8.1, 9.1
Backfire through the exhaust	4.1, 8.1, 9.1
Blue exhaust gases	6.1, 7.1
Black exhaust gases	5.1
Running on (after the ignition is shut off)	3.1, 8.1
Susceptible to moisture	4.1
Engine misfires under load	4.1, 7.1, 8.4, 9.1
Engine misfires at speed	4.1, 8.4
Engine misfires at idle	3.1, 4.1, 5.1, 7.1, 8.4

Sample Section

Test and Procedure	Results and Indications	Proceed to
4.1—Check for spark: Hold each spark plug wire approximately ¼" from ground with gloves or a heavy, dry rag. Crank the engine and observe the spark.	→ If no spark is evident:	→ 4.2
	→ If spark is good in some cases:	→ 4.3
	→ If spark is good in all cases:	→ 4.6

Specific Diagnosis

This section is arranged so that following each test, instructions are given to proceed to another, until a problem is diagnosed.

Section 1—Battery

Test and Procedure	Results and Indications	Proceed to
1.1—Inspect the battery visually for case condition (corrosion, cracks) and water level.	If case is cracked, replace battery:	**1.4**
	If the case is intact, remove corrosion with a solution of baking soda and water (**CAUTION:** *do not get the solution into the battery*), and fill with water:	**1.2**

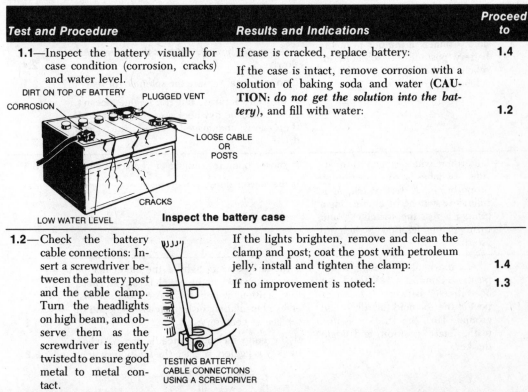

DIRT ON TOP OF BATTERY   PLUGGED VENT

CORROSION

LOOSE CABLE OR POSTS

CRACKS

LOW WATER LEVEL   **Inspect the battery case**

1.2—Check the battery cable connections: Insert a screwdriver between the battery post and the cable clamp. Turn the headlights on high beam, and observe them as the screwdriver is gently twisted to ensure good metal to metal contact.	If the lights brighten, remove and clean the clamp and post; coat the post with petroleum jelly, install and tighten the clamp:	**1.4**
	If no improvement is noted:	**1.3**

TESTING BATTERY CABLE CONNECTIONS USING A SCREWDRIVER

1.3—Test the state of charge of the battery using an individual cell tester or hydrometer.	If indicated, charge the battery. **NOTE:** *If no obvious reason exists for the low state of charge (i.e., battery age, prolonged storage), proceed to:*	**1.4**

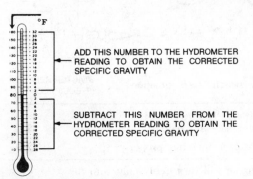

ADD THIS NUMBER TO THE HYDROMETER READING TO OBTAIN THE CORRECTED SPECIFIC GRAVITY

SUBTRACT THIS NUMBER FROM THE HYDROMETER READING TO OBTAIN THE CORRECTED SPECIFIC GRAVITY

Specific Gravity (@ 80° F.)

Minimum	Battery Charge
1.260	100% Charged
1.230	75% Charged
1.200	50% Charged
1.170	25% Charged
1.140	Very Little Power Left
1.110	Completely Discharged

The effects of temperature on battery specific gravity (left) and amount of battery charge in relation to specific gravity (right)

1.4—Visually inspect battery cables for cracking, bad connection to ground, or bad connection to starter.	If necessary, tighten connections or replace the cables:	**2.1**

Section 2—Starting System
See Chapter 3 for service procedures

Test and Procedure	Results and Indications	Proceed to
Note: Tests in Group 2 are performed with coil high tension lead disconnected to prevent accidental starting.		
2.1—Test the starter motor and solenoid: Connect a jumper from the battery post of the solenoid (or relay) to the starter post of the solenoid (or relay).	If starter turns the engine normally:	**2.2**
	If the starter buzzes, or turns the engine very slowly:	**2.4**
	If no response, replace the solenoid (or relay).	**3.1**
	If the starter turns, but the engine doesn't, ensure that the flywheel ring gear is intact. If the gear is undamaged, replace the starter drive.	**3.1**
2.2—Determine whether ignition override switches are functioning properly (clutch start switch, neutral safety switch), by connecting a jumper across the switch(es), and turning the ignition switch to "start".	If starter operates, adjust or replace switch:	**3.1**
	If the starter doesn't operate:	**2.3**
2.3—Check the ignition switch "start" position: Connect a 12V test lamp or voltmeter between the starter post of the solenoid (or relay) and ground. Turn the ignition switch to the "start" position, and jiggle the key.	If the lamp doesn't light or the meter needle doesn't move when the switch is turned, check the ignition switch for loose connections, cracked insulation, or broken wires. Repair or replace as necessary:	**3.1**
	If the lamp flickers or needle moves when the key is jiggled, replace the ignition switch.	**3.3**

Checking the ignition switch "start" position

STARTER RELAY (IF EQUIPPED)

Test and Procedure	Results and Indications	Proceed to
2.4—Remove and bench test the starter, according to specifications in the engine electrical section.	If the starter does not meet specifications, repair or replace as needed:	**3.1**
	If the starter is operating properly:	**2.5**
2.5—Determine whether the engine can turn freely: Remove the spark plugs, and check for water in the cylinders. Check for water on the dipstick, or oil in the radiator. Attempt to turn the engine using an 18″ flex drive and socket on the crankshaft pulley nut or bolt.	If the engine will turn freely only with the spark plugs out, and hydrostatic lock (water in the cylinders) is ruled out, check valve timing:	**9.2**
	If engine will not turn freely, and it is known that the clutch and transmission are free, the engine must be disassembled for further evaluation:	**Chapter 3**

Section 3—Primary Electrical System

Test and Procedure	Results and Indications	Proceed to
3.1—Check the ignition switch "on" position: Connect a jumper wire between the distributor side of the coil and ground, and a 12V test lamp between the switch side of the coil and ground. Remove the high tension lead from the coil. Turn the ignition switch on and jiggle the key.	If the lamp lights:	**3.2**
	If the lamp flickers when the key is jiggled, replace the ignition switch:	**3.3**
	If the lamp doesn't light, check for loose or open connections. If none are found, remove the ignition switch and check for continuity. If the switch is faulty, replace it:	**3.3**

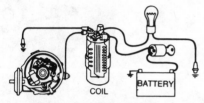

Checking the ignition switch "on" position

3.2—Check the ballast resistor or resistance wire for an open circuit, using an ohmmeter. See Chapter 3 for specific tests.	Replace the resistor or resistance wire if the resistance is zero. **NOTE:** *Some ignition systems have no ballast resistor.*	**3.3**

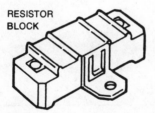

RESISTOR
BLOCK

CALIBRATED
RESISTANCE
LEAD

Two types of resistors

3.3—On point-type ignition systems, visually inspect the breaker points for burning, pitting or excessive wear. Gray coloring of the point contact surfaces is normal. Rotate the crankshaft until the contact heel rests on a high point of the distributor cam and adjust the point gap to specifications. On electronic ignition models, remove the distributor cap and visually inspect the armature. Ensure that the armature pin is in place, and that the armature is on tight and rotates when the engine is cranked. Make sure there are no cracks, chips or rounded edges on the armature.	If the breaker points are intact, clean the contact surfaces with fine emery cloth, and adjust the point gap to specifications. If the points are worn, replace them. On electronic systems, replace any parts which appear defective. If condition persists:	**3.4**

Test and Procedure	Results and Indications	Proceed to
3.4—On point-type ignition systems, connect a dwell-meter between the distributor primary lead and ground. Crank the engine and observe the point dwell angle. On electronic ignition systems, conduct a stator (magnetic pickup assembly) test. See Chapter 3.	On point-type systems, adjust the dwell angle if necessary. **NOTE:** *Increasing the point gap decreases the dwell angle and vice-versa.*	**3.6**
	If the dwell meter shows little or no reading;	**3.5**
	On electronic ignition systems, if the stator is bad, replace the stator. If the stator is good, proceed to the other tests in Chapter 3.	

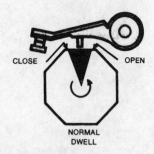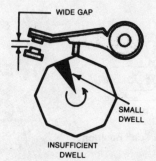

Dwell is a function of point gap

3.5—On the point-type ignition systems, check the condenser for short: connect an ohmeter across the condenser body and the pigtail lead.	If any reading other than infinite is noted, replace the condenser	**3.6**

Checking the condenser for short

3.6—Test the coil primary resistance: On point-type ignition systems, connect an ohmmeter across the coil primary terminals, and read the resistance on the low scale. Note whether an external ballast resistor or resistance wire is used. On electronic ignition systems, test the coil primary resistance as in Chapter 3.	Point-type ignition coils utilizing ballast resistors or resistance wires should have approximately 1.0 ohms resistance. Coils with internal resistors should have approximately 4.0 ohms resistance. If values far from the above are noted, replace the coil.	**4.1**

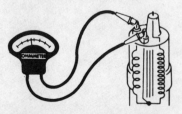

Check the coil primary resistance

Section 4—Secondary Electrical System
See Chapters 2–3 for service procedures

Test and Procedure	Results and Indications	Proceed to
4.1—Check for spark: Hold each spark plug wire approximately ¼″ from ground with gloves or a heavy, dry rag. Crank the engine, and observe the spark.	If no spark is evident:	**4.2**
	If spark is good in some cylinders:	**4.3**
	If spark is good in all cylinders:	**4.6**

Check for spark at the plugs

Test and Procedure	Results and Indications	Proceed to
4.2—Check for spark at the coil high tension lead: Remove the coil high tension lead from the distributor and position it approximately ¼″ from ground. Crank the engine and observe spark. **CAUTION:** *This test should not be performed on engines equipped with electronic ignition.*	If the spark is good and consistent:	**4.3**
	If the spark is good but intermittent, test the primary electrical system starting at 3.3:	**3.3**
	If the spark is weak or non-existent, replace the coil high tension lead, clean and tighten all connections and retest. If no improvement is noted:	**4.4**
4.3—Visually inspect the distributor cap and rotor for burned or corroded contacts, cracks, carbon tracks, or moisture. Also check the fit of the rotor on the distributor shaft (where applicable).	If moisture is present, dry thoroughly, and retest per 4.1:	**4.1**
	If burned or excessively corroded contacts, cracks, or carbon tracks are noted, replace the defective part(s) and retest per 4.1:	**4.1**
	If the rotor and cap appear intact, or are only slightly corroded, clean the contacts thoroughly (including the cap towers and spark plug wire ends) and retest per 4.1:	
	If the spark is good in all cases:	**4.6**
	If the spark is poor in all cases:	**4.5**

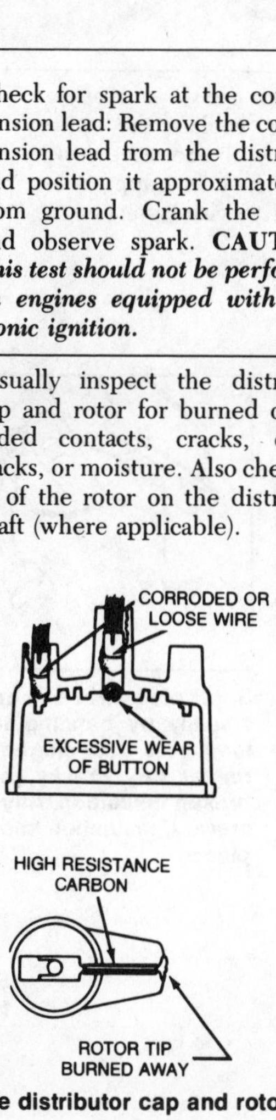

CORRODED OR LOOSE WIRE

EXCESSIVE WEAR OF BUTTON

HIGH RESISTANCE CARBON

ROTOR TIP BURNED AWAY

Inspect the distributor cap and rotor

Test and Procedure	Results and Indications	Proceed to
4.4—Check the coil secondary resistance: On point-type systems connect an ohmmeter across the distributor side of the coil and the coil tower. Read the resistance on the high scale of the ohmmeter. On electronic ignition systems, see Chapter 3 for specific tests.	The resistance of a satisfactory coil should be between 4,000 and 10,000 ohms. If resistance is considerably higher (i.e., 40,000 ohms) replace the coil and retest per 4.1. **NOTE:** *This does not apply to high performance coils.*	

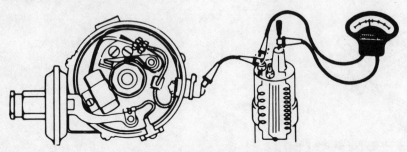

Testing the coil secondary resistance

4.5—Visually inspect the spark plug wires for cracking or brittleness. Ensure that no two wires are positioned so as to cause induction firing (adjacent and parallel). Remove each wire, one by one, and check resistance with an ohmmeter.	Replace any cracked or brittle wires. If any of the wires are defective, replace the entire set. Replace any wires with excessive resistance (over $8000\,\Omega$ per foot for suppression wire), and separate any wires that might cause induction firing.	**4.6**

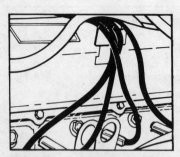

Misfiring can be the result of spark plug leads to adjacent, consecutively firing cylinders running parallel and too close together

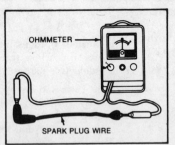

On point-type ignition systems, check the spark plug wires as shown. On electronic ignitions, do not remove the wire from the distributor cap terminal; instead, test through the cap

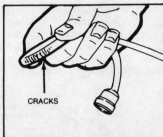

Spark plug wires can be checked visually by bending them in a loop over your finger. This will reveal any cracks, burned or broken insulation. Any wire with cracked insulation should be replaced

4.6—Remove the spark plugs, noting the cylinders from which they were removed, and evaluate according to the color photos in the middle of this book.	See following.	**See following.**

Test and Procedure	Results and Indications	Proceed to
4.7—Examine the location of all the plugs.	The following diagrams illustrate some of the conditions that the location of plugs will reveal.	**4.8**

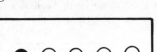

Two adjacent plugs are fouled in a 6-cylinder engine, 4-cylinder engine or either bank of a V-8. This is probably due to a blown head gasket between the two cylinders

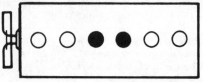

The two center plugs in a 6-cylinder engine are fouled. Raw fuel may be "boiled" out of the carburetor into the intake manifold after the engine is shut-off. Stop-start driving can also foul the center plugs, due to overly rich mixture. Proper float level, a new float needle and seat or use of an insulating spacer may help this problem

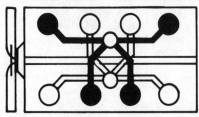

An unbalanced carburetor is indicated. Following the fuel flow on this particular design shows that the cylinders fed by the right-hand barrel are fouled from overly rich mixture, while the cylinders fed by the left-hand barrel are normal

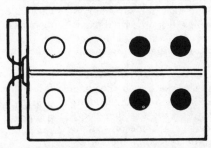

If the four rear plugs are overheated, a cooling system problem is suggested. A thorough cleaning of the cooling system may restore coolant circulation and cure the problem

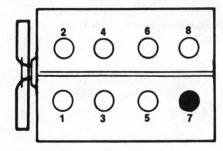

Finding one plug overheated may indicate an intake manifold leak near the affected cylinder. If the overheated plug is the second of two adjacent, consecutively firing plugs, it could be the result of ignition cross-firing. Separating the leads to these two plugs will eliminate cross-fire

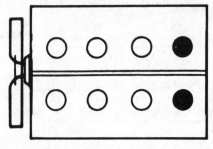

Occasionally, the two rear plugs in large, lightly used V-8's will become oil fouled. High oil consumption and smoky exhaust may also be noticed. It is probably due to plugged oil drain holes in the rear of the cylinder head, causing oil to be sucked in around the valve stems. This usually occurs in the rear cylinders first, because the engine slants that way

Test and Procedure	Results and Indications	Proceed to
4.8—Determine the static ignition timing. Using the crankshaft pulley timing marks as a guide, locate top dead center on the compression stroke of the number one cylinder.	The rotor should be pointing toward the No. 1 tower in the distributor cap, and, on electronic ignitions, the armature spoke for that cylinder should be lined up with the stator.	4.8
4.9—Check coil polarity: Connect a voltmeter negative lead to the coil high tension lead, and the positive lead to ground (**NOTE:** *Reverse the hook-up for positive ground systems*). Crank the engine momentarily. **Checking coil polarity**	If the voltmeter reads up-scale, the polarity is correct: If the voltmeter reads down-scale, reverse the coil polarity (switch the primary leads):	5.1 5.1

Section 5—Fuel System
See Chapter 4 for service procedures

Test and Procedure	Results and Indications	Proceed to
5.1—Determine that the air filter is functioning efficiently: Hold paper elements up to a strong light, and attempt to see light through the filter.	Clean permanent air filters in solvent (or manufacturer's recommendation), and allow to dry. Replace paper elements through which light cannot be seen:	5.2
5.2—Determine whether a flooding condition exists: Flooding is identified by a strong gasoline odor, and excessive gasoline present in the throttle bore(s) of the carburetor. **If the engine floods repeatedly, check the choke butterfly flap**	If flooding is not evident: If flooding is evident, permit the gasoline to dry for a few moments and restart. If flooding doesn't recur: If flooding is persistent:	5.3 5.7 5.5
5.3—Check that fuel is reaching the carburetor: Detach the fuel line at the carburetor inlet. Hold the end of the line in a cup (not styrofoam), and crank the engine. **Check the fuel pump by disconnecting the output line (fuel pump-to-carburetor) at the carburetor and operating the starter briefly**	If fuel flows smoothly: If fuel doesn't flow (**NOTE:** *Make sure that there is fuel in the tank*), or flows erratically:	5.7 5.4

Test and Procedure	Results and Indications	Proceed to
5.4—Test the fuel pump: Disconnect all fuel lines from the fuel pump. Hold a finger over the input fitting, crank the engine (with electric pump, turn the ignition or pump on); and feel for suction.	If suction is evident, blow out the fuel line to the tank with low pressure compressed air until bubbling is heard from the fuel filler neck. Also blow out the carburetor fuel line (both ends disconnected):	5.7
	If no suction is evident, replace or repair the fuel pump:	5.7
	NOTE: *Repeated oil fouling of the spark plugs, or a no-start condition, could be the result of a ruptured vacuum booster pump diaphragm, through which oil or gasoline is being drawn into the intake manifold (where applicable).*	
5.5—Occasionally, small specks of dirt will clog the small jets and orifices in the carburetor. With the engine cold, hold a flat piece of wood or similar material over the carburetor, where possible, and crank the engine.	If the engine starts, but runs roughly the engine is probably not run enough. If the engine won't start:	5.9
5.6—Check the needle and seat: Tap the carburetor in the area of the needle and seat.	If flooding stops, a gasoline additive (e.g., Gumout) will often cure the problem:	5.7
	If flooding continues, check the fuel pump for excessive pressure at the carburetor (according to specifications). If the pressure is normal, the needle and seat must be removed and checked, and/or the float level adjusted:	5.7
5.7—Test the accelerator pump by looking into the throttle bores while operating the throttle.	If the accelerator pump appears to be operating normally:	5.8
	If the accelerator pump is not operating, the pump must be reconditioned. Where possible, service the pump with the carburetor(s) installed on the engine. If necessary, remove the carburetor. Prior to removal:	5.8

Check for gas at the carburetor by looking down the carburetor throat while someone moves the accelerator

Test and Procedure	Results and Indications	Proceed to
5.8—Determine whether the carburetor main fuel system is functioning: Spray a commercial starting fluid into the carburetor while attempting to start the engine.	If the engine starts, runs for a few seconds, and dies:	5.9
	If the engine doesn't start:	6.1

Test and Procedure	Results and Indications	Proceed to
5.9—Uncommon fuel system malfunctions: See below:	If the problem is solved:	6.1
	If the problem remains, remove and recondition the carburetor.	

Condition	Indication	Test	Prevailing Weather Conditions	Remedy
Vapor lock	Engine will not restart shortly after running.	Cool the components of the fuel system until the engine starts. Vapor lock can be cured faster by draping a wet cloth over a mechanical fuel pump.	Hot to very hot	Ensure that the exhaust manifold heat control valve is operating. Check with the vehicle manufacturer for the recommended solution to vapor lock on the model in question.
Carburetor icing	Engine will not idle, stalls at low speeds.	Visually inspect the throttle plate area of the throttle bores for frost.	High humidity, 32–40° F.	Ensure that the exhaust manifold heat control valve is operating, and that the intake manifold heat riser is not blocked.
Water in the fuel	Engine sputters and stalls; may not start.	Pump a small amount of fuel into a glass jar. Allow to stand, and inspect for droplets or a layer of water.	High humidity, extreme temperature changes.	For droplets, use one or two cans of commercial gas line anti-freeze. For a layer of water, the tank must be drained, and the fuel lines blown out with compressed air.

Section 6—Engine Compression
See Chapter 3 for service procedures

6.1—Test engine compression: Remove all spark plugs. Block the throttle wide open. Insert a compression gauge into a spark plug port, crank the engine to obtain the maximum reading, and record.	If compression is within limits on all cylinders:	7.1
	If gauge reading is extremely low on all cylinders:	6.2
	If gauge reading is low on one or two cylinders: (If gauge readings are identical and low on two or more adjacent cylinders, the head gasket must be replaced.)	6.2

Checking compression

6.2—Test engine compression (wet): Squirt approximately 30 cc. of engine oil into each cylinder, and retest per 6.1.	If the readings improve, worn or cracked rings or broken pistons are indicated:	See Chapter 3
	If the readings do not improve, burned or excessively carboned valves or a jumped timing chain are indicated: NOTE: *A jumped timing chain is often indicated by difficult cranking.*	7.1

CHILTON'S
AUTO BODY
REPAIR TIPS

Tools and Materials • Step-by-Step Illustrated Procedures
How To Repair Dents, Scratches and Rust Holes
Spray Painting and Refinishing Tips

With a little practice, basic body repair procedures can be mastered by any do-it-yourself mechanic. The step-by-step repairs shown here can be applied to almost any type of auto body repair.

TOOLS & MATERIALS

You may already have basic tools, such as hammers and electric drills. Other tools unique to body repair — body hammers, grinding attachments, sanding blocks, dent puller, half-round plastic file and plastic spreaders — are relatively inexpensive and can be obtained wherever auto parts or auto body repair parts are sold. Portable air compressors and paint spray guns can be purchased or rented.

Auto Body Repair Kits

The best and most often used products are available to the do-it-yourselfer in kit form, from major manufacturers of auto body repair products. The same manufacturers also merchandise the individual products for use by pros.

Kits are available to make a wide variety of repairs, including holes, dents and scratches and fiberglass, and offer the advantage of buying the materials you'll need for the job. There is little waste or chance of materials going bad from not being used. Many kits may also contain basic body-working tools such as body files, sanding blocks and spreaders. Check the contents of the kit before buying your tools.

BODY REPAIR TIPS

Safety

Many of the products associated with auto body repair and refinishing contain toxic chemicals. Read all labels before opening containers and store them in a safe place and manner.

• Wear eye protection (safety goggles) when using power tools or when performing any operation that involves the removal of any type of material.

• Wear lung protection (disposable mask or respirator) when grinding, sanding or painting.

Sanding

1 Sand off paint before using a dent puller. When using a non-adhesive sanding disc, cover the back of the disc with an overlapping layer or two of masking tape and trim the edges. The disc will last considerably longer.

2 Use the circular motion of the sanding disc to grind *into* the edge of the repair. Grinding or sanding away from the jagged edge will only tear the sandpaper.

3 Use the palm of your hand flat on the panel to detect high and low spots. Do not use your fingertips. Slide your hand slowly back and forth.

WORKING WITH BODY FILLER

Mixing The Filler

Cleanliness and proper mixing and application are extremely important. Use a clean piece of plastic or glass or a disposable artist's palette to mix body filler.

1 Allow plenty of time and follow directions. No useful purpose will be served by adding more hardener to make it cure (set-up) faster. Less hardener means more curing time, but the mixture dries harder; more hardener means less curing time but a softer mixture.

2 Both the hardener and the filler should be thoroughly kneaded or stirred before mixing. Hardener should be a solid paste and dispense like thin toothpaste. Body filler should be smooth, and free of lumps or thick spots.

Getting the proper amount of hardener in the filler is the trickiest part of preparing the filler. Use the same amount of hardener in cold or warm weather. For contour filler (thick coats), a bead of hardener twice the diameter of the filler is about right. There's about a 15% margin on either side, but, if in doubt use less hardener.

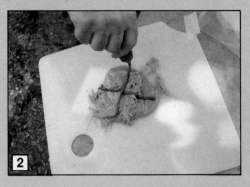

3 Mix the body filler and hardener by wiping across the mixing surface, picking the mixture up and wiping it again. Colder weather requires longer mixing times. Do not mix in a circular motion; this will trap air bubbles which will become holes in the cured filler.

Applying The Filler

1 For best results, filler should not be applied over 1/4" thick.

Apply the filler in several coats. Build it up to above the level of the repair surface so that it can be sanded or grated down.

The first coat of filler must be pressed on with a firm wiping motion.

Apply the filler in one direction only. Working the filler back and forth will either pull it off the metal or trap air bubbles.

REPAIRING DENTS

Before you start, take a few minutes to study the damaged area. Try to visualize the shape of the panel before it was damaged. If the damage is on the left fender, look at the right fender and use it as a guide. If there is access to the panel from behind, you can reshape it with a body hammer. If not, you'll have to use a dent puller. Go slowly and work the metal a little at a time. Get the panel as straight as possible before applying filler.

1 This dent is typical of one that can be pulled out or hammered out from behind. Remove the headlight cover, headlight assembly and turn signal housing.

2 Drill a series of holes ½ the size of the end of the dent puller along the stress line. Make some trial pulls and assess the results. If necessary, drill more holes and try again. Do not hurry.

3 If possible, use a body hammer and block to shape the metal back to its original contours. Get the metal back as close to its original shape as possible. Don't depend on body filler to fill dents.

4 Using an 80-grit grinding disc on an electric drill, grind the paint from the surrounding area down to bare metal. Use a new grinding pad to prevent heat buildup that will warp metal.

5 The area should look like this when you're finished grinding. Knock the drill holes in and tape over small openings to keep plastic filler out.

6 Mix the body filler (see Body Repair Tips). Spread the body filler evenly over the entire area (see Body Repair Tips). Be sure to cover the area completely.

7 Let the body filler dry until the surface can just be scratched with your fingernail. Knock the high spots from the body filler with a body file ("Cheesegrater"). Check frequently with the palm of your hand for high and low spots.

8 Check to be sure that trim pieces that will be installed later will fit exactly. Sand the area with 40-grit paper.

9 If you wind up with low spots, you may have to apply another layer of filler.

10 Knock the high spots off with 40-grit paper. When you are satisfied with the contours of the repair, apply a thin coat of filler to cover pin holes and scratches.

11 Block sand the area with 40-grit paper to a smooth finish. Pay particular attention to body lines and ridges that must be well-defined.

12 Sand the area with 400 paper and then finish with a scuff pad. The finished repair is ready for priming and painting (see Painting Tips).

Materials and photos courtesy of Ritt Jones Auto Body, Prospect Park, PA.

REPAIRING RUST HOLES

There are many ways to repair rust holes. The fiberglass cloth kit shown here is one of the most cost efficient for the owner because it provides a strong repair that resists cracking and moisture and is relatively easy to use. It can be used on large and small holes (with or without backing) and can be applied over contoured areas. Remember, however, that short of replacing an entire panel, no repair is a guarantee that the rust will not return.

1 Remove any trim that will be in the way. Clean away all loose debris. Cut away all the rusted metal. But be sure to leave enough metal to retain the contour or body shape.

2 Grind away all traces of rust with a 24-grit grinding disc. Be sure to grind back 3-4 inches from the edge of the hole down to bare metal and be sure all traces of paint, primer and rust are removed.

3 Block sand the area with 80 or 100 grit sandpaper to get a clear, shiny surface and feathered paint edge. Tap the edges of the hole inward with a ball peen hammer.

4 If you are going to use release film, cut a piece about 2-3″ larger than the area you have sanded. Place the film over the repair and mark the sanded area on the film. Avoid any unnecessary wrinkling of the film.

5 Cut 2 pieces of fiberglass matte to match the shape of the repair. One piece should be about 1″ smaller than the sanded area and the second piece should be 1″ smaller than the first. Mix enough filler and hardener to saturate the fiberglass material (see Body Repair Tips).

6 Lay the release sheet on a flat surface and spread an even layer of filler, large enough to cover the repair. Lay the smaller piece of fiberglass cloth in the center of the sheet and spread another layer of filler over the fiberglass cloth. Repeat the operation for the larger piece of cloth.

7 Place the repair material over the repair area, with the release film facing outward. Use a spreader and work from the center outward to smooth the material, following the body contours. Be sure to remove all air bubbles.

8 Wait until the repair has dried tack-free and peel off the release sheet. The ideal working temperature is 60°-90° F. Cooler or warmer temperatures or high humidity may require additional curing time. Wait longer, if in doubt.

9 Sand and feather-edge the entire area. The initial sanding can be done with a sanding disc on an electric drill if care is used. Finish the sanding with a block sander. Low spots can be filled with body filler; this may require several applications.

10 When the filler can just be scratched with a fingernail, knock the high spots down with a body file and smooth the entire area with 80-grit. Feather the filled areas into the surrounding areas.

11 When the area is sanded smooth, mix some topcoat and hardener and apply it directly with a spreader. This will give a smooth finish and prevent the glass matte from showing through the paint.

12 Block sand the topcoat smooth with finishing sandpaper (200 grit), and 400 grit. The repair is ready for masking, priming and painting (see Painting Tips).

Materials and photos courtesy Marson Corporation, Chelsea, Massachusetts

PAINTING TIPS

Preparation

1 SANDING — Use a 400 or 600 grit wet or dry sandpaper. Wet-sand the area with a $1/4$ sheet of sandpaper soaked in clean water. Keep the paper wet while sanding. Sand the area until the repaired area tapers into the original finish.

2 CLEANING — Wash the area to be painted thoroughly with water and a clean rag. Rinse it thoroughly and wipe the surface dry until you're sure it's completely free of dirt, dust, fingerprints, wax, detergent or other foreign matter.

3 MASKING — Protect any areas you don't want to overspray by covering them with masking tape and newspaper. Be careful not get fingerprints on the area to be painted.

4 PRIMING — All exposed metal should be primed before painting. Primer protects the metal and provides an excellent surface for paint adhesion. When the primer is dry, wet-sand the area again with 600 grit wet-sandpaper. Clean the area again after sanding.

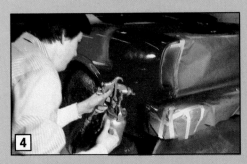

Painting Techniques

Paint applied from either a spray gun or a spray can (for small areas) will provide good results. Experiment on an old piece of metal to get the right combination before you begin painting.

SPRAYING VISCOSITY (SPRAY GUN ONLY) — Paint should be thinned to spraying viscosity according to the directions on the can. Use only the recommended thinner or reducer and the same amount of reduction regardless of temperature.

AIR PRESSURE (SPRAY GUN ONLY) — This is extremely important. Be sure you are using the proper recommended pressure.

TEMPERATURE — The surface to be painted should be approximately the same temperature as the surrounding air. Applying warm paint to a cold surface, or vice versa, will completely upset the paint characteristics.

THICKNESS — Spray with smooth strokes. In general, the thicker the coat of paint, the longer the drying time. Apply several thin coats about 30 seconds apart. The paint should remain wet long enough to flow out and no longer; heavier coats will only produce sags or wrinkles. Spray a light (fog) coat, followed by heavier color coats.

DISTANCE — The ideal spraying distance is 8″-12″ from the gun or can to the surface. Shorter distances will produce ripples, while greater distances will result in orange peel, dry film and poor color match and loss of material due to overspray.

OVERLAPPING — The gun or can should be kept at right angles to the surface at all times. Work to a wet edge at an even speed, using a 50% overlap and direct the center of the spray at the lower or nearest edge of the previous stroke.

RUBBING OUT (BLENDING) FRESH PAINT — Let the paint dry thoroughly. Runs or imperfections can be sanded out, primed and repainted.

Don't be in too big a hurry to remove the masking. This only produces paint ridges. When the finish has dried for at least a week, apply a small amount of fine grade rubbing compound with a clean, wet cloth. Use lots of water and blend the new paint with the surrounding area.

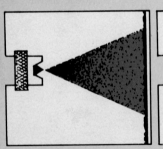

WRONG

Thin coat. Stroke too fast, not enough overlap, gun too far away.

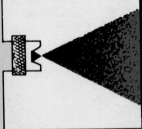

CORRECT

Medium coat. Proper distance, good stroke, proper overlap.

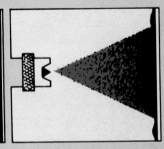

WRONG

Heavy coat. Stroke too slow, too much overlap, gun too close.

Section 7—Engine Vacuum
See Chapter 3 for service procedures

Test and Procedure	Results and Indications	Proceed to
7.1—Attach a vacuum gauge to the intake manifold beyond the throttle plate. Start the engine, and observe the action of the needle over the range of engine speeds.	See below.	**See below**

INDICATION: normal engine in good condition

Proceed to: 8.1

Normal engine
Gauge reading: steady, from 17–22 in./Hg.

INDICATION: sticking valves or ignition miss

Proceed to: 9.1, 8.3

Sticking valves
Gauge reading: intermittent fluctuation at idle

INDICATION: late ignition or valve timing, low compression, stuck throttle valve, leaking carburetor or manifold gasket

Proceed to: 6.1

Incorrect valve timing
Gauge reading: low (10–15 in./Hg) but steady

INDICATION: improper carburetor adjustment or minor intake leak.

Proceed to: 7.2

Carburetor requires adjustment
Gauge reading: drifting needle

INDICATION: ignition miss, blown cylinder head gasket, leaking valve or weak valve spring

Proceed to: 8.3, 6.1

Blown head gasket
Gauge reading: needle fluctuates as engine speed increases

INDICATION: burnt valve or faulty valve clearance. Needle will fall when defective valve operates

Proceed to: 9.1

Burnt or leaking valves
Gauge reading: steady needle, but drops regularly

INDICATION: choked muffler, excessive back pressure in system

Proceed to: 10.1

Clogged exhaust system
Gauge reading: gradual drop in reading at idle

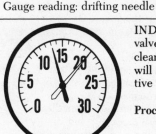

INDICATION: worn valve guides

Proceed to: 9.1

Worn valve guides
Gauge reading: needle vibrates excessively at idle, but steadies as engine speed increases

White pointer = steady gauge hand

Black pointer = fluctuating gauge hand

Test and Procedure	Results and Indications	Proceed to
7.2—Attach a vacuum gauge per 7.1, and test for an intake manifold leak. Squirt a small amount of oil around the intake manifold gaskets, carburetor gaskets, plugs and fittings. Observe the action of the vacuum gauge.	If the reading improves, replace the indicated gasket, or seal the indicated fitting or plug: If the reading remains low:	**8.1** **7.3**
7.3—Test all vacuum hoses and accessories for leaks as described in 7.2. Also check the carburetor body (dashpots, automatic choke mechanism, throttle shafts) for leaks in the same manner.	If the reading improves, service or replace the offending part(s): If the reading remains low:	**8.1** **6.1**

Section 8—Secondary Electrical System
See Chapter 2 for service procedures

Test and Procedure	Results and Indications	Proceed to
8.1—Remove the distributor cap and check to make sure that the rotor turns when the engine is cranked. Visually inspect the distributor components.	Clean, tighten or replace any components which appear defective.	**8.2**
8.2—Connect a timing light (per manufacturer's recommendation) and check the dynamic ignition timing. Disconnect and plug the vacuum hose(s) to the distributor if specified, start the engine, and observe the timing marks at the specified engine speed.	If the timing is not correct, adjust to specifications by rotating the distributor in the engine: (Advance timing by rotating distributor opposite normal direction of rotor rotation, retard timing by rotating distributor in same direction as rotor rotation.)	**8.3**
8.3—Check the operation of the distributor advance mechanism(s): To test the mechanical advance, disconnect the vacuum lines from the distributor advance unit and observe the timing marks with a timing light as the engine speed is increased from idle. If the mark moves smoothly, without hesitation, it may be assumed that the mechanical advance is functioning properly. To test vacuum advance and/or retard systems, alternately crimp and release the vacuum line, and observe the timing mark for movement. If movement is noted, the system is operating.	If the systems are functioning: If the systems are not functioning, remove the distributor, and test on a distributor tester:	**8.4** **8.4**
8.4—Locate an ignition miss: With the engine running, remove each spark plug wire, one at a time, until one is found that doesn't cause the engine to roughen and slow down.	When the missing cylinder is identified:	**4.1**

Section 9—Valve Train
See Chapter 3 for service procedures

Test and Procedure	Results and Indications	Proceed to
9.1—Evaluate the valve train: Remove the valve cover, and ensure that the valves are adjusted to specifications. A mechanic's stethoscope may be used to aid in the diagnosis of the valve train. By pushing the probe on or near push rods or rockers, valve noise often can be isolated. A timing light also may be used to diagnose valve problems. Connect the light according to manufacturer's recommendations, and start the engine. Vary the firing moment of the light by increasing the engine speed (and therefore the ignition advance), and moving the trigger from cylinder to cylinder. Observe the movement of each valve.	Sticking valves or erratic valve train motion can be observed with the timing light. The cylinder head must be disassembled for repairs.	**See Chapter 3**
9.2—Check the valve timing: Locate top dead center of the No. 1 piston, and install a degree wheel or tape on the crankshaft pulley or damper with zero corresponding to an index mark on the engine. Rotate the crankshaft in its direction of rotation, and observe the opening of the No. 1 cylinder intake valve. The opening should correspond with the correct mark on the degree wheel according to specifications.	If the timing is not correct, the timing cover must be removed for further investigation.	**See Chapter 3**

Section 10—Exhaust System

Test and Procedure	Results and Indications	Proceed to
10.1—Determine whether the exhaust manifold heat control valve is operating: Operate the valve by hand to determine whether it is free to move. If the valve is free, run the engine to operating temperature and observe the action of the valve, to ensure that it is opening.	If the valve sticks, spray it with a suitable solvent, open and close the valve to free it, and retest. If the valve functions properly: If the valve does not free, or does not operate, replace the valve:	**10.2** **10.2**
10.2—Ensure that there are no exhaust restrictions: Visually inspect the exhaust system for kinks, dents, or crushing. Also note that gases are flowing freely from the tailpipe at all engine speeds, indicating no restriction in the muffler or resonator.	Replace any damaged portion of the system:	**11.1**

Section 11—Cooling System
See Chapter 3 for service procedures

Test and Procedure	Results and Indications	Proceed to
11.1—Visually inspect the fan belt for glazing, cracks, and fraying, and replace if necessary. Tighten the belt so that the longest span has approximately ½″ play at its mid-point under thumb pressure (see Chapter 1).	Replace or tighten the fan belt as necessary:	**11.2**

Checking belt tension

11.2—Check the fluid level of the cooling system.	If full or slightly low, fill as necessary:	**11.5**
	If extremely low:	**11.3**
11.3—Visually inspect the external portions of the cooling system (radiator, radiator hoses, thermostat elbow, water pump seals, heater hoses, etc.) for leaks. If none are found, pressurize the cooling system to 14–15 psi.	If cooling system holds the pressure:	**11.5**
	If cooling system loses pressure rapidly, reinspect external parts of the system for leaks under pressure. If none are found, check dipstick for coolant in crankcase. If no coolant is present, but pressure loss continues:	**11.4**
	If coolant is evident in crankcase, remove cylinder head(s), and check gasket(s). If gaskets are intact, block and cylinder head(s) should be checked for cracks or holes.	
	If the gasket(s) is blown, replace, and purge the crankcase of coolant:	**12.6**
	NOTE: *Occasionally, due to atmospheric and driving conditions, condensation of water can occur in the crankcase. This causes the oil to appear milky white. To remedy, run the engine until hot, and change the oil and oil filter.*	
11.4—Check for combustion leaks into the cooling system: Pressurize the cooling system as above. Start the engine, and observe the pressure gauge. If the needle fluctuates, remove each spark plug wire, one at a time, noting which cylinder(s) reduce or eliminate the fluctuation.	Cylinders which reduce or eliminate the fluctuation, when the spark plug wire is removed, are leaking into the cooling system. Replace the head gasket on the affected cylinder bank(s).	

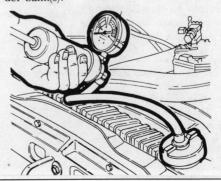

Pressurizing the cooling system

Test and Procedure	Results and Indications	Proceed to
11.5—Check the radiator pressure cap: Attach a radiator pressure tester to the radiator cap (wet the seal prior to installation). Quickly pump up the pressure, noting the point at which the cap releases.	If the cap releases within ± 1 psi of the specified rating, it is operating properly:	**11.6**
	If the cap releases at more than ± 1 psi of the specified rating, it should be replaced:	**11.6**

Checking radiator pressure cap

Test and Procedure	Results and Indications	Proceed to
11.6—Test the thermostat: Start the engine cold, remove the radiator cap, and insert a thermometer into the radiator. Allow the engine to idle. After a short while, there will be a sudden, rapid increase in coolant temperature. The temperature at which this sharp rise stops is the thermostat opening temperature.	If the thermostat opens at or about the specified temperature:	**11.7**
	If the temperature doesn't increase: (If the temperature increases slowly and gradually, replace the thermostat.)	**11.7**
11.7—Check the water pump: Remove the thermostat elbow and the thermostat, disconnect the coil high tension lead (to prevent starting), and crank the engine momentarily.	If coolant flows, replace the thermostat and retest per 11.6:	**11.6**
	If coolant doesn't flow, reverse flush the cooling system to alleviate any blockage that might exist. If system is not blocked, and coolant will not flow, replace the water pump.	

Section 12—Lubrication
See Chapter 3 for service procedures

Test and Procedure	Results and Indications	Proceed to
12.1—Check the oil pressure gauge or warning light: If the gauge shows low pressure, or the light is on for no obvious reason, remove the oil pressure sender. Install an accurate oil pressure gauge and run the engine momentarily.	If oil pressure builds normally, run engine for a few moments to determine that it is functioning normally, and replace the sender.	—
	If the pressure remains low:	**12.2**
	If the pressure surges:	**12.3**
	If the oil pressure is zero:	**12.3**
12.2—Visually inspect the oil: If the oil is watery or very thin, milky, or foamy, replace the oil and oil filter.	If the oil is normal:	**12.3**
	If after replacing oil the pressure remains low:	**12.3**
	If after replacing oil the pressure becomes normal:	—

Test and Procedure	Results and Indications	Proceed to
12.3—Inspect the oil pressure relief valve and spring, to ensure that it is not sticking or stuck. Remove and thoroughly clean the valve, spring, and the valve body.	If the oil pressure improves: If no improvement is noted:	— **12.4**
12.4—Check to ensure that the oil pump is not cavitating (sucking air instead of oil): See that the crankcase is neither over nor underfull, and that the pickup in the sump is in the proper position and free from sludge.	Fill or drain the crankcase to the proper capacity, and clean the pickup screen in solvent if necessary. If no improvement is noted:	**12.5**
12.5—Inspect the oil pump drive and the oil pump:	If the pump drive or the oil pump appear to be defective, service as necessary and retest per 12.1: If the pump drive and pump appear to be operating normally, the engine should be disassembled to determine where blockage exists:	**12.1** **See Chapter 3**
12.6—Purge the engine of ethylene glycol coolant: Completely drain the crankcase and the oil filter. Obtain a commercial butyl cellosolve base solvent, designated for this purpose, and follow the instructions precisely. Following this, install a new oil filter and refill the crankcase with the proper weight oil. The next oil and filter change should follow shortly thereafter (1000 miles).		

TROUBLESHOOTING EMISSION CONTROL SYSTEMS

See Chapter 4 for procedures applicable to individual emission control systems used on specific combinations of engine/transmission/model.

TROUBLESHOOTING THE CARBURETOR
See Chapter 4 for service procedures

Carburetor problems cannot be effectively isolated unless all other engine systems (particularly ignition and emission) are functioning properly and the engine is properly tuned.

Condition	Possible Cause
Engine cranks, but does not start	1. Improper starting procedure 2. No fuel in tank 3. Clogged fuel line or filter 4. Defective fuel pump 5. Choke valve not closing properly 6. Engine flooded 7. Choke valve not unloading 8. Throttle linkage not making full travel 9. Stuck needle or float 10. Leaking float needle or seat 11. Improper float adjustment
Engine stalls	1. Improperly adjusted idle speed or mixture **Engine hot** 2. Improperly adjusted dashpot 3. Defective or improperly adjusted solenoid 4. Incorrect fuel level in fuel bowl 5. Fuel pump pressure too high 6. Leaking float needle seat 7. Secondary throttle valve stuck open 8. Air or fuel leaks 9. Idle air bleeds plugged or missing 10. Idle passages plugged **Engine Cold** 11. Incorrectly adjusted choke 12. Improperly adjusted fast idle speed 13. Air leaks 14. Plugged idle or idle air passages 15. Stuck choke valve or binding linkage 16. Stuck secondary throttle valves 17. Engine flooding—high fuel level 18. Leaking or misaligned float
Engine hesitates on acceleration	1. Clogged fuel filter 2. Leaking fuel pump diaphragm 3. Low fuel pump pressure 4. Secondary throttle valves stuck, bent or misadjusted 5. Sticking or binding air valve 6. Defective accelerator pump 7. Vacuum leaks 8. Clogged air filter 9. Incorrect choke adjustment (engine cold)
Engine feels sluggish or flat on acceleration	1. Improperly adjusted idle speed or mixture 2. Clogged fuel filter 3. Defective accelerator pump 4. Dirty, plugged or incorrect main metering jets 5. Bent or sticking main metering rods 6. Sticking throttle valves 7. Stuck heat riser 8. Binding or stuck air valve 9. Dirty, plugged or incorrect secondary jets 10. Bent or sticking secondary metering rods. 11. Throttle body or manifold heat passages plugged 12. Improperly adjusted choke or choke vacuum break.
Carburetor floods	1. Defective fuel pump. Pressure too high. 2. Stuck choke valve 3. Dirty, worn or damaged float or needle valve/seat 4. Incorrect float/fuel level 5. Leaking float bowl

Condition	Possible Cause
Engine idles roughly and stalls	1. Incorrect idle speed 2. Clogged fuel filter 3. Dirt in fuel system or carburetor 4. Loose carburetor screws or attaching bolts 5. Broken carburetor gaskets 6. Air leaks 7. Dirty carburetor 8. Worn idle mixture needles 9. Throttle valves stuck open 10. Incorrectly adjusted float or fuel level 11. Clogged air filter
Engine runs unevenly or surges	1. Defective fuel pump 2. Dirty or clogged fuel filter 3. Plugged, loose or incorrect main metering jets or rods 4. Air leaks 5. Bent or sticking main metering rods 6. Stuck power piston 7. Incorrect float adjustment 8. Incorrect idle speed or mixture 9. Dirty or plugged idle system passages 10. Hard, brittle or broken gaskets 11. Loose attaching or mounting screws 12. Stuck or misaligned secondary throttle valves
Poor fuel economy	1. Poor driving habits 2. Stuck choke valve 3. Binding choke linkage 4. Stuck heat riser 5. Incorrect idle mixture 6. Defective accelerator pump 7. Air leaks 8. Plugged, loose or incorrect main metering jets 9. Improperly adjusted float or fuel level 10. Bent, misaligned or fuel-clogged float 11. Leaking float needle seat 12. Fuel leak 13. Accelerator pump discharge ball not seating properly 14. Incorrect main jets
Engine lacks high speed performance or power	1. Incorrect throttle linkage adjustment 2. Stuck or binding power piston 3. Defective accelerator pump 4. Air leaks 5. Incorrect float setting or fuel level 6. Dirty, plugged, worn or incorrect main metering jets or rods 7. Binding or sticking air valve 8. Brittle or cracked gaskets 9. Bent, incorrect or improperly adjusted secondary metering rods 10. Clogged fuel filter 11. Clogged air filter 12. Defective fuel pump

TROUBLESHOOTING FUEL INJECTION PROBLEMS

Each fuel injection system has its own unique components and test procedures, for which it is impossible to generalize. Refer to Chapter 4 of this Repair & Tune-Up Guide for specific test and repair procedures, if the vehicle is equipped with fuel injection.

TROUBLESHOOTING ELECTRICAL PROBLEMS
See Chapter 5 for service procedures

For any electrical system to operate, it must make a complete circuit. This simply means that the power flow from the battery must make a complete circle. When an electrical component is operating, power flows from the battery to the component, passes through the component causing it to perform its function (lighting a light bulb), and then returns to the battery through the ground of the circuit. This ground is usually (but not always) the metal part of the car or truck on which the electrical component is mounted.

Perhaps the easiest way to visualize this is to think of connecting a light bulb with two wires attached to it to the battery. If one of the two wires attached to the light bulb were attached to the negative post of the battery and the other were attached to the positive post of the battery, you would have a complete circuit. Current from the battery would flow to the light bulb, causing it to light, and return to the negative post of the battery.

The normal automotive circuit differs from this simple example in two ways. First, instead of having a return wire from the bulb to the battery, the light bulb returns the current to the battery through the chassis of the vehicle. Since the negative battery cable is attached to the chassis and the chassis is made of electrically conductive metal, the chassis of the vehicle can serve as a ground wire to complete the circuit. Secondly, most automotive circuits contain switches to turn components on and off as required.

Every complete circuit from a power source must include a component which is using the power from the power source. If you were to disconnect the light bulb from the wires and touch the two wires together (don't do this) the power supply wire to the component would be grounded before the normal ground connection for the circuit.

Because grounding a wire from a power source makes a complete circuit—less the required component to use the power—this phenomenon is called a short circuit. Common causes are: broken insulation (exposing the metal wire to a metal part of the car or truck), or a shorted switch.

Some electrical components which require a large amount of current to operate also have a relay in their circuit. Since these circuits carry a large amount of current, the thickness of the wire in the circuit (gauge size) is also greater. If this large wire were connected from the component to the control switch on the instrument panel, and then back to the component, a voltage drop would occur in the circuit. To prevent this potential drop in voltage, an electromagnetic switch (relay) is used. The large wires in the circuit are connected from the battery to one side of the relay, and from the opposite side of the relay to the component. The relay is normally open, preventing current from passing through the circuit. An additional, smaller, wire is connected from the relay to the control switch for the circuit. When the control switch is turned on, it grounds the smaller wire from the relay and completes the circuit. This closes the relay and allows current to flow from the battery to the component. The horn, headlight, and starter circuits are three which use relays.

It is possible for larger surges of current to pass through the electrical system of your car or truck. If this surge of current were to reach an electrical component, it could burn it out. To prevent this, fuses, circuit breakers or fusible links are connected into the current supply wires of most of the major electrical systems. When an electrical current of excessive power passes through the component's fuse, the fuse blows out and breaks the circuit, saving the component from destruction.

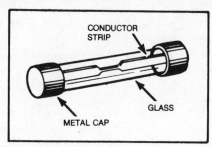

Typical automotive fuse

A circuit breaker is basically a self-repairing fuse. The circuit breaker opens the circuit the same way a fuse does. However, when either the short is removed from the circuit or the surge subsides, the circuit breaker resets itself and does not have to be replaced as a fuse does.

A fuse link is a wire that acts as a fuse. It is normally connected between the starter relay and the main wiring harness. This connection is usually under the hood. The fuse link (if installed) protects all the

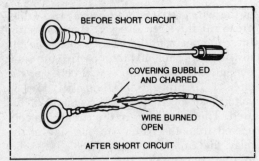

BEFORE SHORT CIRCUIT

COVERING BUBBLED
AND CHARRED

WIRE BURNED
OPEN

AFTER SHORT CIRCUIT

Most fusible links show a charred, melted insulation when they burn out

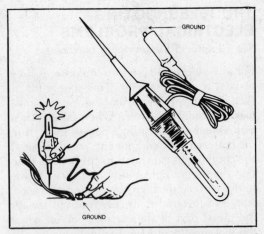

GROUND

GROUND

The test light will show the presence of current when touched to a hot wire and grounded at the other end

chassis electrical components, and is the probable cause of trouble when none of the electrical components function, unless the battery is disconnected or dead.

Electrical problems generally fall into one of three areas:

1. The component that is not functioning is not receiving current.

2. The component itself is not functioning.

3. The component is not properly grounded.

The electrical system can be checked with a test light and a jumper wire. A test light is a device that looks like a pointed screwdriver with a wire attached to it and has a light bulb in its handle. A jumper wire is a piece of insulated wire with an alligator clip attached to each end.

If a component is not working, you must follow a systematic plan to determine which of the three causes is the villain.

1. Turn on the switch that controls the inoperable component.

2. Disconnect the power supply wire from the component.

3. Attach the ground wire on the test light to a good metal ground.

4. Touch the probe end of the test light to the end of the power supply wire that was disconnected from the component. If the component is receiving current, the test light will go on.

NOTE: *Some components work only when the ignition switch is turned on.*

If the test light does not go on, then the problem is in the circuit between the battery and the component. This includes all the switches, fuses, and relays in the system. Follow the wire that runs back to the battery. The problem is an open circuit between the

battery and the component. If the fuse is blown and, when replaced, immediately blows again, there is a short circuit in the system which must be located and repaired. If there is a switch in the system, bypass it with a jumper wire. This is done by connecting one end of the jumper wire to the power supply wire into the switch and the other end of the jumper wire to the wire coming out of the switch. If the test light lights with the jumper wire installed, the switch or whatever was bypassed is defective.

NOTE: *Never substitute the jumper wire for the component, since it is required to use the power from the power source.*

5. If the bulb in the test light goes on, then the current is getting to the component that is not working. This eliminates the first of the three possible causes. Connect the power supply wire and connect a jumper wire from the component to a good metal ground. Do this with the switch which controls the component turned on, and also the ignition switch turned on if it is required for the component to work. If the component works with the jumper wire installed, then it has a bad ground. This is usually caused by the metal area on which the component mounts to the chassis being coated with some type of foreign matter.

6. If neither test located the source of the trouble, then the component itself is defective. Remember that for any electrical system to work, all connections must be clean and tight.

Troubleshooting Basic Turn Signal and Flasher Problems
See Chapter 5 for service procedures

Most problems in the turn signals or flasher system can be reduced to defective flashers or bulbs, which are easily replaced. Occasionally, the turn signal switch will prove defective.

F = Front   R = Rear   ● = Lights off   ○ = Lights on

Condition		Possible Cause
Turn signals light, but do not flash	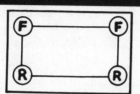	Defective flasher
No turn signals light on either side	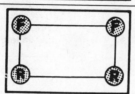	Blown fuse. Replace if defective. Defective flasher. Check by substitution. Open circuit, short circuit or poor ground.
Both turn signals on one side don't work	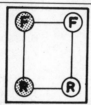	Bad bulbs. Bad ground in both (or either) housings.
One turn signal light on one side doesn't work	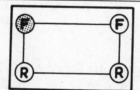	Defective bulb. Corrosion in socket. Clean contacts. Poor ground at socket.
Turn signal flashes too fast or too slowly	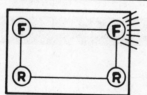	Check any bulb on the side flashing too fast. A heavy-duty bulb is probably installed in place of a regular bulb. Check the bulb flashing too slowly. A standard bulb was probably installed in place of a heavy-duty bulb. Loose connections or corrosion at the bulb socket.
Indicator lights don't work in either direction		Check if the turn signals are working. Check the dash indicator lights. Check the flasher by substitution.
One indicator light doesn't light		On systems with one dash indicator: See if the lights work on the same side. Often the filaments have been reversed in systems combining stoplights with taillights and turn signals. Check the flasher by substitution. On systems with two indicators: Check the bulbs on the same side. Check the indicator light bulb. Check the flasher by substitution.

Troubleshooting Lighting Problems
See Chapter 5 for service procedures

Condition	Possible Cause
One or more lights don't work, but others do	1. Defective bulb(s) 2. Blown fuse(s) 3. Dirty fuse clips or light sockets 4. Poor ground circuit
Lights burn out quickly	1. Incorrect voltage regulator setting or defective regulator 2. Poor battery/alternator connections
Lights go dim	1. Low/discharged battery 2. Alternator not charging 3. Corroded sockets or connections 4. Low voltage output
Lights flicker	1. Loose connection 2. Poor ground. (Run ground wire from light housing to frame) 3. Circuit breaker operating (short circuit)
Lights "flare"—Some flare is normal on acceleration—If excessive, see "Lights Burn Out Quickly"	High voltage setting
Lights glare—approaching drivers are blinded	1. Lights adjusted too high 2. Rear springs or shocks sagging 3. Rear tires soft

Troubleshooting Dash Gauge Problems

Most problems can be traced to a defective sending unit or faulty wiring. Occasionally, the gauge itself is at fault. See Chapter 5 for service procedures.

Condition	Possible Cause
COOLANT TEMPERATURE GAUGE	
Gauge reads erratically or not at all	1. Loose or dirty connections 2. Defective sending unit. 3. Defective gauge. To test a bi-metal gauge, remove the wire from the sending unit. Ground the wire for an instant. If the gauge registers, replace the sending unit. To test a magnetic gauge, disconnect the wire at the sending unit. With ignition ON gauge should register COLD. Ground the wire; gauge should register HOT.
AMMETER GAUGE—TURN HEADLIGHTS ON (DO NOT START ENGINE). NOTE REACTION	
Ammeter shows charge Ammeter shows discharge Ammeter does not move	1. Connections reversed on gauge 2. Ammeter is OK 3. Loose connections or faulty wiring 4. Defective gauge

Condition	Possible Cause

OIL PRESSURE GAUGE

Gauge does not register or is inaccurate	1. On mechanical gauge, Bourdon tube may be bent or kinked. 2. Low oil pressure. Remove sending unit. Idle the engine briefly. If no oil flows from sending unit hole, problem is in engine. 3. Defective gauge. Remove the wire from the sending unit and ground it for an instant with the ignition ON. A good gauge will go to the top of the scale. 4. Defective wiring. Check the wiring to the gauge. If it's OK and the gauge doesn't register when grounded, replace the gauge. 5. Defective sending unit.

ALL GAUGES

All gauges do not operate All gauges read low or erratically All gauges pegged	1. Blown fuse 2. Defective instrument regulator 3. Defective or dirty instrument voltage regulator 4. Loss of ground between instrument voltage regulator and frame 5. Defective instrument regulator

WARNING LIGHTS

Light(s) do not come on when ignition is ON, but engine is not started Light comes on with engine running	1. Defective bulb 2. Defective wire 3. Defective sending unit. Disconnect the wire from the sending unit and ground it. Replace the sending unit if the light comes on with the ignition ON. 4. Problem in individual system 5. Defective sending unit

Troubleshooting Clutch Problems

It is false economy to replace individual clutch components. The pressure plate, clutch plate and throwout bearing should be replaced as a set, and the flywheel face inspected, whenever the clutch is overhauled. See Chapter 6 for service procedures.

Condition	Possible Cause
Clutch chatter	1. Grease on driven plate (disc) facing 2. Binding clutch linkage or cable 3. Loose, damaged facings on driven plate (disc) 4. Engine mounts loose 5. Incorrect height adjustment of pressure plate release levers 6. Clutch housing or housing to transmission adapter misalignment 7. Loose driven plate hub
Clutch grabbing	1. Oil, grease on driven plate (disc) facing 2. Broken pressure plate 3. Warped or binding driven plate. Driven plate binding on clutch shaft
Clutch slips	1. Lack of lubrication in clutch linkage or cable (linkage or cable binds, causes incomplete engagement) 2. Incorrect pedal, or linkage adjustment 3. Broken pressure plate springs 4. Weak pressure plate springs 5. Grease on driven plate facings (disc)

Troubleshooting Clutch Problems (cont.)

Condition	Possible Cause
Incomplete clutch release	1. Incorrect pedal or linkage adjustment or linkage or cable binding 2. Incorrect height adjustment on pressure plate release levers 3. Loose, broken facings on driven plate (disc) 4. Bent, dished, warped driven plate caused by overheating
Grinding, whirring grating noise when pedal is depressed	1. Worn or defective throwout bearing 2. Starter drive teeth contacting flywheel ring gear teeth. Look for milled or polished teeth on ring gear.
Squeal, howl, trumpeting noise when pedal is being released (occurs during first inch to inch and one-half of pedal travel)	Pilot bushing worn or lack of lubricant. If bushing appears OK, polish bushing with emery cloth, soak lube wick in oil, lube bushing with oil, apply film of chassis grease to clutch shaft pilot hub, reassemble. NOTE: Bushing wear may be due to misalignment of clutch housing or housing to transmission adapter
Vibration or clutch pedal pulsation with clutch disengaged (pedal fully depressed)	1. Worn or defective engine transmission mounts 2. Flywheel run out. (Flywheel run out at face not to exceed 0.005″) 3. Damaged or defective clutch components

Troubleshooting Manual Transmission Problems
See Chapter 6 for service procedures

Condition	Possible Cause
Transmission jumps out of gear	1. Misalignment of transmission case or clutch housing. 2. Worn pilot bearing in crankshaft. 3. Bent transmission shaft. 4. Worn high speed sliding gear. 5. Worn teeth or end-play in clutch shaft. 6. Insufficient spring tension on shifter rail plunger. 7. Bent or loose shifter fork. 8. Gears not engaging completely. 9. Loose or worn bearings on clutch shaft or mainshaft. 10. Worn gear teeth. 11. Worn or damaged detent balls.
Transmission sticks in gear	1. Clutch not releasing fully. 2. Burred or battered teeth on clutch shaft, or sliding sleeve. 3. Burred or battered transmission mainshaft. 4. Frozen synchronizing clutch. 5. Stuck shifter rail plunger. 6. Gearshift lever twisting and binding shifter rail. 7. Battered teeth on high speed sliding gear or on sleeve. 8. Improper lubrication, or lack of lubrication. 9. Corroded transmission parts. 10. Defective mainshaft pilot bearing. 11. Locked gear bearings will give same effect as stuck in gear.
Transmission gears will not synchronize	1. Binding pilot bearing on mainshaft, will synchronize in high gear only. 2. Clutch not releasing fully. 3. Detent spring weak or broken. 4. Weak or broken springs under balls in sliding gear sleeve. 5. Binding bearing on clutch shaft, or binding countershaft. 6. Binding pilot bearing in crankshaft. 7. Badly worn gear teeth. 8. Improper lubrication. 9. Constant mesh gear not turning freely on transmission mainshaft. Will synchronize in that gear only.

Condition	Possible Cause
Gears spinning when shifting into gear from neutral	1. Clutch not releasing fully. 2. In some cases an extremely light lubricant in transmission will cause gears to continue to spin for a short time after clutch is released. 3. Binding pilot bearing in crankshaft.
Transmission noisy in all gears	1. Insufficient lubricant, or improper lubricant. 2. Worn countergear bearings. 3. Worn or damaged main drive gear or countergear. 4. Damaged main drive gear or mainshaft bearings. 5. Worn or damaged countergear anti-lash plate.
Transmission noisy in neutral only	1. Damaged main drive gear bearing. 2. Damaged or loose mainshaft pilot bearing. 3. Worn or damaged countergear anti-lash plate. 4. Worn countergear bearings.
Transmission noisy in one gear only	1. Damaged or worn constant mesh gears. 2. Worn or damaged countergear bearings. 3. Damaged or worn synchronizer.
Transmission noisy in reverse only	1. Worn or damaged reverse idler gear or idler bushing. 2. Worn or damaged mainshaft reverse gear. 3. Worn or damaged reverse countergear. 4. Damaged shift mechanism.

TROUBLESHOOTING AUTOMATIC TRANSMISSION PROBLEMS

Keeping alert to changes in the operating characteristics of the transmission (changing shift points, noises, etc.) can prevent small problems from becoming large ones. If the problem cannot be traced to loose bolts, fluid level, misadjusted linkage, clogged filters or similar problems, you should probably seek professional service.

Transmission Fluid Indications

The appearance and odor of the transmission fluid can give valuable clues to the overall condition of the transmission. Always note the appearance of the fluid when you check the fluid level or change the fluid. Rub a small amount of fluid between your fingers to feel for grit and smell the fluid on the dipstick.

If the fluid appears:	It indicates:
Clear and red colored	Normal operation
Discolored (extremely dark red or brownish) or smells burned	Band or clutch pack failure, usually caused by an overheated transmission. Hauling very heavy loads with insufficient power or failure to change the fluid often result in overheating. Do not confuse this appearance with newer fluids that have a darker red color and a strong odor (though not a burned odor).
Foamy or aerated (light in color and full of bubbles)	1. The level is too high (gear train is churning oil) 2. An internal air leak (air is mixing with the fluid). Have the transmission checked professionally.
Solid residue in the fluid	Defective bands, clutch pack or bearings. Bits of band material or metal abrasives are clinging to the dipstick. Have the transmission checked professionally.
Varnish coating on the dipstick	The transmission fluid is overheating

TROUBLESHOOTING DRIVE AXLE PROBLEMS

First, determine when the noise is most noticeable.

Drive Noise: Produced under vehicle acceleration.

Coast Noise: Produced while coasting with a closed throttle.

Float Noise: Occurs while maintaining constant speed (just enough to keep speed constant) on a level road.

External Noise Elimination

It is advisable to make a thorough road test to determine whether the noise originates in the rear axle or whether it originates from the tires, engine, transmission, wheel bearings or road surface. Noise originating from other places cannot be corrected by servicing the rear axle.

ROAD NOISE

Brick or rough surfaced concrete roads produce noises that seem to come from the rear axle. Road noise is usually identical in Drive or Coast and driving on a different type of road will tell whether the road is the problem.

TIRE NOISE

Tire noise can be mistaken as rear axle noise, even though the tires on the front are at fault. Snow tread and mud tread tires or tires worn unevenly will frequently cause vibrations which seem to originate elsewhere; *temporarily, and for test purposes only,* inflate the tires to 40–50 lbs. This will significantly alter the noise produced by the tires, but will not alter noise from the rear axle. Noises from the rear axle will normally cease at speeds below 30 mph on coast, while tire noise will continue at lower tone as speed is decreased. The rear axle noise will usually change from drive conditions to coast conditions, while tire noise will not. Do not forget to lower the tire pressure to normal after the test is complete.

ENGINE/TRANSMISSION NOISE

Determine at what speed the noise is most pronounced, then stop in a quiet place. With the transmission in Neutral, run the engine through speeds corresponding to road speeds where the noise was noticed. Noises produced with the vehicle standing still are coming from the engine or transmission.

FRONT WHEEL BEARINGS

Front wheel bearing noises, sometimes confused with rear axle noises, will not change when comparing drive and coast conditions. While holding the speed steady, lightly apply the footbrake. This will often cause wheel bearing noise to lessen, as some of the weight is taken off the bearing. Front wheel bearings are easily checked by jacking up the wheels and spinning the wheels. Shaking the wheels will also determine if the wheel bearings are excessively loose.

REAR AXLE NOISES

Eliminating other possible sources can narrow the cause to the rear axle, which normally produces noise from worn gears or bearings. Gear noises tend to peak in a narrow speed range, while bearing noises will usually vary in pitch with engine speeds.

Noise Diagnosis

The Noise Is:	Most Probably Produced By:
1. Identical under Drive or Coast	Road surface, tires or front wheel bearings
2. Different depending on road surface	Road surface or tires
3. Lower as speed is lowered	Tires
4. Similar when standing or moving	Engine or transmission
5. A vibration	Unbalanced tires, rear wheel bearing, unbalanced driveshaft or worn U-joint
6. A knock or click about every two tire revolutions	Rear wheel bearing
7. Most pronounced on turns	Damaged differential gears
8. A steady low-pitched whirring or scraping, starting at low speeds	Damaged or worn pinion bearing
9. A chattering vibration on turns	Wrong differential lubricant or worn clutch plates (limited slip rear axle)
10. Noticed only in Drive, Coast or Float conditions	Worn ring gear and/or pinion gear

Troubleshooting Steering & Suspension Problems

Condition	Possible Cause
Hard steering (wheel is hard to turn)	1. Improper tire pressure 2. Loose or glazed pump drive belt 3. Low or incorrect fluid 4. Loose, bent or poorly lubricated front end parts 5. Improper front end alignment (excessive caster) 6. Bind in steering column or linkage 7. Kinked hydraulic hose 8. Air in hydraulic system 9. Low pump output or leaks in system 10. Obstruction in lines 11. Pump valves sticking or out of adjustment 12. Incorrect wheel alignment
Loose steering (too much play in steering wheel)	1. Loose wheel bearings 2. Faulty shocks 3. Worn linkage or suspension components 4. Loose steering gear mounting or linkage points 5. Steering mechanism worn or improperly adjusted 6. Valve spool improperly adjusted 7. Worn ball joints, tie-rod ends, etc.
Veers or wanders (pulls to one side with hands off steering wheel)	1. Improper tire pressure 2. Improper front end alignment 3. Dragging or improperly adjusted brakes 4. Bent frame 5. Improper rear end alignment 6. Faulty shocks or springs 7. Loose or bent front end components 8. Play in Pitman arm 9. Steering gear mountings loose 10. Loose wheel bearings 11. Binding Pitman arm 12. Spool valve sticking or improperly adjusted 13. Worn ball joints
Wheel oscillation or vibration transmitted through steering wheel	1. Low or uneven tire pressure 2. Loose wheel bearings 3. Improper front end alignment 4. Bent spindle 5. Worn, bent or broken front end components 6. Tires out of round or out of balance 7. Excessive lateral runout in disc brake rotor 8. Loose or bent shock absorber or strut
Noises (see also "Troubleshooting Drive Axle Problems")	1. Loose belts 2. Low fluid, air in system 3. Foreign matter in system 4. Improper lubrication 5. Interference or chafing in linkage 6. Steering gear mountings loose 7. Incorrect adjustment or wear in gear box 8. Faulty valves or wear in pump 9. Kinked hydraulic lines 10. Worn wheel bearings
Poor return of steering	1. Over-inflated tires 2. Improperly aligned front end (excessive caster) 3. Binding in steering column 4. No lubrication in front end 5. Steering gear adjusted too tight
Uneven tire wear (see "How To Read Tire Wear")	1. Incorrect tire pressure 2. Improperly aligned front end 3. Tires out-of-balance 4. Bent or worn suspension parts

HOW TO READ TIRE WEAR

The way your tires wear is a good indicator of other parts of the suspension. Abnormal wear patterns are often caused by the need for simple tire maintenance, or for front end alignment.

Excessive wear at the center of the tread indicates that the air pressure in the tire is consistently too high. The tire is riding on the center of the tread and wearing it prematurely. Occasionally, this wear pattern can result from outrageously wide tires on narrow rims. The cure for this is to replace either the tires or the wheels.

This type of wear usually results from consistent under-inflation. When a tire is under-inflated, there is too much contact with the road by the outer treads, which wear prematurely. When this type of wear occurs, and the tire pressure is known to be consistently correct, a bent or worn steering component or the need for wheel alignment could be indicated.

Feathering is a condition when the edge of each tread rib develops a slightly rounded edge on one side and a sharp edge on the other. By running your hand over the tire, you can usually feel the sharper edges before you'll be able to see them. The most common causes of feathering are incorrect toe-in setting or deteriorated bushings in the front suspension.

When an inner or outer rib wears faster than the rest of the tire, the need for wheel alignment is indicated. There is excessive camber in the front suspension, causing the wheel to lean too much putting excessive load on one side of the tire. Misalignment could also be due to sagging springs, worn ball joints, or worn control arm bushings. Be sure the vehicle is loaded the way it's normally driven when you have the wheels aligned.

Cups or scalloped dips appearing around the edge of the tread almost always indicate worn (sometimes bent) suspension parts. Adjustment of wheel alignment alone will seldom cure the problem. Any worn component that connects the wheel to the suspension can cause this type of wear. Occasionally, wheels that are out of balance will wear like this, but wheel imbalance usually shows up as bald spots between the outside edges and center of the tread.

Second-rib wear is usually found only in radial tires, and appears where the steel belts end in relation to the tread. It can be kept to a minimum by paying careful attention to tire pressure and frequently rotating the tires. This is often considered normal wear but excessive amounts indicate that the tires are too wide for the wheels.

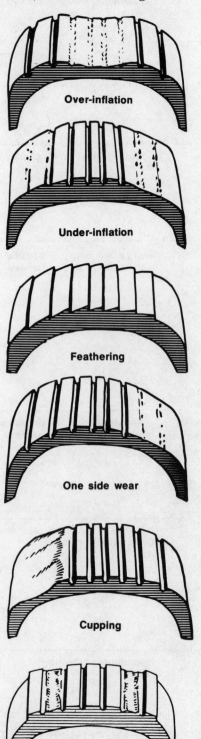

Over-inflation

Under-inflation

Feathering

One side wear

Cupping

Second-rib wear

Troubleshooting Disc Brake Problems

Condition	Possible Cause
Noise—groan—brake noise emanating when slowly releasing brakes (creep-groan)	Not detrimental to function of disc brakes—no corrective action required. (This noise may be eliminated by slightly increasing or decreasing brake pedal efforts.)
Rattle—brake noise or rattle emanating at low speeds on rough roads, (front wheels only).	1. Shoe anti-rattle spring missing or not properly positioned. 2. Excessive clearance between shoe and caliper. 3. Soft or broken caliper seals. 4. Deformed or misaligned disc. 5. Loose caliper.
Scraping	1. Mounting bolts too long. 2. Loose wheel bearings. 3. Bent, loose, or misaligned splash shield.
Front brakes heat up during driving and fail to release	1. Operator riding brake pedal. 2. Stop light switch improperly adjusted. 3. Sticking pedal linkage. 4. Frozen or seized piston. 5. Residual pressure valve in master cylinder. 6. Power brake malfunction. 7. Proportioning valve malfunction.
Leaky brake caliper	1. Damaged or worn caliper piston seal. 2. Scores or corrosion on surface of cylinder bore.
Grabbing or uneven brake action—Brakes pull to one side	1. Causes listed under "Brakes Pull". 2. Power brake malfunction. 3. Low fluid level in master cylinder. 4. Air in hydraulic system. 5. Brake fluid, oil or grease on linings. 6. Unmatched linings. 7. Distorted brake pads. 8. Frozen or seized pistons. 9. Incorrect tire pressure. 10. Front end out of alignment. 11. Broken rear spring. 12. Brake caliper pistons sticking. 13. Restricted hose or line. 14. Caliper not in proper alignment to braking disc. 15. Stuck or malfunctioning metering valve. 16. Soft or broken caliper seals. 17. Loose caliper.
Brake pedal can be depressed without braking effect	1. Air in hydraulic system or improper bleeding procedure. 2. Leak past primary cup in master cylinder. 3. Leak in system. 4. Rear brakes out of adjustment. 5. Bleeder screw open.
Excessive pedal travel	1. Air, leak, or insufficient fluid in system or caliper. 2. Warped or excessively tapered shoe and lining assembly. 3. Excessive disc runout. 4. Rear brake adjustment required. 5. Loose wheel bearing adjustment. 6. Damaged caliper piston seal. 7. Improper brake fluid (boil). 8. Power brake malfunction. 9. Weak or soft hoses.

Troubleshooting Disc Brake Problems (cont.)

Condition	Possible Cause
Brake roughness or chatter (pedal pumping)	1. Excessive thickness variation of braking disc. 2. Excessive lateral runout of braking disc. 3. Rear brake drums out-of-round. 4. Excessive front bearing clearance.
Excessive pedal effort	1. Brake fluid, oil or grease on linings. 2. Incorrect lining. 3. Frozen or seized pistons. 4. Power brake malfunction. 5. Kinked or collapsed hose or line. 6. Stuck metering valve. 7. Scored caliper or master cylinder bore. 8. Seized caliper pistons.
Brake pedal fades (pedal travel increases with foot on brake)	1. Rough master cylinder or caliper bore. 2. Loose or broken hydraulic lines/connections. 3. Air in hydraulic system. 4. Fluid level low. 5. Weak or soft hoses. 6. Inferior quality brake shoes or fluid. 7. Worn master cylinder piston cups or seals.

Troubleshooting Drum Brakes

Condition	Possible Cause
Pedal goes to floor	1. Fluid low in reservoir. 2. Air in hydraulic system. 3. Improperly adjusted brake. 4. Leaking wheel cylinders. 5. Loose or broken brake lines. 6. Leaking or worn master cylinder. 7. Excessively worn brake lining.
Spongy brake pedal	1. Air in hydraulic system. 2. Improper brake fluid (low boiling point). 3. Excessively worn or cracked brake drums. 4. Broken pedal pivot bushing.
Brakes pulling	1. Contaminated lining. 2. Front end out of alignment. 3. Incorrect brake adjustment. 4. Unmatched brake lining. 5. Brake drums out of round. 6. Brake shoes distorted. 7. Restricted brake hose or line. 8. Broken rear spring. 9. Worn brake linings. 10. Uneven lining wear. 11. Glazed brake lining. 12. Excessive brake lining dust. 13. Heat spotted brake drums. 14. Weak brake return springs. 15. Faulty automatic adjusters. 16. Low or incorrect tire pressure.

Condition	Possible Cause
Squealing brakes	1. Glazed brake lining. 2. Saturated brake lining. 3. Weak or broken brake shoe retaining spring. 4. Broken or weak brake shoe return spring. 5. Incorrect brake lining. 6. Distorted brake shoes. 7. Bent support plate. 8. Dust in brakes or scored brake drums. 9. Linings worn below limit. 10. Uneven brake lining wear. 11. Heat spotted brake drums.
Chirping brakes	1. Out of round drum or eccentric axle flange pilot.
Dragging brakes	1. Incorrect wheel or parking brake adjustment. 2. Parking brakes engaged or improperly adjusted. 3. Weak or broken brake shoe return spring. 4. Brake pedal binding. 5. Master cylinder cup sticking. 6. Obstructed master cylinder relief port. 7. Saturated brake lining. 8. Bent or out of round brake drum. 9. Contaminated or improper brake fluid. 10. Sticking wheel cylinder pistons. 11. Driver riding brake pedal. 12. Defective proportioning valve. 13. Insufficient brake shoe lubricant.
Hard pedal	1. Brake booster inoperative. 2. Incorrect brake lining. 3. Restricted brake line or hose. 4. Frozen brake pedal linkage. 5. Stuck wheel cylinder. 6. Binding pedal linkage. 7. Faulty proportioning valve.
Wheel locks	1. Contaminated brake lining. 2. Loose or torn brake lining. 3. Wheel cylinder cups sticking. 4. Incorrect wheel bearing adjustment. 5. Faulty proportioning valve.
Brakes fade (high speed)	1. Incorrect lining. 2. Overheated brake drums. 3. Incorrect brake fluid (low boiling temperature). 4. Saturated brake lining. 5. Leak in hydraulic system. 6. Faulty automatic adjusters.
Pedal pulsates	1. Bent or out of round brake drum.
Brake chatter and shoe knock	1. Out of round brake drum. 2. Loose support plate. 3. Bent support plate. 4. Distorted brake shoes. 5. Machine grooves in contact face of brake drum (Shoe Knock). 6. Contaminated brake lining. 7. Missing or loose components. 8. Incorrect lining material. 9. Out-of-round brake drums. 10. Heat spotted or scored brake drums. 11. Out-of-balance wheels.

Troubleshooting Drum Brakes (cont.)

Condition	Possible Cause
Brakes do not self adjust	1. Adjuster screw frozen in thread. 2. Adjuster screw corroded at thrust washer. 3. Adjuster lever does not engage star wheel. 4. Adjuster installed on wrong wheel.
Brake light glows	1. Leak in the hydraulic system. 2. Air in the system. 3. Improperly adjusted master cylinder pushrod. 4. Uneven lining wear. 5. Failure to center combination valve or proportioning valve.

Mechanic's Data

General Conversion Table

Multiply By	To Convert	To	
		LENGTH	
2.54	Inches	Centimeters	.3937
25.4	Inches	Millimeters	.03937
30.48	Feet	Centimeters	.0328
.304	Feet	Meters	3.28
.914	Yards	Meters	1.094
1.609	Miles	Kilometers	.621
		VOLUME	
.473	Pints	Liters	2.11
.946	Quarts	Liters	1.06
3.785	Gallons	Liters	.264
.016	Cubic inches	Liters	61.02
16.39	Cubic inches	Cubic cms.	.061
28.3	Cubic feet	Liters	.0353
		MASS (Weight)	
28.35	Ounces	Grams	.035
.4536	Pounds	Kilograms	2.20
—	To obtain	From	Multiply by

Multiply By	To Convert	To	
		AREA	
.645	Square inches	Square cms.	.155
.836	Square yds.	Square meters	1.196
		FORCE	
4.448	Pounds	Newtons	.225
.138	Ft./lbs.	Kilogram/meters	7.23
1.36	Ft./lbs.	Newton-meters	.737
.112	In./lbs.	Newton-meters	8.844
		PRESSURE	
.068	Psi	Atmospheres	14.7
6.89	Psi	Kilopascals	.145
		OTHER	
1.104	Horsepower (DIN)	Horsepower (SAE)	.9861
.746	Horsepower (SAE)	Kilowatts (KW)	1.34
1.60	Mph	Km/h	.625
.425	Mpg	Km/1	2.35
—	To obtain	From	Multiply by

Tap Drill Sizes

National Coarse or U.S.S.

Screw & Tap Size	Threads Per Inch	Use Drill Number
No. 5	40	39
No. 6	32	36
No. 8	32	29
No. 10	24	25
No. 12	24	17
1/4	20	8
5/16	18	F
3/8	16	5/16
7/16	14	U
1/2	13	27/64
9/16	12	31/64
5/8	11	17/32
3/4	10	21/32
7/8	9	49/64

National Coarse or U.S.S.

Screw & Tap Size	Threads Per Inch	Use Drill Number
1	8	7/8
1 1/8	7	63/64
1 1/4	7	1 7/64
1 1/2	6	1 11/32

National Fine or S.A.E.

Screw & Tap Size	Threads Per Inch	Use Drill Number
No. 5	44	37
No. 6	40	33
No. 8	36	29
No. 10	32	21

National Fine or S.A.E.

Screw & Tap Size	Threads Per Inch	Use Drill Number
No. 12	28	15
1/4	28	3
6/16	24	1
3/8	24	Q
7/16	20	W
1/2	20	29/64
9/16	18	33/64
5/8	18	37/64
3/4	16	11/16
7/8	14	13/16
1 1/8	12	1 3/64
1 1/4	12	1 11/64
1 1/2	12	1 27/64

Drill Sizes In Decimal Equivalents

Inch	Decimal	Wire & Letter	mm
1/64	.0156		.39
	.0157		.4
	.0160	78	
	.0165		.42
	.0173		.44
	.0177		.45
	.0180	77	
	.0181		.46
	.0189		.48
	.0197		.5
	.0200	76	
	.0210	75	
	.0217		.55
	.0225	74	
	.0236		.6
	.0240	73	
	.0250	72	
	.0256		.65
	.0260	71	
	.0276		.7
	.0280	70	
	.0292	69	
	.0295		.75
	.0310	68	
1/32	.0312		.79
	.0315		.8
	.0320	67	
	.0330	66	
	.0335		.85
	.0350	65	
	.0354		.9
	.0360	64	
	.0370	63	
	.0374		.95
	.0380	62	
	.0390	61	
	.0394		1.0
	.0400	60	
	.0410	59	
	.0413		1.05
	.0420	58	
	.0430	57	
	.0433		1.1
	.0453		1.15
	.0465	56	
3/64	.0469		1.19
	.0472		1.2
	.0492		1.25
	.0512		1.3
	.0520	55	
	.0531		1.35
	.0550	54	
	.0551		1.4
	.0571		1.45
	.0591		1.5
	.0595	53	
	.0610		1.55
1/16	.0625		1.59
	.0630		1.6
	.0635	52	
	.0650		1.65
	.0669		1.7
	.0670	51	
	.0689		1.75
	.0700	50	
	.0709		1.8
	.0728		1.85
	.0730	49	
	.0748		1.9
	.0760	48	
	.0768		1.95
5/64	.0781		1.98
	.0785	47	
	.0787		2.0
	.0807		2.05
	.0810	46	
	.0820	45	
	.0827		2.1
	.0846		2.15
	.0860	44	
	.0866		2.2
	.0886		2.25
	.0890	43	
	.0906		2.3
	.0925		2.35
	.0935	42	
3/32	.0938		2.38
	.0945		2.4
	.0960	41	
	.0965		2.45
	.0980	40	
	.0981		2.5
	.0995	39	
	.1015	38	
	.1024		2.6
	.1040	37	
	.1063		2.7
	.1065	36	
	.1083		2.75
7/64	.1094		2.77
	.1100	35	
	.1102		2.8
	.1110	34	
	.1130	33	
	.1142		2.9
	.1160	32	
	.1181		3.0
	.1200	31	
	.1220		3.1
1/8	.1250		3.17
	.1260		3.2
	.1280		3.25
	.1285	30	
	.1299		3.3
	.1339		3.4
	.1360	29	
	.1378		3.5
	.1405	28	
9/64	.1406		3.57
	.1417		3.6
	.1440	27	
	.1457		3.7
	.1470	26	
	.1476		3.75
	.1495	25	
	.1496		3.8
	.1520	24	
	.1535		3.9
	.1540	23	
5/32	.1562		3.96
	.1570	22	
	.1575		4.0
	.1590	21	
	.1610	20	
	.1614		4.1
	.1654		4.2
	.1660	19	
	.1673		4.25
	.1693		4.3
	.1695	18	
11/64	.1719		4.36
	.1730	17	
	.1732		4.4
	.1770	16	
	.1772		4.5
	.1800	15	
	.1811		4.6
	.1820	14	
	.1850	13	
	.1850		4.7
	.1870		4.75
3/16	.1875		4.76
	.1890		4.8
	.1890	12	
	.1910	11	
	.1929		4.9
	.1935	10	
	.1960	9	
	.1969		5.0
	.1990	8	
	.2008		5.1
	.2010	7	
13/64	.2031		5.16
	.2040	6	
	.2047		5.2
	.2055	5	
	.2067		5.25
	.2087		5.3
	.2090	4	
	.2126		5.4
	.2130	3	
7/32	.2188		5.5
	.2205		5.6
	.2210	2	
	.2244		5.7
	.2264		5.75
	.2280	1	
	.2283		5.8
	.2323		5.9
15/64	.2344		5.95
	.2340	A	
	.2362		6.0
	.2380	B	
	.2402		6.1
	.2420	C	
	.2441		6.2
	.2460	D	
	.2461		6.25
	.2480		6.3
1/4	.2500	E	6.35
	.2520		6.
	.2559		6.5
	.2570	F	
	.2598		6.6
	.2610	G	
	.2638		6.7
17/64	.2656		6.74
	.2657		6.75
	.2660	H	
	.2677		6.8
	.2717		6.9
	.2720	I	
	.2756		7.0
	.2770	J	
	.2795		7.1
	.2810	K	
9/32	.2812		7.14
	.2835		7.2
	.2854		7.25
	.2874		7.3
	.2900	L	
	.2913		7.4
	.2950	M	
	.2953		7.5
19/64	.2969		7.54
	.2992		7.6
	.3020	N	
	.3031		7.7
	.3051		7.75
	.3071		7.8
	.3110		7.9
5/16	.3125		7.93
	.3150		8.0
	.3160	O	
	.3189		8.1
	.3228		8.2
	.3230	P	
	.3248		8.25
	.3268		8.3
21/64	.3281		8.33
	.3307		8.4
	.3320	Q	
	.3346		8.5
	.3386		8.6
	.3390	R	
	.3425		8.7
11/32	.3438		8.73
	.3445		8.75
	.3465		8.8
	.3480	S	
	.3504		8.9
	.3543		9.0
	.3580	T	
	.3583		9.1
23/64	.3594		9.12
	.3622		9.2
	.3642		9.25
	.3661		9.3
	.3680	U	
	.3701		9.4
	.3740		9.5
3/8	.3750		9.52
	.3770	V	
	.3780		9.6
	.3819		9.7
	.3839		9.75
	.3858		9.8
	.3860	W	
	.3898		9.9
25/64	.3906		9.92
	.3937		10.0
	.3970	X	
	.4040	Y	
13/32	.4062		10.31
	.4130	Z	
	.4134		10.5
27/64	.4219		10.71
	.4331		11.0
7/16	.4375		11.11
	.4528		11.5
29/64	.4531		11.51
15/32	.4688		11.90
	.4724		12.0
31/64	.4844		12.30
	.4921		12.5
1/2	.5000		12.70
	.5118		13.0
33/64	.5156		13.09
17/32	.5312		13.49
	.5315		13.5
35/64	.5469		13.89
	.5512		14.0
9/16	.5625		14.28
	.5709		14.5
37/64	.5781		14.68
	.5906		15.0
19/32	.5938		15.08
39/64	.6094		15.47
	.6102		15.5
5/8	.6250		15.87
	.6299		16.0
41/64	.6406		16.27
	.6496		16.5
21/32	.6562		16.66
	.6693		17.0
43/64	.6719		17.06
11/16	.6875		17.46
	.6890		17.5
45/64	.7031		17.85
	.7087		18.0
23/32	.7188		18.25
	.7283		18.5
47/64	.7344		18.65
	.7480		19.0
3/4	.7500		19.05
49/64	.7656		19.44
	.7677		19.5
25/32	.7812		19.84
	.7874		20.0
51/64	.7969		20.24
	.8071		20.5
13/16	.8125		20.63
	.8268		21.0
53/64	.8281		21.03
27/32	.8438		21.43
	.8465		21.5
55/64	.8594		21.82
	.8661		22.0
7/8	.8750		22.22
	.8858		22.5
57/64	.8906		22.62
	.9055		23.0
29/32	.9062		23.01
59/64	.9219		23.41
	.9252		23.5
15/16	.9375		23.81
	.9449		24.0
61/64	.9531		24.2
	.9646		24.5
31/32	.9688		24.6
	.9843		25.0
63/64	.9844		25.0
1	1.0000		25.4

Index

Chilton's Repair & Tune-Up Guides

The Complete line covers domestic cars, imports, trucks, vans, RV's and 4-wheel drive vehicles.

RTUG Title	Part No.
AMC 1975-82	7199
Covers all U.S. and Canadian models	
Aspen/Volare 1976-80	6637
Covers all U.S. and Canadian models	
Audi 1970-73	5902
Covers all U.S. and Canadian models.	
Audi 4000/5000 1978-81	7028
Covers all U.S. and Canadian models including turbocharged and diesel engines	
Barracuda/Challenger 1965-72	5807
Covers all U.S. and Canadian models	
Blazer/Jimmy 1969-82	6931
Covers all U.S. and Canadian 2- and 4-wheel drive models, including diesel engines	
BMW 1970-82	6844
Covers U.S. and Canadian models	
Buick/Olds/Pontiac 1975-85	7308
Covers all U.S. and Canadian full size rear wheel drive models	
Cadillac 1967-84	7462
Covers all U.S. and Canadian rear wheel drive models	
Camaro 1967-81	6735
Covers all U.S. and Canadian models	
Camaro 1982-85	7317
Covers all U.S. and Canadian models	
Capri 1970-77	6695
Covers all U.S. and Canadian models	
Caravan/Voyager 1984-85	7482
Covers all U.S. and Canadian models	
Century/Regal 1975-85	7307
Covers all U.S. and Canadian rear wheel drive models, including turbocharged engines	
Champ/Arrow/Sapporo 1978-83	7041
Covers all U.S. and Canadian models	
Chevette/1000 1976-86	6836
Covers all U.S. and Canadian models	
Chevrolet 1968-85	7135
Covers all U.S. and Canadian models	
Chevrolet 1968-79 Spanish	7082
Chevrolet/GMC Pick-Ups 1970-82 Spanish	7468
Chevrolet/GMC Pick-Ups and Suburban 1970-86	6936
Covers all U.S. and Canadian 1/2, 3/4 and 1 ton models, including 4-wheel drive and diesel engines	
Chevrolet LUV 1972-81	6815
Covers all U.S. and Canadian models	
Chevrolet Mid-Size 1964-86	6840
Covers all U.S. and Canadian models of 1964-77 Chevelle, Malibu and Malibu SS; 1974-77 Laguna; 1978-85 Malibu; 1970-86 Monte Carlo; 1964-84 El Camino, including diesel engines	
Chevrolet Nova 1986	7658
Covers all U.S. and Canadian models	
Chevy/GMC Vans 1967-84	6930
Covers all U.S. and Canadian models of 1/2, 3/4, and 1 ton vans, cutaways, and motor home chassis, including diesel engines	
Chevy S-10 Blazer/GMC S-15 Jimmy 1982-85	7383
Covers all U.S. and Canadian models	
Chevy S-10/GMC S-15 Pick-Ups 1982-85	7310
Covers all U.S. and Canadian models	
Chevy II/Nova 1962-79	6841
Covers all U.S. and Canadian models	
Chrysler K- and E-Car 1981-85	7163
Covers all U.S. and Canadian front wheel drive models	
Colt/Challenger/Vista/Conquest 1971-85	7037
Covers all U.S. and Canadian models	
Corolla/Carina/Tercel/Starlet 1970-85	7036
Covers all U.S. and Canadian models	
Corona/Cressida/Crown/Mk.II/Camry/Van 1970-84	7044
Covers all U.S. and Canadian models	

RTUG Title	Part No.
Corvair 1960-69	6691
Covers all U.S. and Canadian models	
Corvette 1953-62	6576
Covers all U.S. and Canadian models	
Corvette 1963-84	6843
Covers all U.S. and Canadian models	
Cutlass 1970-85	6933
Covers all U.S. and Canadian models	
Dart/Demon 1968-76	6324
Covers all U.S. and Canadian models	
Datsun 1961-72	5790
Covers all U.S. and Canadian models of Nissan Patrol; 1500, 1600 and 2000 sports cars; Pick-Ups; 410, 411, 510, 1200 and 240Z	
Datsun 1973-80 Spanish	7083
Datsun/Nissan F-10, 310, Stanza, Pulsar 1977-86	7196
Covers all U.S. and Canadian models	
Datsun/Nissan Pick-Ups 1970-84	6816
Covers all U.S and Canadian models	
Datsun/Nissan Z & ZX 1970-86	6932
Covers all U.S. and Canadian models	
Datsun/Nissan 1200, 210, Sentra 1973-86	7197
Covers all U.S. and Canadian models	
Datsun/Nissan 200SX, 510, 610, 710, 810, Maxima 1973-84	7170
Covers all U.S. and Canadian models	
Dodge 1968-77	6554
Covers all U.S. and Canadian models	
Dodge Charger 1967-70	6486
Covers all U.S. and Canadian models	
Dodge/Plymouth Trucks 1967-84	7459
Covers all 1/2, 3/4, and 1 ton 2- and 4-wheel drive U.S. and Canadian models, including diesel engines	
Dodge/Plymouth Vans 1967-84	6934
Covers all 1/2, 3/4, and 1 ton U.S. and Canadian models of vans, cutaways and motor home chassis	
D-50/Arrow Pick-Up 1979-81	7032
Covers all U.S. and Canadian models	
Fairlane/Torino 1962-75	6320
Covers all U.S. and Canadian models	
Fairmont/Zephyr 1978-83	6965
Covers all U.S. and Canadian models	
Fiat 1969-81	7042
Covers all U.S. and Canadian models	
Fiesta 1978-80	6846
Covers all U.S. and Canadian models	
Firebird 1967-81	5996
Covers all U.S. and Canadian models	
Firebird 1982-85	7345
Covers all U.S. and Canadian models	
Ford 1968-79 Spanish	7084
Ford Bronco 1966-83	7140
Covers all U.S. and Canadian models	
Ford Bronco II 1984	7408
Covers all U.S. and Canadian models	
Ford Courier 1972-82	6983
Covers all U.S. and Canadian models	
Ford/Mercury Front Wheel Drive 1981-85	7055
Covers all U.S. and Canadian models Escort, EXP, Tempo, Lynx, LN-7 and Topaz	
Ford/Mercury/Lincoln 1968-85	6842
Covers all U.S. and Canadian models of FORD Country Sedan, Country Squire, Crown Victoria, Custom, Custom 500, Galaxie 500, LTD through 1982, Ranch Wagon, and XL; MERCURY Colony Park, Commuter, Marquis through 1982, Gran Marquis, Monterey and Park Lane; LINCOLN Continental and Towne Car	
Ford/Mercury/Lincoln Mid-Size 1971-85	6696
Covers all U.S. and Canadian models of FORD Elite, 1983-85 LTD, 1977-79 LTD II, Ranchero, Torino, Gran Torino, 1977-85 Thunderbird; MERCURY 1972-85 Cougar,	

continued on next page

RTUG Title	Part No.	RTUG Title	Part No.
1983-85 Marquis, Montego, 1980-85 XR-7; LINCOLN 1982-85 Continental, 1984-85 Mark VII, 1978-80 Versailles		**Mercedes-Benz 1974-84** Covers all U.S. and Canadian models	6809
Ford Pick-Ups 1965-86 Covers all $1/2$, $3/4$ and 1 ton, 2- and 4-wheel drive U.S. and Canadian pick-up, chassis cab and camper models, including diesel engines	6913	**Mitsubishi, Cordia, Tredia, Starion, Galant 1983-85** Covers all U.S. and Canadian models	7583
Ford Pick-Ups 1965-82 Spanish	7469	**MG 1961-81** Covers all U.S. and Canadian models	6780
Ford Ranger 1983-84 Covers all U.S. and Canadian models	7338	**Mustang/Capri/Merkur 1979-85** Covers all U.S. and Canadian models	6963
Ford Vans 1961-86 Covers all U.S. and Canadian $1/2$, $3/4$ and 1 ton van and cutaway chassis models, including diesel engines	6849	**Mustang/Cougar 1965-73** Covers all U.S. and Canadian models	6542
		Mustang II 1974-78 Covers all U.S. and Canadian models	6812
GM A-Body 1982-85 Covers all front wheel drive U.S. and Canadian models of BUICK Century, CHEVROLET Celebrity, OLDSMOBILE Cutlass Ciera and PONTIAC 6000	7309	**Omni/Horizon/Rampage 1978-84** Covers all U.S. and Canadian models of DODGE omni, Miser, 024, Charger 2.2; PLYMOUTH Horizon, Miser, -TC3, TC3 Tourismo; Rampage	6845
GM C-Body 1985 Covers all front wheel drive U.S. and Canadian models of BUICK Electra Park Avenue and Electra T-Type, CADILLAC Fleetwood and deVille, OLDSMOBILE 98 Regency and Regency Brougham	7587	**Opel 1971-75** Covers all U.S. and Canadian models	6575
		Peugeot 1970-74 Covers all U.S. and Canadian models	5982
		Pinto/Bobcat 1971-80 Covers all U.S. and Canadian models	7027
GM J-Car 1982-85 Covers all U.S. and Canadian models of BUICK Skyhawk, CHEVROLET Cavalier, CADILLAC Cimarron, OLDSMOBILE Firenza and PONTIAC 2000 and Sunbird	7059	**Plymouth 1968-76** Covers all U.S. and Canadian models	6552
		Pontiac Fiero 1984-85 Covers all U.S. and Canadian models	7571
GM N-Body 1985-86 Covers all U.S. and Canadian models of front wheel drive BUICK Somerset and Skylark, OLDSMOBILE Calais, and PONTIAC Grand Am	7657	**Pontiac Mid-Size 1974-83** Covers all U.S. and Canadian models of Ventura, Grand Am, LeMans, Grand LeMans, GTO, Phoenix, and Grand Prix	7346
		Porsche 924/928 1976-81 Covers all U.S. and Canadian models	7048
GM X-Body 1980-85 Covers all U.S. and Canadian models of BUICK Skylark, CHEVROLET Citation, OLDSMOBILE Omega and PONTIAC Phoenix	7049	**Renault 1975-85** Covers all U.S. and Canadian models	7165
		Roadrunner/Satellite/Belvedere/GTX 1968-73 Covers all U.S. and Canadian models	5821
GM Subcompact 1971-80 Covers all U.S. and Canadian models of BUICK Skyhawk (1975-80), CHEVROLET Vega and Monza, OLDSMOBILE Starfire, and PONTIAC Astre and 1975-80 Sunbird	6935	**RX-7 1979-81** Covers all U.S. and Canadian models	7031
		SAAB 99 1969-75 Covers all U.S. and Canadian models	5988
		SAAB 900 1979-85 Covers all U.S. and Canadian models	7572
Granada/Monarch 1975-82 Covers all U.S. and Canadian models	6937	**Snowmobiles 1976-80** Covers Arctic Cat, John Deere, Kawasaki, Polaris, Ski-Doo and Yamaha	6978
Honda 1973-84 Covers all U.S. and Canadian models	6980	**Subaru 1970-84** Covers all U.S. and Canadian models	6982
International Scout 1967-73 Covers all U.S. and Canadian models	5912	**Tempest/GTO/LeMans 1968-73** Covers all U.S. and Canadian models	5905
Jeep 1945-87 Covers all U.S. and Canadian CJ-2A, CJ-3A, CJ-3B, CJ-5, CJ-6, CJ-7, Scrambler and Wrangler models	6817	**Toyota 1966-70** Covers all U.S. and Canadian models of Corona, MkII, Corolla, Crown, Land Cruiser, Stout and Hi-Lux	5795
		Toyota 1970-79 Spanish	7467
Jeep Wagoneer, Commando, Cherokee, Truck 1957-86 Covers all U.S. and Canadian models of Wagoneer, Cherokee, Grand Wagoneer, Jeepster, Jeepster Commando, J-100, J-200, J-300, J-10, J20, FC-150 and FC-170	6739	**Toyota Celica/Supra 1971-85** Covers all U.S. and Canadian models	7043
		Toyota Trucks 1970-85 Covers all U.S. and Canadian models of pick-ups, Land Cruiser and 4Runner	7035
		Valiant/Duster 1968-76 Covers all U.S. and Canadian models	6326
Laser/Daytona 1984-85 Covers all U.S. and Canadian models	7563	**Volvo 1956-69** Covers all U.S. and Canadian models	6529
Maverick/Comet 1970-77 Covers all U.S. and Canadian models	6634	**Volvo 1970-83** Covers all U.S. and Canadian models	7040
Mazda 1971-84 Covers all U.S. and Canadian models of RX-2, RX-3, RX-4, 808, 1300, 1600, Cosmo, GLC and 626	6981	**VW Front Wheel Drive 1974-85** Covers all U.S. and Canadian models	6962
		VW 1949-71 Covers all U.S. and Canadian models	5796
Mazda Pick-Ups 1972-86 Covers all U.S. and Canadian models	7659	**VW 1970-79 Spanish**	7081
Mercedes-Benz 1959-70 Covers all U.S. and Canadian models	6065	**VW 1970-81** Covers all U.S. and Canadian Beetles, Karmann Ghia, Fastback, Squareback, Vans, 411 and 412	6837
Mereceds-Benz 1968-73 Covers all U.S. and Canadian models	5907		

Chilton's Repair & Tune-Up Guides are available at your local retailer or by mailing a check or money order for **$13.95** plus **$3.25** to cover postage and handling to:

Chilton Book Company
Dept. DM
Radnor, PA 19089

NOTE: When ordering be sure to include your name & address, book part No. & title.